C000134133

'… vivid images, layer upon
eyewitness feel … Sophie's Jour
inspirational story, with a little
strength of character in sharp

Courier ~~Mail~~

'This is a book that will at times put a lump in your throat …
[it] is a sheer joy to read … Read it and recommend it
to others.'
Newcastle Herald

'Let me give you a word of warning before you pick up this
book. Make sure you read it in private and make sure you have
nowhere to go … Sophie's inspirational story has given so
many other people strength. I can guarantee it won't be
gathering dust on your bedside table. It's a page turner.'
Today Show's Kelly Connolly

'It's the most inspirational book I've ever read'
Singer and Australian Idol winner Guy Sebastian

sophie's
JOURNEY

SALLY COLLINGS

HarperCollins*Publishers*

HarperCollins_Publishers_

First published in Australia in 2007
This edition published in 2008
by HarperCollins_Publishers_ Australia Pty Limited
ABN 36 009 913 517
www.harpercollins.com.au

HarperCollins_Publishers_
25 Ryde Road, Pymble, Sydney NSW 2073, Australia
31 View Road, Glenfield, Auckland 10, New Zealand
1–A, Hamilton House, Connaught Place, New Delhi – 110 001, India
77–85 Fulham Palace Road, London W6 8JB, United Kingdom
2 Bloor Street East, 20th Floor, Toronto, Ontario M4W 1A8, Canada
10 East 53rd Street, New York NY 10022, United States of America

National Library of Australia Cataloguing-in-Publication data:

Collings, Sally.
Sophie's journey / author, Sally Collings.
Pymble, N.S.W. : HarperCollins Publishers, 2008.
978 0 7322 8553 1 (pbk.)
Delezio, Sophie, 2001– .
Traffic accident victims – New South Wales – Biography.
613.69092

Cover and internal design by Matt Stanton
Front and back cover photographs: Mark Mawson Photography
Author photograph: Patrick McKenna
Additional interviewing: Kate Rossmanith
Typeset in ACaslon by Kirby Jones
Printed and bound in Australia by Griffin Press

79gsm Bulky Paperback White used by HarperCollins_Publishers_ is a natural, recyclable
product made from wood grown in a combination of sustainable plantation and regrowth
forests. It also contains up to a 20% portion of recycled fibre. The manufacturing processes
conform to the environmental regulations in Tasmania, the place of manufacture.

5 4 3 2 1   08 09 10 11

This book is for Mum and Dad — I wish you could have been here to see it.

Sally Collings

contents

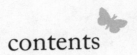

foreword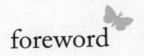

Monday, 15 December 2003. The day Sophie's world changed forever — her 'day of difference'.

That night I remember holding my kids that little bit closer and wondering how anyone could survive such a tragedy.

Three years later and Sophie's quiet resilience has answered that question triumphantly — a story of extraordinary determination in the face of adversity.

It is also an incredible story of cutting-edge medicine, administered with love and skill by some of the world's finest clinicians — many of them tempered in the aftermath of Bali.

Above all, it's the story of how this broken little girl was sustained by the collective will of a nation as her life hung in a traumatic balance.

All but the coldest and most empty hearts will have an enduring place for Sophie Delezio and her winning smile.

We remain humbled by the remarkable, life-affirming story which is 'Sophie's Journey'.

MORRIS IEMMA
PREMIER OF NEW SOUTH WALES
OCTOBER 2006

This book is to thank the teams that support our family and all families of children with a medical condition. We hope it gives an understanding of what happens behind the walls of a children's hospital and how lives and futures are impacted.

This book also recognises the unsung heroes and acknowledges the incredible compassion directed to our family from both the professional and public sectors. We hope that it makes a difference in your life, as our work for Day of Difference does for us.

RON DELEZIO AND CAROLYN MARTIN

introduction

The first time I saw Sophie Delezio was in school. I'd been chatting with her teacher, and we looked in at Sophie's classroom for a few minutes. Sensing someone coming into the room, most of the children turned around. Sophie's gaze was bold, quizzical and assessing. It was definitely the once-over! Then she and the rest of the kids turned their attention back to the story their teacher was reading.

Sophie stood out. Not just because of her injuries, which are extreme and impossible to ignore, but because she has a presence — you might even say a charisma. Would she have been like that if she had not been through so much? I can't say — though some of the people speaking in this book give their view.

Ten days before Christmas, on 15 December 2003, a car crashed into the Roundhouse Childcare Centre in the Sydney suburb of Fairlight. By some kind of miracle, no one was killed, but Sophie Delezio was trapped beneath the car and suffered third-degree burns to 85 per cent of her body. She lost both feet, some fingers, and her right ear — yet she survived. The public took Sophie to their hearts, touched by her tragedy and the strength she demonstrated in her battle to live. Two and a half years later, on 5 May 2006, the unthinkable happened — Sophie was hit by a car on a pedestrian crossing. She was left with a brain injury, punctured lungs, nine broken ribs, a broken jaw, a broken collarbone and fractures in her spine. Once again doctors told Sophie's parents that she might die. Yet again, she defied the odds and survived.

This book describes Sophie's journey, through the words of the many people who have supported her, helped her and loved her — friends and family, hospital staff, emergency workers and high-profile supporters. The voices of Sophie's parents, Ron Delezio and Carolyn Martin, also run through the book, describing the twists and turns of their journey so far. It is a spoken story as much as a written story.

Sophie's Journey is more than the moving account of a little girl struck by two tragic accidents and a survival that some call miraculous. This book is not just about Sophie. It is about every child who goes to hospital, every parent who fears losing their child. It's about everyone who experiences pain and who is supported by the love of their friends and family. It's also about the teams of people behind the scenes — emergency workers, hospital staff, home carers — who make each step in this long journey a little easier.

In the hospitals they say, 'We have many Sophies'. That doesn't make Sophie's story any less remarkable and significant, but it brings home the fact that there are other children who suffer injury and illness and beat the odds. Sophie's plastic surgeon, Peter Hayward, pays tribute to the many other patients of his who survive despite losing limbs, organs and brain function: 'Their lives are struggles, they are deathly ill; are they brave? They are all brave; they are all as brave as Sophie.'

But there is something special about Sophie. In this book you'll see her as a fighter who moves beyond obstacles, who lives in the moment, and who has a robust spirit that allows her to transcend physical adversity. There is also the 'Sophie effect': the way in which the community feels that Sophie is their little girl and responds to her struggles and triumphs in a remarkably passionate way. She has become 'our Sophie'.

I expected this to be a moving and uplifting story about the misfortune of a little girl. It is much more than that. Sophie's experience of two major life-threatening events is more than what could be considered 'fair' for anyone. It's not surprising that this book has moved beyond simply the recounting of an accident, a burn and a brave child. On hearing Sophie's story, most people are drawn to reflect on the fragility of existence, the presence or absence of God, the choice between life and death, the resilience of children.

This is a book of many voices. As you read it, you'll notice that not everyone agrees. For some of the hospital staff, Sophie was the most profoundly injured patient they had ever seen. Others say they had seen worse. Some friends see a bright future for Sophie; others see a troubled path. Even apparent matters of fact — how quickly the fire engines arrived at the fire, what Sophie's skin feels like — are recalled quite differently. Those contradictions have not been smoothed away, because each person has their own truth, and together they build a bigger picture. There are themes that come up again and again throughout *Sophie's Journey*: of strength and spirit; the power of a community to support a family and the power of a family to support a child; the deep connections that link people; the good that can come from a desperate situation.

Not every voice is here. Some people connected with Sophie didn't want to relive the events of the past few years; some have had enough of the public spotlight, preferring to heal privately. There are names that do not appear in this book because we have respected those decisions.

For Sophie's parents, Ron and Carolyn, this book is an opportunity to thank the community for the generosity of their support: 'It was a hugely humbling experience, so we had to learn how to accept that and say thank you. We know we are extraordinarily lucky with the opportunities we've been presented, the enormous care and love people gave to us, and we accept that generosity because we know how fragile life is — and it can be gone in an instant.' Ron and Carolyn's lives have been profoundly affected by the events of the past few years. Originally trained as a kindergarten teacher, before Sophie's accident Carolyn was a property adviser in real estate and was about to purchase her own property management company; now, she is a director of the Day of Difference Foundation and is Sophie's principal carer as well as running their household. Ron formerly ran a plastic machinery import company and travelled extensively across Australia and overseas. Since the Roundhouse accident he has dedicated himself to setting up the Day of Difference Foundation and acting as its chairman.

The people who most inspire us are often the ones who have suffered most. Nelson Mandela, emerging from 27 years in prison to lead South Africa to democracy; Aron Ralston, cutting off his own arm to survive after a rock-climbing accident; Sara Henderson, left with a mountain of debt on a remote cattle station in the Australian outback when her husband died. Their pain makes them who they are and gives them something to tell the world. We benefit from their adversity, in a way. But would we wish their misfortune on these people? Would we wish anything like it on ourselves? Sophie and her family have not escaped pain, but they have moved beyond it, and in that they inspire us all.

I've been privileged to speak to some remarkable people in the course of writing this book, and I've been moved to tears and uplifted by their stories. I hope you are too.

1

Fire at the Roundhouse

It is just after one o'clock on a Monday afternoon, 15 December 2003 — ten days before Christmas. In the Sydney suburb of Fairlight it is a bright, clear summer's day; children sleep on mattresses at the Roundhouse Childcare Centre. They always have a nap after lunch, but today is special. Santa is coming. It's not easy to settle down, but one by one the 13 children in the Possum Room soften into sleep. One of the last to close their eyes is Sophie Delezio. She is two and a half.

Ron Delezio and Carolyn Martin
SOPHIE'S PARENTS

Carolyn: The Roundhouse was a really calm and contented place. At two years of age, the children were just starting to form friendships. It was a small preschool class, a close-knit little group.

Ron: We still don't understand how the accident happened. The only explanation we had from the police was that the car was going along the road, then all of a sudden it did a complete 90-degree turn, hit the window and landed on top of Sophie. I can't see how that happened.

Carolyn: Because of the nature of the police enquiry we were never privy to any discussion of the event. We had no idea of the sheer enormity of the teams involved until we read stories in the paper. Someone would come up to me and say, 'My husband works with the ambulance officers who were involved with the accident'. I was at Mary MacKillop Chapel in 2005 and a nun came up to me and said a relation of hers had been involved in the accident — and I had no idea.

I always felt the parents from the Roundhouse felt a degree of protectiveness towards us; they wanted to make sure everything was all right for us. Out of all the children in that accident, Sophie was the most severely injured. They all have a sense it could have been their child. In that group, asleep in an area this big — it could have been any of them.

Amanda Zimmerman

CHILDCARE WORKER,
ROUNDHOUSE CHILDCARE CENTRE IN FAIRLIGHT

Amanda Zimmerman was the childcare worker in charge of the two- and three-year-olds in the Possum Room. When the car came through the doors, it came straight towards her at head height. She took one step back; it missed her by centimetres.

Sophie had a strong will always, even when she was in the baby room. She had the fighting spirit from day one. On the day of the accident, because Santa was coming that afternoon, she was the last one to go to sleep. She kept on saying, 'My Santa is coming, my Santa is coming'. She wasn't upset, but she was being told she had to go to sleep because of the Christmas party — 'If you don't do it you won't be able to see Santa, because you need to rest'. All the parents come in and we do a concert and then Santa comes. The children just go berserk because it is so exciting. Some of them get intimidated by it, but she wouldn't have been.

I was getting stuff ready outside, cleaning up and getting plates for parents to put food on. I was walking back inside when I heard a bang outside and a car came straight at me. I heard the glass smashing first of all. It was weird because the driver had his lights on and I could see him in the car. He was looking straight ahead and the car just followed through to my head. I just moved back a step and it landed.

I could hear the kids screaming straight away. Everything was dark, all the curtains were shut. That was the problem: the smoke couldn't get out, even though there were glass doors you could open from the outside. The screen doors were jammed — his car went straight into them. Because it was pitch-black it was hard to see anything, all you could hear were the tyres on the lino spinning around. I went straight down and ran and got one of the kids who was closest to me. I had to crawl to pick him up and I took him out the back. Then I came back in to try to get another child, but I couldn't even see by that stage, with the smoke ... I don't know whether I pulled out another child or not then. I literally had to go in on my knees and feel around for them because they were all on the ground.

I went outside and tried to open the [glass] doors. A man had jumped the fence and we were trying to open them. Then I got one of our A frames to try to smash the glass but I couldn't do it, so he did it. As he was doing that, the driver walked out of the babies' room. Because he had blood on his face I thought that I'd hit glass into his face; I thought he was just somebody coming to help, even though only a minute had gone past. He walked out and lay down next to the sandpit.

Laura — the girl I work with — and Marg and the others had been pulling babies out as well. Then I got something to tie around my face and I got down on my hands and knees to try to pull some kids out. I got one girl out and brought her back through and then I went back in. But the car kept revving, and the people who were in there, you couldn't even see them but they were shouting, 'It's going to explode'. The tyres were just spinning the whole time. So I would crawl back out and then it would calm down again; I don't know why, at this stage the flames were already up to the roof of the room. And then I would get back down again and crawl back in.

Amanda sounded the fire alarm before going back into the room.

All the kids in the other room — the Gumnuts, the older children — had already been taken out by the teachers anyway. We practised it so many times, the kids just instinctively walked over to where they were meant to be. Our cook rang the fire brigade. We heard the siren and we pulled the fire extinguisher off the wall. I couldn't get the pin out of it, just because I was panicking. I gave it to one of the men from across the road and he started to use it. It didn't do anything anyway because of the type of fire it was. Then I ran around to try to jump over the wall on the other side to the babies' room, because there were five children trapped in there. I knew there was at least one child under the car the whole time; I knew that someone was under there, but I couldn't see them because of the way the car was sitting. It was wedged up on one of the room dividers, and that's why the tyres were spinning at the back. When I first started crawling across, you could see at that level but by the second time I went across, I could see hardly anything.

The smoke was so bad; there was a guy there and I said, 'You've got to pull them up' so we tried to pull the children up over the wall from that side — he pulled them out and was taking them out. Then I ran back around the other side; Marg had said there were some babies in the cot room, which is the back of our room — you can only get into it from one door. I got on my knees and grabbed another man; we crawled in and tried to shake the cots to see if the babies were in there. There was no noise, but you couldn't see anything. The next thing I remember there was a fireman there — I could see someone with a mask on. I could hear one of the guys in our room, he was virtually trying to lift the car at one stage and he was screaming. He was the one who was yelling that it was going to explode.

I went back over the other side near our screen doors and there was a policeman there. I dragged him in and said, 'You have to go in and get the kids out'. I dragged him through the door and came back out; I couldn't go in there any more. Then he came out and he looked sick already. I thought, 'What are you doing, why aren't you doing your job?' which is horrible, because no one wants to be put in that situation. Then all of a sudden the doors were opened and the car must have been extinguished and they were starting to lift the car. We'd got everybody out but I can't remember it, I haven't been able to remember ... I remember having Layla and another child, Liam, on the ground next to me, next to the ambulance. They had blood on them and were burnt. But I don't remember how I got them out, I don't remember doing it.

Just telling you about it now, it seems like three-quarters of an hour, an hour, with all that was happening — but it wasn't, it was quick. To me it felt that it took ages for the fire brigade to come, but apparently it was only six minutes or something. I remember being outside and seeing people jump the fence and looking across the road, seeing a news person filming without even coming in to help. I don't know how they got there; this was even before the firemen got there. It was disgusting.

When the emergency services got there, the doors were opened and the car was extinguished and they were lifting it up and someone pushed me away from the door. I didn't even see who was under the car because I was told to leave. I didn't know if it was two children, four children ... I didn't even get word that it was Sophie because they took her out the front and I was out the back. Then I started running back and forth to try and count all the children from the roll and work out who was missing. There were people everywhere. People trying to help you were just getting in the way. You had people shouting, 'Where is my mobile phone?' and 'Who's got my sunglasses?'

Once I'd done the list, Sophie was the only one I couldn't account for so I had to tell the police.

In any disaster, there are the obvious victims — in the case of the Roundhouse accident, the children who were injured. But for everyone who was there, the accident isn't over when the ambulances and fire engines leave. There is a legacy, different for each of those involved.

After the accident I would wake up at night and have to run to the window because I couldn't breathe. I had to have counselling for a year, on and off. I was a bridesmaid in my husband's sister's wedding and I had to plan to try to make it through the day. We had thousands of arguments about it, because he believed I should just get over it, as men do.

We were called in to go and get work ready [the Roundhouse reopened in January 2004]. We were cleaning toys that were just melted with smoke, which was horrific — the smell of burning rubber was in everything. I had to leave work, I couldn't stand it any more — the parents would look at me and start crying.

I didn't see the news, I didn't want to know. It is not because I don't care. I felt sorry for Sophie; we visited her in hospital and that was one of the hardest things I've ever had to do. I felt so guilty. I felt I should have been able to lift up the car. Afterwards you see things — you could have moved this, I didn't go fast enough, I wasn't quick enough ...

With the second accident, I felt obligated — I thought, 'Gosh, I should send them something'. But there is a part of me that says I don't want to be involved any more. It wrecked lives, staff, boyfriends, partners, relationships with other staff members ... I just think it's done now.

The Roundhouse Childcare Centre sits a little back from Balgowlah Road, a leafy, winding road. It is flanked by a park, tennis courts and a bowling club, forming a green band beside a road that is busy enough — but still a suburban street, not a major thoroughfare. Fairlight itself is set back from Sydney's northern beaches, behind its more famous sister, Manly. It's a quiet, pretty place, with a strong community feel. People walk a lot — to the ferry, the shops, the beach. It's a place where you might spend your whole life, raise a family, grow old. You don't look for disaster there.

Belinda Glynn

LIVES ACROSS THE ROAD FROM THE ROUNDHOUSE CHILDCARE CENTRE IN FAIRLIGHT

Belinda Glynn was one of the first on the scene. At first, she couldn't tell where the accident had happened — standing outside, there was no sign of a car inside the childcare centre.

I remember the kindy teacher going on about this car and I didn't think it was an actual car, because you couldn't tell from the outside. The kindy looked fine as I was crossing the road but when those doors came down and I saw there was a car I was completely shocked; it was unbelievable.

Then I think I just went with the flow. When someone handed a child to me I can still remember the face on that little girl and the shock that she was in. All she said was, 'Oh, my dress is wet', like she was going to get in trouble for it. What struck me were the guys going back into the kindy. The smoke was really thick, it literally burnt the inside of your nostrils. The visuals were overwhelming — the car, the flames, the smoke. Then the noise of the car accelerating faster and faster and this whining pitch; it just felt like it was going to explode. And you saw all this smoke and what you'd heard and smelt and saw was so overwhelming. The smoke was getting blacker and blacker and more acrid, yet these guys could continually go back in — and these were the lay [untrained] guys.

Manly is generally a community where you get to know people — on different levels of course — but you do recognise locals. The driver [Donald McNeall] was an old guy who had been around for quite some time. He was completely catatonic, just didn't look very good. I think I basically went into shock as well. I was thinking, 'Oh my God, I hope he doesn't die'. The guys came out and dropped him at my feet, literally. I just turned him on his side because I was a little bit concerned about airways. I didn't know what to do, I had no first aid training. Looking back now it's quite comical — there were arms and legs splayed out like he was going to be drawn and quartered. He was in a zombie-like state, he wasn't aware of what was going on. I've never seen anybody like that before; he was aware that the ambulance guy was trying to give him a needle or take his blood pressure and he was trying to push it [the equipment] away, but he was completely 'not at home'.

When I was with the driver I looked back towards the kindy; I was extremely angry and extremely distressed because it was like I was frozen. I was with the driver, I couldn't do anything but I could see all these firemen standing around. They didn't case the building or come round to the back, and in fact somebody called out, 'Hey, there is a fire here, get over here' and then the fire chief said, 'Hey, you two, go put the flames out'. The whole thing was very surreal.

I did go back into the kindy — not all the way in, because I couldn't get all the way in, I couldn't see anything. The car was going to explode; maybe if I'd seen a child — I can remember looking under the car and not seeing anything, and I can remember thinking if there was a child under there, I couldn't even see. How those lay guys just kept going back into that kindy, I have no idea. They were finding kids in cupboards and stuff like that. There were a few guys who I've never seen again; I don't know who they are, they have never been recognised. All I can say is it's like a fireman going up the stairs to 9/11 — it really felt like that car was going to explode. You couldn't breathe, you couldn't see, it sounded horrible, it looked horrible. How they found those kids in cupboards — I don't know whether they had prior experience but I really have no idea how they kept going back in. I always thought if I was ever in a position to help I would put my life on the line, but it makes you realise . . . I don't know whether it is a failing, a weakness or a soft spot, but the reality of things makes you realise where your boundaries are. I haven't got the words to describe how those guys did it; it was literally . . . as if they had superhero qualities. It was totally going against your instincts of self-preservation. Maybe if you could see someone in distress, but to see nothing — to this day, I just don't know how they did it.

In a way that whole experience provided me with a gift and I guess those emotional and spiritual gifts don't come without a price. Physically I went into post-traumatic stress disorder — my arms went on the blink and all sorts of weird things. I think that was because of not being able to help in the situation. While I was holding the driver I felt so angry at the firemen, supposedly for not doing their job, that I felt helpless. I'm not blaming the fireys [firemen], but that was my perception of events — I want to state that really clearly. But because my arms went on the blink it then jeopardised my job and I went into this spiral of *oh poor me*. When I parallel it to Sophie — she's always been a fighter, you look at the trauma she went through. But then I realised that the arms wasn't necessarily a physical thing ... There is a lot of strength that comes from your mind. Some people have an innately higher level of mental strength, when your body is weak, to pull the rest of you through — maybe it is a spiritual thing. I look at Sophie and think, 'My God, she is only a little girl, but it is one of her characteristics'.

They say as you go through life if you don't get the lesson the first time it will keep coming back; if it's not a lesson, it's a truth or whatever. When I was with the driver and I was looking at the fireys I was so angry, so angry; and it took me a little while to realise that I held this thing in my body ...

When I think of the two accidents, I just think, 'Has Sophie decided she is going to be the beacon to point people's awareness in these areas, to save further pain to other people?' You know, some of the guys out in the surf [Belinda is a surfer] say, 'There mustn't be a God for that to happen'. I would prefer to believe that there is a lot of good that has come out of it. Sophie is like a hero, with those super strengths. It makes people rise to the occasion, brings the community closer together, brings people out of themselves to think of other things. I think we probably need more of that these days. One of the dads from the kindy is out in the surf; we recognise each other, so it's brought that kind of connection.

Wade Laverack
FIREFIGHTER, MANLY FIRE STATION

Gordon Boath
FIRE INSPECTOR, MANLY FIRE STATION

Wade Laverack was the firefighter who pulled Sophie from beneath the burning car. Here, he reads from the report he wrote just after the incident, and recalls his experience of that day. Gordon Boath was the senior officer in charge at the Roundhouse fire.

Wade: '13:26 Monday 15 December 2003. 24 Station Manly responded to a call via 000 to a school alight. Close to arrival at the incident smoke could be seen emitting from the building. Upon arrival I was wearing full breathing apparatus' — what is referred to as full PPE, full protective clothing — gloves, flash hood, helmet. The reason we had all that on is that as we were coming down the hill from the fire station to the kindergarten, we could see that there was quite a lot of black smoke emitting from the incident, which meant that there was something acrid burning.

Gordon: The darker the smoke, the more likely that hydrocarbons are involved. Black smoke coming from a house indicates that the furniture is on fire. With car fires you get very black acrid smoke from burning tyres and car paints or parts.

Wade: When we pulled up at the front of the Roundhouse first indications were that the front wall had collapsed. At that stage neither Tony [a senior firefighter], myself or Dennis, who was the operational commander, the New South Wales Fire

Brigades Incident Commander, knew that there was a car inside. My initial thoughts were that there had been an explosion of some type, perhaps a gas line.

'I then ran around to the back of the premises with Senior Firefighter Tony Farrell, who was my partner in the back of the fire appliance.' We work as a team. There was Tony Farrell and myself in the rear, the station commander (he was in the front relaying messages at that stage), and Steven Barnwell. He was the driver and he's just as important a part of the crew as well — he got us there and his first job was to start organising water for the fire to be extinguished.

'Upon entering the grounds of the centre we were approached by a distressed staff member indicating that children were still trapped inside.' We ran around the side to the rear of the centre and there was a wire fence about 5 foot [1.6 metres] high. When we got round the back I could see that there was a car or something within the building confines. There was a staff member there who was quite frantic and she was reiterating that children were still trapped inside. 'We climbed over the fence then entered the building through a broken glass door at the rear of the building.' There were two big sliding glass doors; the impact had pushed those doors out and the glass was shattered everywhere on the ground. Upon entering Tony and I commenced search and rescue and discovered a vehicle had crashed through the front wall. As soon as we could see there was a car we could analyse what was going on. Once we have people reported the main priority is search and rescue to make sure those people are out of the fire before we even start worrying about putting the fire out.

Gordon: In a buddy system you've got people going in with air cylinders on; for every person inside with an air cylinder on there has to be a second person outside. Because Tony and Wade had gone in to conduct a search and rescue there was another truck at Manly which responded behind the normal fire engine. It's a ladder truck, it doesn't have a pump on it, and there are two firefighters on that. They put on their air cylinders on arrival to act as the backup crew; if something happened to Tony and Wade they could go in and rescue them. There are always two stations that respond to every call of a reported structure fire, which this one was. Manly was the first arriving crew; Dennis Goldsworthy, the station officer who was the initial incident controller, sent an urgent message — what we call a red message. He asked for a second alarm, being the code for which four stations and a rescue unit respond — that equates to about 20 firefighters. Within a space of seven minutes we had something like ten firefighters on the scene, so you could commit more and more crews to the search and rescue operation as those crews arrived. But the original two were Tony and Wade. On the grand scale of things it wasn't that big a fire but because of the life hazard, it required sufficient resources so all hands could be on deck for a search and rescue.

Wade: 'Approximately five male civilians already inside the building assisting alerted Tony and myself that children were trapped under the vehicle.' When we went through the back glass doors there were civilians already in there attempting to help get the kids out. When the car crashed through the window the petrol line underneath the sub frame of the vehicle ignited — caused by friction when the vehicle crashed over the brick retaining wall before crashing through the window. The rear tyre started burning, which developed into a fire at the rear of the vehicle. When we got there black acrid smoke was emitting from the burning tyre and car parts. Those civilians who were in there were in danger, as that smoke was getting very, very thick — in other words, it was very dangerous to be inhaling it. We had our air sets on so we were right for a while; the building was quickly filling with smoke.

'Upon lying down beside the vehicle I could see the feet of a child.' An ambulance officer was just behind me at this point, but being low to the ground he was not inhaling the black acrid smoke. The other civilians were still standing up; they were all yelling out that the kids were underneath. Sophie was towards the middle of the car, towards the driver's side. At this point I noticed petrol dripping from the damaged fuel line and igniting the carpet, so the other burns which Sophie had were caused by the petrol dripping out. The carpet had started to catch on fire and that was burning up against her as well. I yelled out to the guys that they had to lift the car; the wheel had burned down to the rim so the car was on an angle. I could see her but I just couldn't get my hands close enough to grab her. The other side of the car was pinned up against lockers, so there were no avenues to get under the other side.

All I could see was a very charred body and I thought she was deceased. The civilians lifted the car; I got underneath, grabbed Sophie's leg and pulled her out. I had an ambulance officer right behind me and we went straight outside. She was face down; when I dragged her out from under the vehicle, I threw her against me and she started screaming, really screaming, so I knew then that she was alive. I thought, 'Well, she might get out of this'.

I carried Sophie outside with the ambulance officer behind me. When I got outside we dowsed Sophie in water but because there were still a lot of unaccounted children at that stage and the place was filling up with smoke very rapidly, I left the ambulance officer with Sophie and I returned to the building to continue search and rescue. Tony had got one of the girls out from the front and we then went back in together. At this stage the rear of the vehicle was well alight so it was getting very smoke-logged. I ordered the civilians who were still inside the building outside, otherwise they were going to become casualties as well. Tony and I recommenced search and rescue, concentrating on the rear of the vehicle, removing debris — the impact of the vehicle crushed cupboards, glass, bricks and furniture; debris was everywhere, making it hard to climb over. Tony went around to the driver's side that was up against what looked like lockers; there was a young girl who had hidden in one of the cupboards, and Tony got her out. When kids get scared they will try to hide anywhere where they feel safe. At the rear of the vehicle I uncovered another child who was covered in debris — he was not visible until I started lifting furniture and so on; he had lacerations to his legs and was naturally in severe shock. He was under the rear of the vehicle's boot, on the opposite side to the burning tyre (the burning tyre was on the rear passenger side, where the petrol line runs). I lay under the rear of the vehicle to remove more debris to ensure his legs weren't pinned by the weight of the vehicle. They weren't pinned, so I dragged the child out and left the building. There were still unaccounted children so I left the child there in the care of a civilian, a nurse. Tony and I returned to further search and rescue.

'24 Station Ladder crew had started firefighting operations on the burning vehicle' — they'd come in through the window where the car had come in and they'd started putting the fire out. They were concentrating on that and we were making sure there were no more kids involved. Additional firefighter crews arrived and we commenced to jack the left rear of the vehicle to check for any further casualties. At this stage most of the fire was out while we were making sure there weren't any deceased personnel under the car. I assisted in the stabilisation of the vehicle and rendering the area safe. I left the building and reported my actions to the incident controller and assisted in general salvage operations.

After that, I was dripping in sweat and I was hot and thirsty. Not only myself but Tony and 24 Ladder Crew, and Steve, who was the pump driver, had been running around doing all the work outside, and I think we all sat down after it.

Gordon: The chaplain came out, plus critical incident support. Everybody was sitting in the shade with refreshments and they had a debrief — a counselling session for the firefighters and other emergency services and anybody else who was involved.

Wade: I didn't expect Sophie to live, not when I heard she had 82 per cent burns. I could tell straight away when I picked her up that she had severe burns — the only unburned skin was her face and I could see that her clothes had melted onto her. I assessed that she was suffering third-degree burns so I assumed then that she wasn't going to make it. Afterward we sat down and we all just looked at each other and thought, 'This is intense'. Anything that involves kids is probably the most traumatic. I think any firefighter, any policeman, any ambulance officer who deals with children is always going to be somewhat emotional about it.

Sophie was lying face down and that was the only reason she survived. She was breathing what fresh air was available. The intensity of the fire was going over her back; if she had been face up she would have been breathing all the fire gases — hydrocarbons and so on. When you start breathing them in your time's very limited because your throat starts swelling up. So she was very lucky that she was face down. One thing I noticed when I took her out, the only part of her that was recognisable as a child was her face. I pretty well assumed that she would lose her feet because of the extent of the burns; the flesh was coming off the bone. She was past the pain barrier [having third-degree burns] — she would have just been clinging to life.

I did catch up with her once after the event at the Roundhouse. Ron gave me a call and I went down to their house. I organised a fire engine for the visit and one of the other guys came with me and I had a cup of coffee with them. When she found out there was a fire engine out the front, she thought that was great — and her brother for that matter and all the neighbourhood! She was sitting up and having a drive, and her brother [Mitchell] was up there, and I think Ron and Carolyn got up there as well. To see her recovering from the burns was great.

Gordon: The intervention of the centre staff putting the emergency plans into place to get the kids out and evacuate and start the rescue process, the intervention of the fire brigade and members of the public, meant that the injuries were limited. If there hadn't been that level of response then the possibility of fatalities and more serious injuries was very real.

Wade: All the services worked together: ambulance crews arrived, paramedics arrived, CareFlight arrived, police arrived, and everyone did their job to the nth degree. The police were terrific in coordinating the crowds outside, the ambulance officers were terrific in treating not only Sophie but numerous other kids. There were a lot of injuries sustained by other children — lacerations, cuts. The incident had the potential to have had fatalities. I don't know what sort of speed the car would have been doing when it went over the wall, but it's a miracle — the tyres must have just gone between those children lying on the floor sleeping. Had the car not ignited it would have just been rescuing kids from under a car; they might have just had exhaust burns. It was just some sort of miracle that no kids were killed.

Trudy Wise

A LONG-TERM FRIEND OF SOPHIE'S PARENTS, RON AND CAROLYN

Trudy helped handle the barrage of media enquiries following the accident.

The team at the Roundhouse were wonderful: kind and very protective. I spoke quite often to them when they were getting lots of media enquiries. And I think while we all were having our own issues dealing with the accident, when I spoke to the

Roundhouse team I was reminded of how much this had affected them. One of the women there endangered her own life to help save the children, she went back into the burning building to try again to get them out.

They opened the centre again in January. When I spoke to them in January they were still trying to clean smoke off all the toys. Can you imagine the stress of cleaning up the accident scene? Can you imagine what they must have gone through when it came time to put the children down for their sleep time when the centre reopened? They probably still go through it every day. The emotional strain was enormous for the whole team and they had ongoing issues trying to counsel their employees and children for a long time — it might still go on, for all I know.

They are heroes to me.

Dave Simmons
INSPECTOR AND DUTY OFFICER, MANLY POLICE

At any major incident or disaster in New South Wales, a police officer takes on the role of coordinating the responses of all of the emergency services and support agencies to combat and manage the initial event — deciding where the ambulances should set up the triage, where the uninjured victims should be accommodated and where the public and the media may be permitted to view the action without interfering with the emergency services, and overseeing the establishment of the perimeters for the emergency scene. Dave Simmons took that role at the Roundhouse accident.

When I arrived, there were police, ambulance, fire brigade, centre staff, some parents and bystanders in the immediate area. It would have been ten to 15 minutes after the incident occurred; smoke was still issuing from the building. I went to the front of the place, acquainted myself with what actually happened, then looked at the lie of the land, how I wanted to set it up. There is a certain procedure of how you set up the agencies with enough room to give them scope to do what they do best.

I immediately knew by the sheer scope of it that we would probably declare it an emergency incident. I have a tabard that goes over my jacket that says who I am — just in case there are two or three senior police, so that all the emergency services personnel know who is taking the role on. Senior members of the other major combat agencies also put on special tabards so everyone knows who's who in the zoo. At this stage it was all pretty jumbled; people were still arriving, there were police still trying to lift up the vehicle and check what was underneath. I went to the senior ambulance person at the scene and said, 'Give me a status'. At that time I believed that several people were killed and there would have been multiple major injuries, just by the sheer scope of what I saw in front of me. He told me there was at least one missing, at least three seriously injured and most of the other people were being transported or awaiting transport. I asked where he wanted his triage. I then told police to set up perimeters — there is an inner perimeter that lets in whoever is doing the combating and an outer perimeter to keep everybody else out. More and more police were coming, more and more fire brigade, more and more ambulance and of course the onlookers were coming, plus I still had the teachers, and some parents who were trying to assist. I declared a certain area the command post and basically I stood there. I called over the senior fire officer and asked him what area he wanted. Tape was put around that area and things started to get stabilised.

At a rough count we had 20 police officers on the scene. I was lucky that I had another inspector there and several sergeants. The inspector became the police commander; I asked him to find out how many victims there were. We were lucky in that the kindergarten had kept an accurate list of who was there that day and they had already commenced roll call; there was still one person missing. Later on we found out that one person got double-counted at one end and wasn't counted at another end, so they thought three persons had been severely injured, but in fact there was only two. It was still a worry because it meant we had to keep going back into the building and checking. Children have a predisposition, when they are worried, to get into a corner or a tight place; they easily could have gone into a cupboard or behind mattresses. There was still a fire, mattresses were still smoking and letting off fumes; they were being pulled out one by one and stacked. We then had a problem having to transport too many people and not enough ambulance personnel, so for the first time in my coordination career we had police driving ambulances and an ambulance officer in the back of the ambulance with the patient.

We also had a police helicopter coming to the area; one of the children got airlifted out, so we had to have a designated landing area. It had to be close enough so you don't have a long transport by vehicle to the plane, but not be in the way as well. Nobody at that point thought about doing any investigation as to how [the incident] happened, it was all about getting the situation stabilised; that policing stuff comes later.

Everyone was doing their job and doing it well — and I mean everybody, including the staff. It was amazing, their professionalism. Even the way they marshalled the children — the ones who were okay — out to one side and started singing nursery rhymes. They kept them in one area, not too far away but far enough not to be in the way, and kept them amused and involved them until their parents came along. That took a lot of pressure off the combat agencies. You have two main problems when you have anything like that: one is combating the incident itself; the second is the people who come along just to look. They either want to be involved or want to know what is happening and basically they are a hindrance. Any major incident like that, people gather; some of them have a vested interest, but a lot of people driving their cars would just stop, look and obstruct.

Now everything was working and being organised. The fire brigade were doing their job well, they had control of the fire, the car and fuel; ambulance had a good handle on their triage and getting the children out of the place; the school had a very good handle on working with them. But although I asked several times, I think it was about an hour into it before I would believe and had it confirmed to me that nobody had been killed and there were only two seriously injured people. For the first hour I did not believe any reports coming to me saying they all got out. I wasn't satisfied that we got off as lightly as we did.

I went to Granville [train disaster] when I was a very junior police officer; I also had something to do with the Boral gas explosions at St Peters. I've been involved in a lot of crime [scenes]; my background is communication and emergency management. This was horrific, it was unusual, it involved a lot of young children and that was why it took me an hour to believe no one had been killed. To this day I still don't know how that car turned and went through that small window. I understand the issues raised in the police investigation of the collision, but I believe a stunt car driver couldn't do what the driver of the car managed to do. I've got to support the planners of the area; nobody would ever have envisaged that the car, travelling in the direction it was, would have turned to that degree and angle, around a telegraph pole, through a window some 4 foot [1.3 metres] off the ground and done what it did. It was beyond imagination that it could happen.

2
The golden hour

In trauma care they talk about the 'golden hour': the first hour immediately after an accident is vital in terms of whether someone lives or dies. There is no doubt that Sophie would have died had she not had rapid access to high-quality care. The first challenge was keeping this critically ill child stable as she was moved from the scene of the accident, to the ambulance, to Royal North Shore Hospital — and then on to specialist care at The Children's Hospital at Westmead.

Carolyn Martin
SOPHIE'S MOTHER

There are certain things that people say that stay with you. When I arrived at North Shore, [paediatrician] Jonny Taitz said to me, 'Your daughter has been in an accident, she looks like she has been in the Bali bombings'. People say that was a bit brutal, but it gave me an immediate reference. It gave me a picture in my mind — it was a catastrophic accident, not just a broken arm. I needed to know the scale.

Dr Louise Northcott

PAEDIATRICIAN, THE CHILDREN'S HOSPITAL AT WESTMEAD

In one of the many remarkable coincidences (or twists of fate) that mark Sophie's story, paediatrician Louise Northcott lives up the road from the Roundhouse. She was on the scene within minutes and travelled with Sophie in the ambulance to Royal North Shore Hospital, about 12 km away.

I heard the crash and thought to myself, 'I hope that it's not the childcare centre'. I opened my back door, looked out and the childcare centre was on fire, so I ran down the road. The ambulance had already arrived — the ambulance station is only 200 metres away. I identified one of the ambulance drivers and said, 'I'm a paediatrician, can I help?' — despite the fact I was in shorts and thongs and a singlet.

Sophie was in the back of the ambulance in the bed with oxygen on. It was very obvious she was significantly injured, even though she was still talking and interacting with us. I was going to try to put a line in for some fluid resuscitation but the ambulance guys redirected me; they didn't have any lines small enough for small children, so we used an intraosseous needle — something I'd been taught about but never actually used. I think that was one of the things that really helped us help Sophie — that was a really good choice on the part of the ambulance driver.

As soon as the second ambulance arrived on the scene we were free to go with Sophie. We were trying to make a decision as to which hospital we'd go to. I thought we'd be better going to the burns unit at Westmead; the ambulance drivers were keen to take her to Manly. We decided to go to North Shore, which was the nearest paediatric and trauma centre. I thought the doctors there might be more able to cope with her injuries than at Manly, which is a smaller hospital. We irrigated all of her burns with intravenous fluids; there were four bags of sterile water and salty water in the back of the ambulance and we poured them all over her to try to cool the burn. We ended up with the back of the ambulance just soaking. We managed to wet all of the burn that looked like it was potentially going to heal and then she was lying in a little puddle of cold water, which would have helped with her back, but if we had put a lot of water on her we wouldn't have been safe in the back of the ambulance going that fast. We were sliding around quite a lot on the little bit of water that was there.

Sophie was asking for her mother, so we told her some fibs. I don't often lie to patients but I chose this time to tell some small lies. We told Sophie that Carolyn was driving behind us in her car. We actually didn't know Sophie's name at that point; we didn't know how old she was, we didn't know how much she weighed. We had to guess using resuscitation formulas. We took off to North Shore; I still remember going down the hill at Manly Road towards Spit Bridge. The floor was slippery, so we were trying to hang onto her, hang onto the intraosseous line — because you can't tape them in very easily — and we were sliding around the back of the ambulance, so they were really hard conditions to work in. But we managed to give her fluid and pain relief through the intraosseous line and we managed to comfort her a little, I think, and keep talking to her and keep her going. She was quite frightened but she is quite resilient; she was still talking and answering simple questions. She was asking for

Carolyn and we managed to calm her down quite a lot by saying Carolyn was behind us. Once we started driving we'd say, 'Mummy is behind in a car' and she managed to get quite a bit of comfort from that, I think. By the time we'd given her a third dose of morphine, she was much more comfortable.

Sophie was amazing in the ambulance when she was talking to us — 'Where am I, what's happening, where's my mum?'. She was having a look at her hands and was trying to work that out. She certainly wasn't crying but she was in a lot of pain. We tried to do our best with painkillers but she wasn't screaming or anything, she was actually interacting. Most adults would not be able to do that in the situation that Sophie found herself.

Burns go from pink to red to white to black and Sophie had some areas where she was almost charred, so her burns were quite horrific, especially on her back. And her legs were already very badly injured. But she was a very lucky girl, especially because her face was spared; we think she turned away from the burning tyres and put her hands over her face, which protected her windpipe. The real risk after a severe burn is airway compromise; she didn't have any blackness around her mouth, so we knew we had a little bit of time to get her to hospital and we didn't need to intubate her [put a tube down her throat to assist breathing] in the back of the ambulance because she was still talking and breathing okay.

There was a point coming back up Spit Hill when we had to brake fairly hard to avoid a concrete truck. I remember sliding down the back of the ambulance, looking out and seeing the concrete truck. We were on our knees and holding onto her and the access that we had and giving medicine and fluid at the same time, so you needed about five pairs of hands. I think sailing teachers tell you to hold on with one hand and work with the other ... I have done a lot of emergency and neonatal work, but it was the first time I've ever resuscitated somebody out of hospital. It opens your eyes to how hard it is working without your nursing team, your medical team. The paramedics were brilliant and they made some really good suggestions about what would work in that kind of environment. I was new to Australia [Louise is from the UK], I had only been here for two months, and we still managed to work really well together in a team. The international trauma organisations make sure the training we get in the UK is the same as you would get in North America and Australia. Even though we had never met before we could all work together as a team, and I thought that was a huge achievement.

We had been on the phone to North Shore. Sophie had such severe injuries that I wanted the burns surgeons to be there. The normal trauma team — anaesthetists, paediatrician, trauma ED, consultant surgeon — is a team of about six people and nursing staff. At that time we were still thinking about going to Westmead; we got onto the Pacific Highway, and the paramedic said, 'Final decision'. We'd given her several doses of morphine, so we decided we should stop at North Shore. They had their senior burns specialists available and we'd radioed ahead to get the most senior anaesthetists, so when we got there, there was an enormous team of people available for her. I got her onto the bed and the paramedic handed over what we'd done. One of the team said to me, 'Are you her mother?' — I hadn't even thought about her parents, then it hit me. I didn't meet Ron and Carolyn until

Sophie was in intensive care and I thought, 'God, if I was her mother that would just tear your heart out'.

When you are on the handing-over side you step back and that's it, your job is done. I wanted to get stuck in and carry on helping. But I was in casual clothes and I could have been anyone, so it wouldn't have been appropriate. North Shore had a brilliant team of people, plenty of expertise, but it is a bit strange when you are working really hard with someone and you just pass them on to the next team.

The paramedics were very worried about Sophie. They asked if I thought she would survive. It's not a very good thing to admit to, but I did say I thought she had a very minimal chance of survival. They were quite upset and we all had a chat, and then they had to get on with their job. That must be really hard as well, to get back in the ambulance and go to the next job. I had nothing with me; I had run out my back door with nothing, in a pair of shorts — no keys, no wallet. Someone gave me some money and I had to get the bus home. One of the ambulance guys offered me a lift, but people were asking where they were, they needed to be back in circulation; I thought it wouldn't be very fair for me to ask them to drive me home. So I got on the 143 back to Manly. When I got home my back door was wide open from when I had run out and the area was swarming with people. I was so lucky that no one walked into my house.

Probably 48 hours afterwards, Ron gave me a ring. The social worker had passed on my details and he said they would like to talk about what happened at the Roundhouse Centre and in the ambulance. It was at the time when it was touch and go and she was really critically ill; a lot of people, even the intensive care specialist, thought she probably wouldn't survive. I went and met Ron and Carolyn; they wanted to know how Sophie had been, what she said, what we'd done. We went through all that, hoping it was useful, but there was a real concern at the time that the ambulance crew and I might have been the last people to see her alive.

Dr Jonny Taitz

PAEDIATRICIAN AND CLINICAL OPERATIONS ASSISTANT DIRECTOR, SYDNEY CHILDREN'S HOSPITAL

I first encountered Sophie on 15 December 2003; I remember the day well, like most of us. I was working at Royal North Shore Hospital at the time. We got a call, even though I wasn't on call that day; we initially heard that six girls had been badly burned in a car crash somewhere in the Manly area. Fortunately there were only three, but when Sophie arrived, she was the sickest girl I've ever seen. She was severely burned, 85 per cent of her body, she was shut down, she wasn't breathing. The first thing the team had to work on was establishing an airway and getting some drips in, which was very difficult because she was so badly burned, and attend to her basic first aid — resuscitation. That took a number of hours. Because she was so badly burned the only option was The Children's Hospital at Westmead ICU; they are the only place in the state that would take someone so badly burned, so we organised a transfer. Fortunately at RNS we have the adult burns unit for the state and so we used the expertise there, and that probably had a major role in saving her life.

When people burn they become very swollen; that stops the blood supply. Very early on they did fasciotomies, literally cutting through skin and muscle; it is quite horrific but it is probably what saved her life. I informed Ron and Carolyn that their daughter was going to die. We didn't expect her to survive that afternoon, given the severity and extent of her injuries and the type of injuries. Carolyn was in a state of shock. I think Ron was too.

Because of the traffic at that time of the afternoon, we got a helicopter to transfer her to Westmead. We couldn't open the door to the helipad — an ironic part of the afternoon, because everything else to that point had gone well. Sophie was only at North Shore for six to eight hours, no more. We didn't expect her to survive. We counselled the staff — they were very badly affected by this; many of them have kids of their own, myself included, and one was the same age as Sophie, so it hit home quite hard. My colleagues at Westmead were faced with a very similar dilemma for the first weeks; I know they had end-of-life discussions with the Delezios. For me it was that first discussion: 'I'm one of the doctors in the emergency department, I am heading up a team looking after Sophie, the extent of the injuries is horrific, she is extremely badly burnt everywhere except her face, we are having trouble establishing any sort of blood pressure, her pulse is very weak, she is not breathing on her own, she has been anaesthetised, we have given her lots of pain relief, lots of morphine, our surgeons are busy working on her now in the emergency department trying to save her life. Given our experience of these sorts of patients, we wouldn't expect her to survive the afternoon.' It's pretty matter of fact; we say it as empathetically as possible but you need to get those words across to parents.

Dr Carolyn Cooper
Paediatrician, Royal North Shore Hospital

When the ambulance put the call through to Emergency, they'd correctly activated the equivalent of a disaster plan, so they activated staff from all relevant departments to be on site in Emergency when the children were brought in. There were other paediatricians as well as myself, there were nursing staff, anaesthetists, surgical — a whole number of people from different departments. I can recall being told that there'd been an accident in a childcare centre, a fire, and some children had been injured. They didn't know how many children, they didn't have any other details, and I was asked to be down in Emergency.

The first child who came through was Sophie, although at the time we didn't have her name. At that stage we weren't exactly sure of how old she was — it was difficult to tell, but to see a child who's obviously distressed ... She's a strong child; when she came in she was awake, she'd been given some pain relief en route but she was still alert at that point, clearly distressed and clearly had obvious injuries. It hits you, but everyone got working immediately to get the intravenous lines established, to get her comfortable, get appropriate pain relief, sedate her so that the things that needed to happen could happen with minimal delays — it was very much a team approach. At that time no one knew how many children were involved, so there were other teams available to go if another child came though the door.

You meet many people through the emergency department and some are more memorable than others. If there's something very much out of the ordinary, something that you're not anticipating, that does stay with you. Sophie was obviously in some pain even though she had pain relief on the way, but there was that spirit there; she was still alert enough to have that spirit.

We're not a children's hospital so we're not regularly dealing with children who have been in such horrific accidents. The impact of any accident involving a child, or any child who has been well and then suddenly something happens, touches you. When you go home to your own children you'd give them a hug that night because of what you've experienced.

Andrew Berry
NETS AND CHILD FLIGHT MEDICAL CONSULTANT

NETS is the newborn and paediatric emergency transport service in New South Wales. Hospitals get in touch with NETS when a baby or child needs intensive care which isn't available at that hospital. A specialist team is sent out by ambulance, helicopter or aircraft to treat, stabilise and then carefully move the child. NETS also connects clinicians by conference call to discuss the best treatment and the options for transfer or retrieval.

We were called by the Ambulance Service, who had doctors at Royal North Shore Hospital on the line at two o'clock on

15 December. They were dealing with what they described as a major disaster involving a car that had driven into a childcare centre and exploded into flames and there were multiple children involved, possibly as many as eight. We activated a retrieval team from Westmead to go to North Shore immediately in one of our own ambulances. They were there just after half past two and spent just over two hours with Sophie stabilising her for transport.

With any call, we talk through the clinical and operational issues with the staff in the referring hospital, and in parallel make arrangements for teams to travel and aircraft and ambulances to be activated. A doctor in a hospital like Royal North Shore would ring us and say, 'We have a child who's too sick for us, please come and help'. (In this case the initial call happened to go via the Ambulance Service because it was categorised as a disaster.) Those children need a level of care in transit which is comparable to the level of care they're going to receive at the destination, otherwise they go from being in a reasonably sophisticated place to being in an ambulance with some oxygen and that's all, which is a backward step.

Firstly we have to decide how quickly things will happen, and what advice can be given about the treatment that's happening in the referring hospital. To do that we connect a number of people who are ultimately going to be involved in the care of a child, by way of a conference call. We connected the head of Emergency of North Shore with the intensivist at The Children's Hospital at Westmead and a duty burns surgeon who was operating in another hospital at the time — that was Peter Hayward. Teams from NETS were also on the line.

By definition, any disaster is something that overwhelms the normal process. We weren't dealing just with Sophie; we were dealing with what could have been eight children and trying to make judgements about what the priorities were. They weren't all at North Shore, some of them were still in transit by ambulance from the scene and heading towards other hospitals. Sophie sounded like the most seriously injured child so our immediate reaction was to send a team to North Shore for her; we redirected the ambulances with other children that were being sent to smaller hospitals like Manly and Mona Vale to go to North Shore and Sydney Children's Hospital. The Ambulance Service had taken some cases to other hospitals because they made a presumption that North Shore was unable to cope, whereas in fact that wasn't true. If those other children with less severe burns had gone to places like Mona Vale and Manly they would only have needed our teams to move them from those hospitals because they wouldn't have been cared for there anyway. So essentially NETS was doing the choreography, to prevent children needing a second transfer. And NETS was coordinating things with the most senior people in each hospital — in this case the Director of Emergency Medicine at North Shore, the intensivist from The Children's Hospital at Westmead, the Director of Adult Retrieval and the intensive care specialist from Sydney Children's Hospital. We were talking to all these different people to try and deal with all of the children in the most efficient and clinically appropriate way.

The job as a NETS consultant is to have an overview; for the NETS team, their job is to focus on an individual. As on any mission, they went to North Shore with the idea that they would supplement the care being provided already and enhance the care in place, rather than coming in to take over. After stabilisation into the NETS mobile life support system, it was decided to expedite their journey to the burns unit at Westmead by using helicopter transport and Child Flight was sent straight from another NETS mission to complete Sophie's journey from Royal North Shore to Westmead.

Sophie's case represents a real Everest in terms of clinical challenges. She was in a really good place in North Shore, in that she had access to a burns surgeon who deals with children in other parts of his job, and we had all the assets which you would put together to solve a problem — if it was solvable. There were all the challenges of a very serious burns case, but she probably had the best set of circumstances — short of her having this accident right outside the burns unit at Westmead.

Wendy Bladwell
NETS Team Member

We were at the NETS base when we heard that some children had been injured in a childcare centre. Then we received a call saying that Sophie — well, we didn't know her name at the time — needed to be retrieved from Royal North Shore back to the Children's Hospital burns unit, so we were dispatched. The call was triaged through the NETS consultant; they dispatch a team, so Paul Crouchman and I got in an ambulance and drove over to the North Shore Emergency Department.

When we walked into the emergency department there were surgeons, burns staff, theatre staff, trauma staff — just dozens of people surrounding Sophie's bed. I remember thinking, 'How are we ever going to get her stable enough to put her on our stretcher?' When we go to most jobs there might be two or three people surrounding the patient, and we had dozens of people, layers of people with Sophie, performing different procedures. Initially we had to literally stand back, which again is quite unusual — we usually go in and assess the patient after arrival and coordinate from the onset. But with Sophie's case it was very different as there were surgeons performing procedures, and we had to stand back for a long time after we arrived — or certainly what seemed to be a long time, so we were sort of spectators for quite a while before we really got involved. I remember being slowly handed over her care from different people; we had the surgeons telling us what they'd done and the emergency staff telling us what they'd done and nurses telling us important pieces of information.

I remember all the staff performing their roles but at the same time I remember feeling quite strongly that it was an unreal situation, to see a child so badly injured and burned. The best way I can describe it is just like a dream, where everything was blurred — and when you try to wake up your responses are muted. That was how I felt initially: quite alienated, because it was a very unusual and horrific situation to be presented with. I've worked in emergency and intensive care for a long time but this was probably the most horrific burn I've ever seen.

To this day I still remember the smell of burnt skin and hair. We often see burns but not to that extent, not with someone having survived. She almost didn't look like a real person, she was so very badly burned. It just didn't seem real that someone could be that badly burned and still be alive.

Then we received the handover from everybody and very, very slowly and quite meticulously we got her onto a stretcher with monitoring. She was ventilated and she had numerous infusions running to keep her alive, so they were all transferred onto our system. We spent some time making sure we were going to be able to physically move her with some degree of stability. Helicopters have a lot of vibration so we needed to make sure that she was going to be stable enough to be airlifted.

We worked very hard over that hour, constantly adjusting things to maintain her vital signs, keep all her parameters within acceptable levels. Several times we had to intervene when she deteriorated.

I've got a young daughter; she was also in childcare that day, on a busy road. So as a mother of a little girl who happened to be in childcare so that I could be at work, I was just thinking, 'I can't wait to see my own daughter again'. That had a big impact. I'm quite thankful that because we're all so highly trained, a lot of what we did was automatic — not that we did it without thinking, but we could do it without being challenged too much, given all the emotions — mine and those of the other people there.

Because Sophie has such a public life I am often reminded of that day; a lot of the tragic cases that we deal with, you aren't reminded of them again. I wonder how she'll be able to move forward, living always in the moment that she was badly burned and then hit by a car. I worry for her, whether her life will have a sense of normality. I think she's a fighter — that was very evident from the onset, that she was a little fighter and she was quite courageous. People don't usually survive those sorts of injuries. In the emergency room at Royal North Shore there was an almost overwhelming sense of death; I think everyone expected her to die and everyone was totally amazed that she was still alive.

I don't remember the specific things we did, like hanging drips; I just remember the emotional side of it. I remember when Mrs Delezio came into the emergency department for the first time, seeing her daughter lying there, almost unrecognisable to her. As a nurse you don't often get to see [pause] you don't often get to see people so vulnerable. You often see people with lots of masks and lots of protective layers, but that first encounter when Mrs Delezio saw Sophie was really poignant for me. I'll never forget the look in her eyes, the look of pain and fear and helplessness. That first encounter, that's what I remember all these years later. I couldn't tell you what Sophie's heart rate was, but I remember that.

3

In the war zone

About 1000 children are admitted to the paediatric intensive care unit (PICU) at The Children's Hospital at Westmead each year. Their medical conditions range from pneumonia to heart disease, or they may be accident victims, like Sophie. Intensive care requires a level of teamwork beyond belief. Doctors, nurses, social workers, surgeons, specialists: all perform an intricate dance under the conductor's baton of the intensive care specialist. And in the centre is the patient.

Sophie Delezio arrived at Westmead with 85 per cent burns to her body. Her heart arrested on the operating table and again on the ward. No one expected Sophie to live because of the extent of her injuries and the treatments and operations she had to go through; her body was tested to the absolute extreme.

Ron Delezio and Carolyn Martin
Sophie's parents

Carolyn: What impressed us in intensive care — as well as in Emergency at both North Shore and Randwick, where Sophie was taken after her second accident — was that there was a very calm demeanour in a crisis. They all went about what they had to do in an efficient manner, but you never felt unsettled by their stress or agitation. Every one of those children in those beds is critically ill — some are seriously ill, but a lot are critically ill — their lives are hanging by a thread in some cases and there is this calmness.

Ron: The intensivists are a special breed. Jonathan Gillis [intensive care specialist] compared intensive care to a MASH unit [mobile army surgical hospital] in a war zone. You get people coming in with limbs missing, bullet holes — here we are in Sydney and you could be in a MASH unit anywhere in the world.

Brad Ceely

NURSE PRACTITIONER IN THE INTENSIVE CARE UNIT, THE CHILDREN'S HOSPITAL AT WESTMEAD

Brad Ceely admitted Sophie to PICU and was one of the first medical staff to care for her at Westmead.

Sophie came in late one evening. We deal with so many sick children on a day-to-day basis, but the extent of her burns was quite horrific — her feet were completely cooked. They weren't just burnt on the outside, they were burnt right through, they were black pieces of char. Looking at that was quite difficult — and knowing from the beginning she was going to lose her feet.

I know there is lots of stuff in the media saying we wanted to hold back treatment. None of that was unrealistic. Sophie has done fantastically, but for some people that wouldn't be what they want for their child. Ron and Carolyn made an absolutely brave decision and we kept on and I think that is what's made Sophie unique.

When you are having these conversations with families, you are saying, 'The next 20 years is going to look like this', or 'Your life is going to look like this'. Ask the family three days later what the conversation was about and all they are worried about is their child surviving. They are so consumed and that is all they really want. It's not until two years later that they say, 'Wow, this is really what it is about'.

It wasn't just a burn injury for these children, it had been a car, so you are also looking at other things — trauma, broken limbs; you've got spinal precautions in place. The one thing that became apparent was she had quite high pressures in her abdomen because of the skin being burnt and tightening up. Two surgeons had to open up her stomach and expose the bowel, so we could try to relieve the pressure.

When she first came in we allocated two nurses: myself and another nurse. While a patient is in intensive care, it is one-to-one nursing, so all the patients have their own nurse. The thing for me that is most significant is how absolutely devastated her mum was at the time. I remember all her friends saying, 'You have to believe she is such a strong person, she is just about to buy a company' — I think Carolyn was signing papers to buy a company that night of the accident. Yet here was this person in front of my eyes, totally removed from anything that was happening.

For the family, it's an incredibly intense experience — you can't get any more intense. Society is changing and we are becoming more focused on careers; we are always so in control of our existence and our work and our lifestyle. You come to an intensive care setting and you are helpless — there is nothing you can do, you rely on people to give you information and tell you what to do. It is confronting; your whole family changes, everything about you. For families it is a big challenge, because they are putting themselves on the line to go through that learning process and they have no control over the situation, absolutely none. Because of how Carolyn was, I saw that maybe as the biggest challenge.

Every day I come to work and see all this tragedy with children, but I work in an intensive care unit that has 15 beds, which is half the intensive care beds for children across New South Wales — so at the end of the day, most kids are at school having a good time. I don't bog myself down in the whys. For me it is about trying to get them back home, back to having a family, so I am always thinking, 'How I am going to get them home?' as opposed to 'Why did this happen?'. The tragedy has been, it's done — we need to deal with the outcome. It is the outcome Sophie is showing us today — look at where she has come from.

For any family leaving ICU is their first big triumph. In the ICU it is about getting well enough and coming off the ventilator. That is the first time they speak, the first time they say 'mummy', the first time they say 'daddy'. And just knowing they are going to get better, because in ICU they live day to day, hour to hour.

Dr Jonathan Gillis
INTENSIVE CARE SPECIALIST,
THE CHILDREN'S HOSPITAL AT WESTMEAD

Like the conductor of an orchestra, the intensive care specialist coordinates the whole health team in ICU. Their expertise is in life support, but they also take a key role in supporting and involving the parents of each patient. Dr Jonathan Gillis was the intensive care specialist in charge of Sophie's case.

If you judged the world by what came into intensive care you would say there is a war going on outside the ICU doors, because every person who comes in has had something dreadful happen. It is the ward of the unlucky.

For every parent — Sophie's parents or any parents — admission to ICU is a devastating event. Parents come with a mixture of fear, anxiety and hope. The vast majority of parents never cease to amaze me. Most parents would give up their lives for their children innately — not because they are brave, but because it is instinctively what a parent does for their child.

It is difficult coping with tragedy, the uncertainty of what is going to happen. When parents have a critically ill child, they have to hand them over to the care of strangers. They are used to managing everything about them night and day, and suddenly that power is taken away from them. That is very testing. The next thing is the uncertainty — in Sophie's case we didn't know what was going to happen. People are sometimes surprised at that because the image of medicine is that we are very certain, but in fact in these situations it is hard to know what is going to happen.

Ron and Carolyn are good representatives of what a lot of other parents do in the unit. In their time here they were incredibly loving, normal, compassionate parents, who cared for their child, wanted the best for their child and advocated appropriately when they thought things weren't going right, but on the other hand sat down and talked about everything. I am not saying they are better than other parents; they just showed what is good about parenthood in a crisis situation. We have over 100 nurses, many doctors — parents aren't alone in those situations, so their tragedy and their anguish is played out in front of everyone else. That is a very difficult thing for parents and Sophie's parents did that as well as anyone can do it.

Parents who spend a lot of time in intensive care see other tragedies; it is not just their own tragedy. Children do die in our unit and when you are there for a while, you see that. You see what happens to other people and realise that suffering is not purely an individual experience. Sophie's parents did their very best to minimise suffering and help children beyond themselves, which is incredibly noteworthy and praiseworthy.

Sophie's case epitomises the fact it could happen to anyone. Sophie's strength, getting through this — you shouldn't underestimate this, how much suffering and strength is required by the child in this situation.

'Miracle' is not a word we use, but maybe we use other words equivalent to 'miracle'. Public hospital medicine is one of the great altruistic activities in this society. When an extremely sick child like Sophie comes in, everyone works to save her life and to get her better without knowing who she is or where she comes from. It is not done for financial gain, even though of course we all get paid. But the care is delivered in the true sense of public service. That in itself in this society is a miracle.

Karen Upton and Lauren Bradford

Theatre Nurses,
The Children's Hospital at Westmead

The first of many operations for Sophie was the amputation of her feet. Two of the nurses in theatre in that initial operation were Karen Upton and Lauren Bradford.

Karen: That first operation, I'd never ever seen anything like it in my entire career. I've seen extensive burns but never to that degree. And I've never known a theatre to be that silent, to the point where the consultant surgeon is saying, 'For goodness sake, somebody tell a joke'. The whole theatre was in tears with that initial amputation of the feet, it was just horrendous.

Lauren: I'd seen Dr Hayward and he said it was quite bad, but nothing really prepares you for when you see her. Her mum and dad had put a picture up on her bed of her; we had to take the picture away while we were operating because we couldn't cope with the picture and what we were doing. You have to distance yourself to cope with it and then talk about it later.

You know when you get a blister on your finger? That is what it is like over your whole body. You are constantly losing fluids and your acid base is completely out of whack, so it is a credit to the anaesthetists that they performed so many anaesthetics. We had the room temperature turned up so high because burns patients lose a lot of body heat; it was like being in Hawaii, so we were all extremely hot and sweaty. With the visors we couldn't see, we were trying to work quickly, counting sponges … You are working at a very fast pace to maintain minimum blood loss and body temperature, so you don't have much time to think about the actual person until you sit down later.

Karen: Because it was Christmas time I was sitting at home watching carols, of all things, and I just burst into tears. It was just the build-up of emotion I'd kept inside. I think the time it happened took its toll — it is supposed to be a joyous time of celebration and for the people who were working, it was a horrible time in more ways than one.

Lauren: When we had to take part of her ear off, Sophie's dad was saying, 'Can we save the ear?' Dr Hayward was saying, 'She might not make it, you are focusing on the wrong thing', and all he could say was, 'Do you think you can save her ear still?' You just can't cope with the enormity of it; even we couldn't, I don't know how they did it.

Karen: We had another boy and his family come through not that long after Sophie and the tragedy was just as bad; a different situation, but this boy lost his whole family. I can remember when one of the siblings passed away; I was upset but not to the extent I was with Sophie. I think maybe I'd just shut myself down. I felt quite bad that I wasn't reacting the same way as everybody else, but I think I'd seen such horrific injuries. I'll never forget the day they excised her back, to take away the skin that was burnt; I've never seen anything like it in my life. So I think I have been traumatised to that extent, that nothing much else could affect me in that way.

Dr Stephen Jacobe

STAFF SPECIALIST AND MEDICAL DIRECTOR OF THE INTENSIVE
CARE UNIT, THE CHILDREN'S HOSPITAL AT WESTMEAD

Sophie had what we would consider the outer limit of burns that children survive. It is always difficult at that stage, you wonder what is going to happen — it is almost like a fight between good and evil. She was with us for 52 days after the first admission and intensive care is always a dangerous place to be, because children who are there by definition are very sick. There was a lot of intervention, and there were probably many times when Sophie could have died for want of those interventions.

There are children who we believe won't survive and they do; there are others we believe will survive and they don't. Those children who you don't believe will survive and they do — personally, it makes me stop and think; it's a big event when that happens. I guess it's called defying the odds; they are pretty resilient. Without doubt children have an innate resilience — try to keep one still for ten minutes, they just won't stay still; they continue to play and run around and do what children do.

I think Sophie is alive today because a lot of people, including her family, put in a big effort to make sure she remained alive. I don't personally subscribe to the 'divine intervention' connotation of a miracle. Working in intensive care, you see a lot of very sick children get a lot of intense care, and unless that care is meticulous and carried out by people with good intention it may not be successful. Just reading Sophie's initial notes you get an impression of all the people, all the interventions — surgeons coming to visit her, plans being made minute to minute, hour to hour, blood tests, infusions, fluids — it was a big team effort.

Twenty years ago and possibly ten years ago she might not have survived. There is no certainty that all children with 80 per cent burns will survive; some with lesser burns may not survive, but certainly 20 years ago I don't think any children with 80 per cent burns would have survived. If it had happened in a small rural town many hours from medical help, I don't think she would have survived. In trauma they talk about the 'golden hour'; that first hour is vital in terms of whether someone lives or dies. It's hard to say that Sophie was lucky, but she could have died had she not had access to the care that she did.

I went to the Day of Difference [charity established by Ron and Carolyn] ball the other week and saw Sophie up on stage. It is a bit like a *Sliding Doors* experience — you talk to the families initially and say it would be reasonable at this time to stop, but if they take that option the outcome is the death of their child. But when you see children a couple of years later and see them looking well and happy, you see the two potential outcomes.

I'd like to say the lesson we learn from Sophie is not to give up. I wouldn't say, 'Never give up' — that would suggest that no matter how much your child suffers you should continue to allow them to suffer, and I don't believe that is the case. I think sometimes there is a point you should say, 'Enough is enough, you should stop now', but I guess while there is hope you should never give up.

Amy Gaffey

REGISTERED NURSE IN THE INTENSIVE CARE UNIT,
THE CHILDREN'S HOSPITAL AT WESTMEAD

Amy looked after Sophie on her first night in intensive care.

Even though it happened a while ago, things still stick in your head. The other kids we get through with burns or other types of accidents, the situations in which they get their injuries aren't as freakish as Sophie's accident because that is something you would never dream would happen. At the time, my little boy was only eighteen months old. He's in childcare as well — it was just one of those things that could happen to anybody; we are all at risk of something this tragic happening. We see so many things up there in ICU, you are just happy you do go home to your own children.

It still hit hard. You have to be professional and be a nurse, but you can't look like you are not caring; it is really difficult to not let yourself get emotionally involved. It was a situation where none of us could step back and be harsh about it and think, 'No, it's work'. It *was* work and we did what we had to do in intensive care, but we still took Sophie and her family under our wing and supported them. But you can't say to someone, 'I understand what you are going through', because nobody would.

Sophie bounces back — you could never give up on her. There were some times you thought, 'She's not going to get through, there is no way she is going to fight this one' — and she did. Maybe because she was so young — kids bounce back amazingly, whatever adversity they are put up against. Most kids just manage to figure out another way of doing something — if they lose something they had before, they always figure out a way to get moving. When kids are sick, they're sick, and when they are better they are up and running. That is the good thing about nursing kids. Sophie has her days though; she can yell and scream and throw a tantrum just as good as the rest of them, but what child wouldn't? She yelled at me a couple of times in the early days, but we get used to it. We always see the bad stuff; we don't get to see them when they are on the wards and happy, we get them when they are critically sick.

We had Sophie when she was at her sickest in ICU. Stuff that happened up there will always be in my head, but the public don't need to know those details. The main thing that sticks in my mind — apart from looking after her and how sick she was — is just the way her mum and dad handled everything: their faith, having their friends and families coming in, and they all had positive beliefs. They had her favourite music playing — we always had the Wiggles CD playing, always familiar things for her to hear. When children are heavily sedated we still don't know whether they can hear things, so we always encourage parents to bring favourite things in for them. They always had bright things around her, butterflies and beautiful things; you could feel the positiveness in her room. That was one of the good things about looking after her; even though it was awful at some stages, you could feel the love and positiveness in the room. You still do, even now.

Helenne Levy

CLINICAL NURSE SPECIALIST IN THE INTENSIVE CARE UNIT,
THE CHILDREN'S HOSPITAL AT WESTMEAD

When Helenne came on duty for the morning shift, she was the first nurse to look after Sophie during the day. Sophie was in intensive care for over two months — the average stay is three days, so it was a long haul and meant that Helenne and the other ICU staff developed strong ties with Sophie and her family.

We had been listening to the news in our cars and we all knew there had been this horrific accident. I realised that during the day I would somehow end up near Sophie's bedside. As it turned out I was allocated Sophie to look after. The first day, I walked into the room feeling that we were dealing with a desperately critical situation where it was really very unlikely that Sophie would survive, but we had to do everything we could.

I am a parent, but you don't have to be a parent to see the pain and despair in the parents' eyes when they look at their child. You think, 'That could be my child' — or grandchild or neighbour's child or niece or nephew. It takes on a very personal perspective. You see very healthy children who were beautiful and whole turned into something else that their parents don't recognise. Sophie truly was a beautiful child, and still is. Her face was perfect, because she had been lying on her tummy and her body bore the brunt so her face was untouched and so beautiful. We looked at her face and her body, and then looked at this little child in her preschool photo, which we encouraged her parents to put up — it was very hard seeing this child so damaged. In

ICU it is a very high-tech world; we have machinery everywhere and we can't see the children as they really are; we can't see the little child who went to breakfast yesterday morning and then went to preschool. So it is quite profound for us to see a photo of the child that the parents know — you look at the bed, at what we've got now, and look at the pain in the parents' eyes. It is very distressing, but it is good for us to see those pictures so we know who the parents are seeing.

From my perspective there was never any question of what the media called 'turning Sophie off and letting her die'. Her own strength kept her going. We are not veterinarians where we put animals down — we are in the business of saving lives. We kept Sophie going and she continued to live. As one of her primary nurses it was very hurtful to hear on the news that she should be 'allowed to go'. We were much criticised, but within the unit we felt we had no choices. The parents couldn't let go, Sophie didn't let go and we kept going.

It is difficult when they are touch and go. You walk off duty and think, 'I've just been through the most horrific shift, didn't get a loo break, didn't need a loo break because I didn't even have enough to drink to need to go to the loo'. Sophie was often so unstable it was inappropriate to say, 'I'm going to have a cup of tea' — you couldn't do it. Twelve and a half hours of that sort of nursing is just mind-numbing; you come away feeling gut-wrenched by what you've been through.

The critical stage with burns is six weeks down the track, when overwhelming sepsis [infection in the blood] takes over and the children succumb to infection. It was only ten weeks into her admission that we started to feel as though she was going to make it, but we thought she wasn't going to get out of hospital in under a year. As it is, I think she left in about six months. That was a very long time for us to bond with Sophie and her parents. Several of us had the policy of going up to Sophie at the start of the shift and saying, 'Hello Sophie, I'm Helenne, I've come back to look after you'. She was deeply sedated and deeply unconscious, but we always talked to her — 'I'm just going to wash your mouth, Sophie', or 'I'm just going to change one of your dressings'. I wanted Sophie to know my voice and to know my name, and for Ron and Carolyn to appreciate I was treating their child as an intelligent child. Our information was she didn't have a head injury, and we know people who are under deep sedation wake up and have some intrinsic memory of what happened. It just felt as though it added a dimension to Sophie feeling safe. I hoped at some level she knew there was a girl called Helenne who looked after her and would sing little songs to her.

There were many times I picked Carolyn up off the floor, when she was just leaning against the wall and slid down and collapsed. She was in exhausted pain and my heart ached. And Ron, there were always tears in his eyes. To have two parents confronted with this damaged little person that they love and adore, their only little girl — we were looking after three people, not just Sophie. I would frequently say to them when I was on duty, 'Go outside and have coffee, I want you to walk to the garden and get some fresh air; put your mobile phone on and I'll call you if I'm worried'. Initially they wouldn't go, but after a few days Carolyn used to go to the chapel and pray and Ron would stay. After a while they were able to go and do those sorts of things, but it was based on trust — they knew they could rely on any of us calling them back if we were worried. Other than that they didn't leave the hospital.

These situations often fracture families and divorce is a problem. Often one parent blames the other parent for what happened because the child was in one parent's care when the accident happened. But these two parents were not like that, they were so united. When one was crying the other would be strong and when the other one collapsed, their partner would be strong. They helped each other so much, it was almost symbiotic. They were so caring of each other and also at times worried about us. I remember Ron would often say, 'Are you okay?', and I'd say straight out, 'No, I'm not; I'm able to keep going, but we really care that this has happened. Don't think we are just doing a job.' I chose to tell him the truth, not just say, 'Yeah, we're fine' — because we weren't. We could do our job and we weren't sobbing, but frequently there were tears in my eyes when I was looking after Sophie initially.

For a long time after Sophie left ICU there was an emptiness. But we had to let her move on, and the next lot of children came. I will never forget her, ever. I am just one of many; Sophie won't remember me, but I'll always remember her, mainly as a little child who made it against all odds. One day she will dance — Ron used to say, 'She'll be my princess and dance', and we used to look at this little girl who — we were trying to save her life. She survived two horrific accidents; God must have a purpose for her, somewhere there is a challenge and Sophie is going to meet it. She didn't survive for nothing. She survived very damaged, but she survived brave, strong and with a smile and with courage — one of the strongest wills of a child I've ever nursed.

4

A medical miracle

It is comforting to think of medicine as an exact science. The doctors and specialists involved in Sophie's care after the Roundhouse fire are quick to dispel that myth. They are also quick to point out that no one person saved Sophie — it was a team effort in which the nurses and physiotherapists played as big a part as the surgeons. And without strong support from the parents, the efforts of the healthcare professionals would all be for nothing. The word 'miracle' gets used a lot, but for many of the people who cared for Sophie, the miracle was only made possible by the determination of a group of experts who ensured this little girl's survival — however unlikely that seemed at times.

Carolyn Martin
SOPHIE'S MOTHER

The medical team at Westmead were remarkable. Peter Maitz [from Concord Hospital] told me later at a fundraising function, 'We sat down as a team and we made the decision to do something out of the ordinary for this child'. They made that call based on our family and extended family; they saw people around us supporting us, and they knew they had to look outside the square.

Peter Hayward [Sophie's plastic surgeon] is just one of the gorgeous people of the world. When your daughter can die any moment and you are asked whether we should turn off the life support … I said, 'How do you make that decision?' and he said, 'Carolyn, you have to ask yourself, how much can a koala bear?' It was this dreadful scenario. What do you choose, how do you know when to make that decision? His point to us was that she will give us a sign. Later he also said, 'The soul may be willing but the body just not able'. So we waited each day. He seemed to be able to make the complex issues understandable. They were very simple words in a shocking time, but the simplicity of them gave some clarity, and so we had a direction from that point on. Before that we were almost rudderless.

[Anaesthetist] Dave Murrell is wonderful; he saved me. I'm standing in the corridor of ICU bawling my eyes out because Sophie has got her mouth open gasping for ice; she was waiting to go into an operation, and she had been fasted for so long she was desperately dehydrated. And he said, 'Give that child some ice' and 'When is this child being operated on?' He stormed around and spoke to theatres and got things moving. I'll never forget that. She was lying there, this sick, sick child, just gasping. It was ghastly on top of everything else you see your child going through. Dave brought compassion into it.

We got home from hospital in June. We didn't have any other consideration other than getting Sophie well. To us, the event occurred, it is not going to change, let's not focus on why.

Dr Peter Hayward

PLASTIC SURGEON, THE CHILDREN'S HOSPITAL AT WESTMEAD

From the time Sophie came to Westmead, Peter Hayward has been the surgeon responsible for her care. So far, he has operated on her more than 30 times. He will continue to operate on her once or twice every year until she finishes growing.

There is not just one Sophie in my life; for me, Sophie is not a oncer, but the Sophie phenomenon is — I just don't have patients where little old ladies come into my office crying with $50 notes. That dimension I've never seen before.

I think there are a lot of people out there who have taken great comfort from Sophie, enormous numbers of people who see her as a great symbol of hope. But a lot of what has been written and said about Sophie has been people trying to put an adult perspective on it. She is just a child who survived. There is a girl here who had meningococcal septicaemia; she has no nose, no hands, no legs, she had a liver transplant. A boy who was here last week has lost one leg, most of his fingers, is mentally retarded and has chronic renal failure. Their lives are struggles, they are deathly ill; are they brave? They are all brave; they are all as brave as Sophie.

What would make me feel really good is for Sophie to come and see me one day when I was on my deathbed and say, 'You made the right call keeping me alive'. I certainly have a lot of pride in keeping these people alive because it is a technical exercise which requires a lot of dedication on the part of a very large number of people. But there's a modicum of guilt — well,

I wouldn't say guilt, but I would like it verified for me one day by these children that it was worth it. Because it is a bit of a responsibility; I know their parents feel it too.

To me this isn't a rehearsal. People say, 'What is Sophie going to be like as an adolescent, how hard is her life going to be?' But just hang on a minute: if you are an atheist like me, either you are under the ground or above, and it's better, on balance, to be above the ground than underneath it. If Sophie had a really great life between five and 18 and then became chronically depressed and had a terrible life, I would still see merit in that. If you meet Sophie, she is a very happy person. She doesn't have any legs and she's got a lot of physical deformities but she's happy. I can live with that — to me, that's a win. Am I supposed to salvage your life so that every day of the rest of your very long life is absolutely perfect? I don't think so.

I remember two big meetings with the Delezios, case conferences about whether we should go on. I said, 'How much can a koala bear?' and Ron often repeats that to me. It seems to me what you want to hear from your surgeon is, 'Where is the blue sky?' — I'm a blue-sky kind of guy. So I'd say, 'Sophie's had a good day, she is not as septic as she was, her blood pressure is stable, our grafts took from last week'. I tend to say, 'This is what's good, we can build on it'.

We'll probably finish operating on Sophie when she's about 17 or 18. If you look at Sophie's hands and you look at your own hands, the hand has to double in length; the limbs have to double in length, or triple in some cases. The skin grafts simply won't keep pace with that, it is like outgrowing your jeans. They start to get contractures, they say, 'Look, my fingers are tight'. So you have to add on more skin. You can't predict it. You can't look at her neck or her hand or whatever and say, 'That's got a full range of motion, that will be right for the rest of her life'. You can't really do that until she is probably 18, 19, 20. Plus the cosmetic stuff that we want to do, like rebuild her ears, make her a new hairline — a lot of that will get done early in life. We are already working on her hair now.

The reality of it is that the elements of the technique we used with Sophie — the Integra [bioengineered material designed to replace the dermis, the deep inner layer of the skin] and the cultured skin — are far from new. If the skin is the carpet, the Integra is the underfelt — the Integra is artificial. It was patented in the mid to late 1980s and it just didn't take off because it was expensive. Its niche market was the Sophies and at that time, getting a Sophie to survive to make the Integra useful was hard work. Most people burned around 95 per cent were dead. Then in the 1990s the intensive care resuscitation team — which is why Sophie is alive, not me — could say, 'We can keep this child alive for you to have the time to replace their body cells'. Now you go, 'I better have something to put on the surface'. So was it groundbreaking? It was; I don't think there were too many people around the country at the time that badly burned who had been treated with Integra and cultured skin. I don't think any of the Bali victims were — remembering that in the adult world, nobody survives a 95 per cent burn.

If Sophie had been an adult, she'd be dead. By and large, if your age plus your burn percentage exceeds 100, you will die. That means when an 85-year-old woman gets burned in a nursing home because the water is too hot, if her burn is bigger than 15 per cent there is a greater than better chance she will die. As you age, you are dropping off percentage function. At 85 you might have two kidneys but you no longer have double the kidney function needed to live. Your physiological reserve to take shock has quietly slipped out the back door. Sophie came in under that number and that is one of the reasons she is alive. The cutting-edge technology is not a myth, it is true. She was a case of very adept application of technology. That made a big difference, because we didn't have the skin to cover her. Simply put, you have to take off all the dead stuff, so that leaves you skinned. If you stay in that state, you will with 100 per cent certainty die of infection. You have to resurface the patient with — what? You take [skin from] donor sites. A scraping of skin is done with a machine; it takes a shaving as thick as a piece of paper and you then lay that where you want it to take. Skin grafts take the patient's own skin from another site on their body and transplant it onto the damaged area. [The graft is stitched or stapled into position; new blood vessels start growing into the donor skin within 36 hours. Most skin grafts are successful, but in some cases they don't heal well and the grafting needs to be repeated.] But it is a percentage area argument: all Sophie had was one strip of skin, that was it; you've got to cover four limbs, a head and the whole of her back.

If you just had your hands and face burned, they are high priority — these are what get you a job, what makes your living. On Sophie, you've got somebody who will die if you don't get coverage, so you have to go for area. Once we'd made the decision not to withdraw treatment and the decision to go on, then it was just a relentless battle of operating on her and letting her recover from surgery — because the surgery will upset the applecart of intensive care. Lose another couple of units of blood, maybe more, maybe less, add an infection or two along the way, an infected central line [an intravenous tube placed in a large vein near the heart] — it becomes a numbers game. The battle through January was figuring out how we could take Sophie to theatre and get maximum bang for our buck off every anaesthetic. The way it works is, if she is 95 per cent burned, once I've got 40 per cent grafted, then she is only 55 per cent burned — she is a survivor. The patient starts to thrive, they put on weight, their protein comes up, their immune system comes back on line and they are less susceptible to infection. You see this acceleration to health towards the end of the admission.

That's no use to the meningococcal parent — their child has renal failure, they are on ventilators, the whole deck of cards has fallen over, their legs are dead. A lot of these kids would die within minutes of withdrawing therapy. You say to the parents that if you flick those switches it's all over, no pain, your child will never know what happened. But if you ask me to remove the child's legs to save their life, in a week or so you will see that there will never be another opportunity to turn it off again. I don't say it in such pointed terms as that, but you can't revisit that decision. You are left with the aftermath.

But it is effectively impossible for the parents of small children to agree to an NFR [not for resuscitation] order. Most members of the public could do that for an elderly relative. The vast majority of parents simply cannot do it for little children. When you sit down with them, as we did with the Delezios, and say, 'She is going to be missing a couple of legs, she's lost her ear, she's lost fingers on one hand, she's got lung failure, heart failure — we could stop painlessly, quickly and let her go if you wish', parents can virtually never say, 'Yes, do it', but you have to give them the right. It is the hardest choice you are ever going to have to make, but it is not a choice because you are never going to be able to choose.

I try to make the choice conditional. With Sophie I was saying, 'There have been signs of improvement, so if we can let's do some things and see what happens. If Sophie improves, then perhaps she is sending us a message that she is up for this, or at least her body is.'

Sophie was comatose on a ventilator for most of the worst of the worst. I cannot see a logical argument that Sophie's will to live could have been part of it. But when she is off a ventilator and awake she is an excellent patient. Sophie's great strength is that she is able to normalise in periods of good weather between operations and just be happy. Sophie did demonstrate — and her case is very singular in this — an ability to not obsess on what was going on but to just live for that moment. You could say Sophie has a distinct lack of fear about her. She is a very strong example of somebody who is able to find her space in the hurly-burly of a busy hospital and say, 'Yeah, I've got to have a dressing and that's really painful but after that I'm going to watch *Nemo*' — or *The Lion King* or whatever — and get into that space.

I don't think Sophie would be alive without Ron and Carolyn, I really don't. I deal with some difficult parents who make my life a living hell, trying to help their children, and they do that out of a mixture of fear and guilt. If your child is sick you are guilty that you weren't there. I'm quite sure the Delezios will be guilty their whole life that they weren't there to lift the car off her. Subjugated guilt leads to anger; you can't vent your guilt so you get angry with yourself. You can't kill yourself, so ultimately you get angry with people around you — you just have to find an avenue. Usually it is the medical staff. It usually starts around the second week; they go feral, and I try and talk them through their guilt, their disappointment, the stuff that drives it. I never had to do that with the Delezios, not once. That's special.

I think early in the piece they decided this had a meaning. Maybe the fact that their faith was so rock solid, they thought, 'We can do this, we don't understand why but there must be a reason for this; Sophie is going to survive, if we have faith we'll make it'. It has given them a sort of karma they demonstrated throughout the whole thing. And because they demonstrated it, Sophie demonstrated it. You had this horrendous survival situation with relative calm.

Sophie came in at exactly the wrong time of year, at the time of the Christmas shutdown. Some of the heroes of the Sophie story were the nurses who independently rang up and volunteered to do hours whilst they were on holidays, because there weren't enough staff. There were so many competing voices at the time in theatre. I had to say, 'This kid is a winner, let me do this'. If you sent the message, 'I think this child is going to die anyway', then people would not take you seriously. I was asked, 'Have you talked to the parents about not resussing?' — it is a fair question and I was asked it many times.

So if Sophie ever turns around and says, 'What did Hayward ever do for me?' — I think the surgery is just what she would expect a person of my specialty to do. I am the head of the department, I've trained in America, worked in major burns units, worked at Harvard; I should be able to deliver the surgery. If I get in a 747 the guy in the front of the plane should be able to fly it. But I think I was a good and strong advocate in the system, a very compassionate system; that is something that I am proud of.

It is easy to look sleek when all the people behind you are really good. That kid is the most critically injured child I have ever looked after and she is alive — that is due to the triumph of the team and I am immensely proud of that. It's a fantastic thing to be a part of; it must be like training an Olympic soccer team that's gone on to kick the goal. The feeling that you helped get them there, it is exhilarating.

Dr Peter Maitz

MEDICAL DIRECTOR OF THE BURNS UNIT, CONCORD HOSPITAL

One of the country's leading burns specialists is Peter Maitz, who came from Austria in 2000 to establish the New South Wales Severe Burns Injury Service. Peter Hayward called him soon after Sophie was admitted to discuss the options for her treatment.

In theory, we can keep anybody alive. The question is quality of life — will that person ever leave that hospital and if that person leaves the hospital, in what state? I know that sounds a bit politically incorrect but there are patients where we are advising the family not to go ahead with surgical treatment, because once we start, these patients need two dozen operations over six months, will be in ICU, will be drug addicts by the time they come out of ICU because they are constantly on fentanyl [a narcotic drug] and morphine. And we still can't guarantee that they will survive. Medicine is much less a science than people believe. Every person has a different anatomy; there are people who have their heart on the other side of their chest. If I say, 'This is what we can do', well, we can do it but it doesn't mean the outcome is guaranteed, there is no such thing.

The feeling was the family was very supportive of trying to do whatever was medically possible, which is why Peter Hayward rang me. What the Delezio family had to learn is that the medical professionals can do what we know, but the real support and long-term backup has to be provided by the family — we can't do that. I always tell patients that as a surgeon I can transplant skin; it is not a hard procedure. But I can't make that skin heal in — the patient has to heal the skin.

I find it easier to talk to parents of young children than to husbands, daughters, wives, or parents of adults. The parents of young kids are used to having to look after them 24 hours a day. For them to make that commitment seems to be much easier than for someone who is 60 years old: the kids are out doing their own thing and all of a sudden an event like this puts them back into complete dependence on their family.

Peter and I discussed that it was a very good idea to take a small biopsy because Sophie's donor site, which was where we could harvest skin to transplant, was as big as the palm of my hand — that was it, everything else was burnt. The face was only partially burnt, but one would not harvest skin from the face. We took a small biopsy and sent it to our lab. For us it is a routine procedure; Peter and I forgot about this biopsy, we didn't have it in the forefront of our mind. Our concern was to try and excise as much of the burnt skin as possible in the shortest time. Burnt skin will release what are called cytokines into the bloodstream of the patient and these cytokines will make the patient sick, so we wanted to make sure we could debride — cut off the dead tissue — as soon as possible.

Peter started operating on her arms and on her chest and tried to cover as much as he could with skin grafts and other materials which are called Biobrane [a synthetic biological membrane used as a temporary covering over donor sites and excised areas]. All that does is buy her time; you can't leave the tissue exposed, you have to cover it with something. So he covered her arms and chest with Biobrane and then turned to the worst part, which was the back. As we understand it, the engine block of the car came to rest on her back and that is why the back was like a piece of meat on a barbecue, it was just roasted over a long time. Not only was the skin burnt but the structures underneath the skin. It was apparent when we examined the wound that if we debrided it we would be down to muscle and bone.

There is a material designed at Harvard Medical School in Boston called Integra. Originally it was designed to replace the human dermis, which is the deeper layer of the skin — much like leather is the dermis of the cow. Integra has two layers: one layer is made out of all sorts of protein, from shark collagen to bovine tendons, engineered into a thin sponge-like material. A silicon layer is welded on top of it — the sponge is porous, so we need something that is impermeable, otherwise the patient will dry out and not be able to control their body temperature. What that allows us to do is debride the wound, even down to bone and muscle, and use that material to cover the wound; the body will grow into that sponge-like material, but immediately the wound is closed by that silicon layer. Peter Hayward debrided the back, put the Integra on and that wound was closed. Sophie improved, because there was no more burn tissue on her. That all went quite well; the material is prone to infection, but she didn't have a bad infection. At some stage, though, we would have to remove the silicon and put something on that. The Integra covered the neck and shoulders all the way down to her waist — that is 18 per cent of her body surface area, which is quite a large area. And we had only a 3 or 4 per cent donor site.

This is when we remembered — the lab is growing skin, let's see what it looks like. When I talked to my scientists, they said, 'It's fantastic, very good quality'; they had a lot of material there. Unfortunately the literature does not support the use of cultured epithelial autograft [or CEA — taking skin cells from the patient to grow new skin cells in a laboratory] on Integra. Cells need interaction, a little bit like human beings — they don't want to be isolated, so while they have interaction with other cells of the same kind, they also need to be happy interacting with these dermis cells. Now if they don't have any dermis cells, initially these cells will still be alive, under the wound, but eventually they will coil up and fall off; my graft will shear off and die and I will get an open wound. The thought was because we have a small donor site maybe we should just use this donor site to harvest a little bit of skin and mesh it — that is a technique to make it wider; it looks like fish net. When I do that, the skin graft will contain a few dermal elements from the patient and maybe these dermal elements would be enough for the cultured epithelial cells to communicate to them to make them stay. We took Sophie to theatre and removed the silicon, cleaned the wound, took the split thickness skin graft from her available donor site, meshed it very widely, put that on top of the exposed Integra and on top of that, the cultured cells. Everybody was hoping for the best because there was no other option.

My team from the lab was intensely involved: Zhe Li and Sue Taggart. Sue is a nurse who looks after tissue engineered products and the patients who receive them. She did all the dressings and she visited there every day. Sue rang me five days after the operation and said, 'The wound has healed'. Sophie did produce some smaller wounds under the areas and they had to be re-closed, but Peter and I think that what we did saved her life. The surgical part in treating these patients is actually not that large. We rely on the team, especially the burns nurses, to baby our transplants and grafted areas, because if post-operative care is not correct, our operation is for nothing.

I don't think I can say whether Sophie's parents made the right decision. If Sophie will be a happy person; how long she will live; if the family is a happy entity where she wants to live … We are providing a service with the utmost care and knowledge and dedication, but the decisions need to be made by the people affected. We need to educate them and respect their decisions, whatever they are. We certainly respected the Delezios' decision; if it was right or wrong, I don't think it is for us to judge.

Carrie Hopwood

Nursing Unit Manager,
The Children's Hospital at Westmead

As nursing unit manager for the burns unit, Carrie Hopwood's role encompasses both the physical and the psychological side of nursing. She coordinates the care patients receive, as well as supporting her staff, particularly when they are caring for children with devastating injuries like Sophie's.

From the minute you meet the parents you know the journey they have to take, the ups and downs. You can almost visualise that journey, but you can also visualise her walking out that door. I always say to parents that this is what we find easier, because we can see a patient leaving. But in Sophie's case it was really hard to think she would leave hospital. But children are just so resilient and know no boundaries. Adults in similar situations become very depressed and quite morbid about it, whereas children find a way of doing things, whether it be walking on artificial legs or — I've seen a child playing Nintendo with their feet and it is just amazing, whereas I don't think adults adapt so easily.

It was very hard to express how we all felt; the more experienced you become in a trauma role the more comfortable you are with silence and the interaction that goes on and that's how I felt. I said to Ron, 'I'm so sorry; you know that all my staff are thinking of you'. It was one of those moments, I guess.

Sophie's transition to the care-by-parent ward and subsequently her discharge home was so easy — that is something which stands out in my mind. Ron was initially told Sophie would be in hospital a year. I said to him, 'It won't be a year, it could be six months'. When I said that I took a deep breath and thought, 'Oh, was that sensible?' I was going on my experience of children with similar injuries, and I was really pleased that that was exactly what happened, because I can usually predict a patient's journey.

I often have nightmares about situations — not necessarily burns related, but trauma issues. To a certain extent you do listen to the news, you hear about someone being burned. Firstly you hear their age and then you listen to what state they are in, whether they are in New South Wales. Quite often I can go to work on a Monday morning and know what I am going to face, if there is a house fire or something similar. I often am quite stressed on a Sunday night if I know there have been traumas over the weekend. I tend not to read the Sunday papers, I try to avoid the news over the weekend.

Believe it or not [the burns unit has] one of the best retention rates of nurses in the hospital. I attribute that to the fact that we feel very special. The situation with Sophie made us realise the role that we play in helping our children get back into a normal life, and it has made us feel quite proud about what we achieve. We are expert in our field and we have a really good relationship with a team of doctors and people who have worked together for years and years. There is nowhere in Australia where a child could get more treatment. You get a phone call from a GP in Gulargambone or somewhere saying, 'I've got this child here, what do I do?', and you really feel special to be able to help them. We feel Australia comes to us.

Dr David Murrell

ANAESTHETIST, THE CHILDREN'S HOSPITAL AT WESTMEAD

The anaesthetist's job doesn't begin and end in the operating theatre. They also make sure each patient has minimal pain after any procedure. David Murrell got to know Sophie and her family well through the many months and many operations she underwent at Westmead.

I don't think there was a person in the department who didn't care for Sophie, but there were some rather poignant moments that we were all involved in. One I particularly remember was just before Sophie's third birthday. This was several months down the track; she was due to come to theatre on her birthday for some debridement — removal of dead skin and tissue. I got a feeling Sophie's parents were rather hoping she wouldn't go to theatre on her birthday and I remember finding reasons to let her not go to theatre on her birthday. In fact we did cancel it — partly because intensive care beds were a bit tight. Sophie wasn't quite out of the woods but she was certainly getting to the edge, and I think it provided a bit of a break. Some of those moments tended to be a bit of a bridge with the Delezios. I think they knew why we cancelled it, even though from the surgeon's point of view we cancelled it because there wasn't a bed in ICU.

I remember one day on a pain round, Sophie's parents and nurses seemed to be expecting her to go to theatre that day. I was quite sure things were very tight in theatre and they weren't going to have time to do it. It was just normal prioritisation; her trips to theatre took so long we'd wait till we had a good four- or five-hour session. But everybody expected her to go to theatre, she'd been fasted. So I broke away from the pain round and went to theatre and did a bit of sniffing around. I said, 'Are you expecting Sophie today?' and they said, 'No, she's cancelled for today', so I went back and told them. They seemed so grateful to be told that information; people were so caught up with the technical care of Sophie that often those things tended to get overlooked.

There was a particularly moving moment for me when Sophie had her first burns dressing down on the ward. Normally they are just provided with a little bit of sedation, but because of the unique situation she was in we decided to provide general anaesthesia in the burns dressing room, which is a little bit difficult technically. Ron came in; it was the first time he'd seen her burns to the full extent, particularly her limbs, and that was very distressing for him. That was one of the things that we shared together in a way, because I felt part of my job was to support him through that. Week after week those things build up and we understood as much as anybody where they were and what they were going through.

From a medical point of view I wouldn't use the term 'miracle'; I would say 'an unlikely survival'. Technically there were a lot of points where Sophie could have got better, not worse. It's like coming to a T-junction; some patients in intensive care, every time they get to the T-junction they turn left; some patients turn right and they are out in five days, but those people who keep turning left, if they can just get the odd right turn and keep going ... It's good timing, it's good judgement, not doing too much surgery in one day. It was not letting her get too cold, giving her the right amount of blood and fluids, not missing out on the antibiotics when she was in theatre, and attention to detail. And whilst from a lay point of view one can say, 'That's a miracle', when you were there and charting its progress, it is a bit like building a house — an architect has designed it, somebody else who knows how to lay bricks has built it, there is nothing miraculous about it. Sophie's care was a little bit like that; it involved an enormous amount of expertise by a lot of people. Not just surgeons, anaesthetists and nurses, it was the physio, nutrition — nutrition is terribly important after burns; you could say the dietitian played as much a part as we did in many ways.

Through Sophie, we've all learnt never to give up. Not that we would give up but we have learnt that where there is life, you keep going. And you draw strength from people like Ron and Carolyn too. I don't think they ever seriously thought of pulling out.

Siobhan Connelly
BURNS AND PLASTIC SURGERY CLINICAL NURSE SPECIALIST,
THE CHILDREN'S HOSPITAL AT WESTMEAD

When Sophie was admitted to Westmead, Siobhan Connelly was part of the team looking after the long-term patients, starting from admission and going right through to discharge, working on issues such as going back to school, and helping parents learn how to take on the ongoing care for their children. (Siobhan has since left Westmead.)

When Sophie was first brought in, we went up to intensive care, to the first dressing. I look at the wounds; I let intensive care take care of respiration and general life support because I don't like the machines that beep ... So I looked at the wounds and the blood flow to the areas and what sort of condition Sophie was in. I didn't stay very long on that first day, I didn't do a whole dressing; I just had a look, talked to a few people and then moved on from there.

It is very confronting and very difficult for people who aren't in the area. I can look at a wound and see it healed down the track rather than focus on the fact that it is at the acute phase. I was lucky in that I had six or seven years' experience before Sophie came in, and I'd seen a lot of large burns. That's not to say that they don't affect me — Sophie did, especially as she came in when we had four or five children in intensive care and were really pushed to the limits. But you just have to focus on how you are going to help, rather than that these are horrible burns. Unfortunately her fingers couldn't survive and that was very obvious originally, but what we had to do was help her survive to the best of her ability.

When you are talking about wounds, I can say, 'This is what I can do', but when you have someone with pretty much all of their body burned, it keeps you awake at night. With Sophie it did often. You'd question things: are we doing the right thing for her? Especially when they get very sick in that initial period, it is always a questioning game. But if she is strong enough to survive, we are strong enough to support her through it.

With burns, because they've lost so much skin and fluid, it affects every single part of their body; after a 20 or 30 per cent burn it affects all your organs. So every time Sophie survived an operation, every time the skin settled down onto the body after grafting it was a little step forward, but I suppose we weren't starting to cheer for about two months. There are little steps forward, so you have to focus on that.

When they left the hospital we had so many people and so many media there; you just want to push them in their car and let them go. You get a bit protective. At the first Day of Difference dinner, I remember walking past this huge bank of cameras and reporters, and Sophie was sitting in the front like a frightened child and I just wanted to push all the reporters away. But you know, she seems to like it. I think the family would say, 'That's enough' if it was too much for Sophie.

I love the fact that Sophie is such a positive person. Whenever you see her face come on TV you have to laugh. She is the funniest little monkey — I shouldn't call her a monkey, but that is a term of endearment.

Children are amazing. They can survive amputations of both their legs and one of their hands and still sit up and smile and joke around and move on. Sophie is amazing. I don't know why she survived; she is just so strong — which actually strengthens her family. I think if she wasn't coping as well, it would have had a negative effect on her family. But because she is strengthening her family it is coming back in return.

Sarah Clarke

NURSE IN THE BURNS UNIT,
THE CHILDREN'S HOSPITAL AT WESTMEAD

In the time Sophie was on Clubbe Ward [the burns unit at Westmead] Sarah Clarke was part of the team responsible for her day-to-day care.

Initially, large-burns patients are very complicated. There are lots of things going on with all of their body systems; they are very 'busy' patients. From a burns nurse's point of view, primarily what we deal with is the wounds; we do the dressings, which can be every day or every couple of days, it just depends. When you've got a really big burn it takes a long time to do a burns dressing, it can take a good two to three hours. You have to take the whole dressing off; we clean the wound, we wash the wound, we debride any bits of dead skin and then once all of that is done, we wrap them back up. It is no different to a little burn on the arm in terms of the treatment, but obviously it is much more painful when it is the whole body. And you have to be very careful that they don't get too cold, because they don't have their skin. In the bathrooms down here we have special heat lights to keep the room very hot. Up in ICU they generally have a temperature probe which is constantly monitoring their temperature. As soon as it starts coming down, we do things like warm all the water that we wet the dressing with, use warm blankets and wrap them up.

Sophie was a lovely patient; I really enjoyed looking after her. She is a very happy little girl, despite her circumstances, she could always come out with a smile. She was quite young, and things definitely hurt her and things were very painful. But even when she was very sick you could see that underlying personality, and as she got better we just saw more and more of her personality every day.

There is a lot going on for a large-burns patient like Sophie; a lot of physiotherapy, and all of that sort of stuff is painful, and it has to be done every single day. So there was probably never a day when nothing horrible or painful would happen. But at the same time there were good parts to every day; there were certainly rest periods, and play therapy time where it would just be fun and every member of the team would try to make it as fun as possible, or turn it into a bit of a game. That's what you do with children, but it doesn't mean it doesn't hurt.

When you've done this for a while you know the end will come and you know why you are doing things — physio, for example, and the importance of sitting a patient up and getting them to walk. If you just said, 'We won't do it because it hurts them', they would never be able to sit up again, they would never be able to walk again. So you have the knowledge that what you are doing has a good outcome, even though it seems really awful at the time.

Dr John Collins

HEAD OF THE PAIN AND PALLIATIVE CARE SERVICE, THE
CHILDREN'S HOSPITAL AT WESTMEAD

There's no getting away from pain in a hospital. Dr John Collins is responsible for acute pain management (when children have to undergo painful procedures), chronic pain (mostly working with outpatients) and palliative care (working with children with progressive, fatal illnesses).

My most vivid memory of Sophie relates to her phantom limb pain. She had severe pain in the sites where her limbs were previously located and I was involved in the medication and management of the phantom pain. It is very common after amputation. It used to be thought to be uncommon in children, but surveys have revealed it is just as common as in adults.

Sophie also had difficulty sleeping at night. This is not uncommon with children who have been in the intensive care environment; the day–night cycle gets totally disturbed because of all the sedation and so on. The art of it all is to try to work out the cause and treat appropriately. Besides a disrupted sleep cycle, was there pain or anxiety — problems that can cause insomnia in children — was it just the transition, the foreign environment? I think the transition from the intensive care environment was a very distressing time for Sophie. It is not unusual for some children to have sleeping difficulties.

I was also involved with Sophie's pain management after her discharge from the intensive care unit. She had been receiving strong pain medication — opioids, we call them — for a very long period of time. When we are reducing the medications it can precipitate drug withdrawal and all sorts of very unpleasant symptoms. So we are judicious in how we decrease those doses in children — you can't just stop them abruptly. I would touch base with Sophie's family and supervise the decreasing drug doses over time. That seemed to take forever because she was sick for an incredibly long time; she also had had an enormous number of painful procedures.

Sophie was a dear child and very sweet, a very engaging young patient. Likewise her parents are very engaging. You could not help but be compassionate to them for the amount of suffering they were undergoing. This was the most awful thing that could happen to any person really. But they were amazing, in capital letters, absolutely amazing. Very striking and strong in some way; I know they have a very deep religious faith and maybe that is the explanation. They were extraordinarily brave in

Sophie visits Santa with her brother, Mitchell, just days before the accident at the Roundhouse Childcare Centre that caused her horrific injuries.

A peaceful scene at the Roundhouse Childcare Centre at Fairlight, Sydney, where Sophie's first accident took place in 2003.

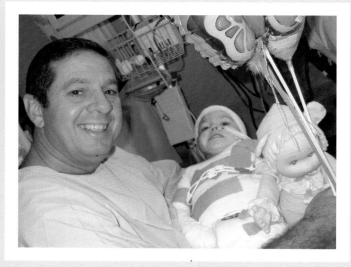

Ron with daughter Sophie in The Children's Hospital at Westmead two months after the Roundhouse accident, surrounded by balloons and toys from well-wishers.

Music therapist, Fiona Lamb (left), and play therapist, Michelle Driver, with Sophie at Sydney Children's Hospital.

Plastic Surgeon Dr Peter Hayward talks to the media about the skin culturing and grafting processes used for Sophie, just before her release from The Children's Hospital at Westmead in June 2004. *(Newspix/Jeff Herbert)*

Dr Peter Maitz, Medical Director of the burns unit at Concord Hospital, shows the bioengineered skin that was used on Sophie's injuries. *(Newspix/ James Horan)*

Sophie leaves The Children's Hospital at Westmead in June 2004, with her parents, Carolyn and Ron, and brother, Mitchell.
(Newspix/Jim Trifyllis)

Sophie and Carolyn (with Madeline) promoting purple wristbands for the Day of Difference Foundation.

Maree Thomas is Sophie's 'fairy godmother', and takes great pleasure in bringing magic into Sophie's life. Here, Sophie has a tissue expander on her head to increase her hairline after an operation.

Sophie enjoys a pony ride on holiday in Byron Bay. In one of the many generous gestures from their supporters, the Delezios were invited to stay at a resort owned by a friend.

As enthusiastic Sydney Swans supporters, Sophie and her family enjoy opportunities such as meeting Swans star Michael O'Loughlin.

Mitchell and Sophie with their grandfather Allan Martin and their aunt Ann-Louise de La Poype.

Carolyn's parents, Allan and Joy Martin, on their 50th wedding anniversary in 2005. Allan and Joy have moved from New Zealand to be closer to Sophie and her family.

Ron's parents, Frank and Mary Delezio, believe that Sophie's survival is nothing short of a miracle.

Sophie and Mitchell in their Power Rangers outfits. Mitchell is Sophie's hero as well as her brother.

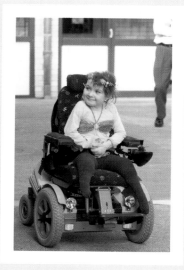

Sophie takes her new wheelchair for a test run. The electric wheelchair helps Sophie to get around quickly and independently.

the context of all sorts of stuff — the possibility she might die, living with the unknown, complications that occurred, coping with her pain management and supporting her through that, being her advocate — consummate advocates of the best kind.

Megan Cluff
CLINICAL NURSE CONSULTANT IN PAIN AND PALLIATIVE CARE, THE CHILDREN'S HOSPITAL AT WESTMEAD

Also part of the pain and palliative care team, Megan Cluff saw Sophie at least once most days, providing sedation and analgesia for painful procedures.

I think Sophie's was one of the largest burns that we have seen in the hospital. She is in a group of her own. With the extent of the injury, typically you would have ups and downs — just when you think you are getting on top of things something would drag it back down.

Unfortunately even once you heal from a burn, the pain doesn't stop. Sophie is quite young and going through huge growth periods. She had ongoing operations for the growing of skin on her scalp; every time she was requiring pain medicine.

Most of my contact was with Ron and Carolyn, because Sophie was so young: [we relied on] their interpretation of what Sophie was going through and how we could help, did they think it was pain, did they think she was just fed up with lying in bed because she is a toddler and would prefer to be running around? Although we are happy to give medication if she is uncomfortable, you don't want to give medication if it can be easily fixed with distraction or play therapy or even getting her out of the room. Once Sophie was awake she was a great little talker, so a lot of the day-to-day management was talking to Sophie and finding out how she felt, and making sure the parents agreed.

Meeting Ron and Carolyn in intensive care, having such a horrific thing happen to their child, they were just always composed. Not that other parents ask unsensible questions, but they just seemed to ask sensible questions, and really got the gist of things well. Because of that they were able to speak so beautifully for Sophie, to get the best out of the hospital for their daughter.

As Sophie was getting better and looking like she was going home, my role changed: trying to give them all the information they needed so they could manage at home, and speak on her behalf to other people who would become involved in her life. Like what happens if she is in pain at school? — this is the best thing to use; this is the best way to go about it; this is the point when you call us. The Delezios are very eloquent in teaching other people about that.

I was pregnant at the time with my first child. I went on maternity leave and came back to work and Sophie was still here. The feelings you have watching a family go through that, being a parent and not being a parent, are completely different. It is very emotional. I think we all try to be a bit stoical, to not show the parents you are upset, but at times you probably should show you really feel for them and what their child is going through. You can see the hurt in them so it hurts you.

Sophie is just like any other little toddler, full of life, full of energy. That is why I love working here — nothing gets kids down. Sophie had everything thrown at her and yet at the end she still had a smile.

Sophie is an amazingly positive child. We see children with ongoing illnesses, injuries, palliative care — often it just gets on top of them and you have to help them out psychologically and use medications to help them get up. She never needed any of that — through play therapy she had a bit of psychological help, but she never needed any medication to make her happy. She has an extraordinary ability to rise above.

All of us whinge about little things. And then you see this gorgeous face on the television smiling and getting on with life and you think, 'Well, if she's able to do that, I've just got to pick myself up a bit more'.

Dr Gary Sholler

PAEDIATRIC CARDIOLOGIST,
THE CHILDREN'S HOSPITAL AT WESTMEAD

While Sophie was in ICU, she developed a series of infections — not unusual for children who are in intensive care for a long time. Infections in the heart can develop, so cardiologist Gary Sholler helped in Sophie's care.

At one phase of Sophie's treatment her circulation was not as strong or as robust as people thought it ought to be, so we looked at her heart and found that she had some mild dysfunction of the heart muscle as well as an area of the heart which had some conditional material on it. We didn't know if that was an infection or a blood clot — both of those things were possible, but she was managed as if it were an infection. Fortunately as her general condition improved, her heart muscle improved, but the area of abnormal material within the heart itself persisted.

There is a bit of luck that follows her around as well as the bad luck she has had, so fortunately things improved by themselves; we didn't need to do anything special in the way of additional treatments. Even after she left hospital she kept coming back and I could see this material inside the heart gradually getting better and better and eventually disappearing.

Sophie has a verve and robustness of soul that allowed her to transcend some of the physical things that were happening to her. Children do that a bit better than adults, and she managed that more than some children could in extraordinarily adverse circumstances. That would be my snapshot of her — she managed as a personality to develop and exist within the war that was going on around her body.

There are physical things that can't be overcome by spirit, but there is no doubt that an ability to move beyond those physical problems — or not be distracted by them — plays a really important role. We are all connected together by a thread as we travel through our life's journey, so the ability to connect with that thread, in spite of what else goes on around you, has a lot to do with moving on to the next part of your life.

I think it is the simplicity of the connection you make with the child — that transparent honesty of dealing with children — that has always been attractive to me [in paediatric work]. The one thing you never do with a child is patronise them; what you do is talk to them and all you ever do when you talk to a child is learn, so that has always been what's motivated me. The other thing is that, in the area of complex cardiac problems, you can make a big difference. If you can make something better you can make things better for a long time; in a way you can make a life happen — and that can be a long life. It means the consequences of things not going well can be pretty substantial. Someone like Sophie is just starting to travel the consequences of what's happened but I sense that her own spirit is such that she will not be impaired by that; the body is a finite thing.

No child exists in isolation from their family and their parents, and no child who is under assault in their physical condition is able to survive without the structure that family supports can offer them. It seemed to me that Sophie's parents have tried to see the obstacles that Sophie has faced as obstacles to be overcome and to be moved around, not obstacles to obstruct and prevent. They seemed to see something beyond where they were at that point in time; perhaps that's where Sophie gets that part of her.

5

One of a kind

The Children's Hospital at Westmead lies 26 km west of Sydney, reached by car along a fairly bleak motorway. But the hospital itself is surrounded by attractive gardens where parents and staff can find a reprieve from their struggle. The hospital foyer features a gigantic wooden 'artwork' — half sculpture, half seat, where adults sit and wait and children clamber.

In Sophie's time at Westmead there were rarely easy days, even for the professionals there who are used to caring for sick children. To the social workers, therapists, volunteers and support staff there, Sophie was one of many — but also one of a kind, her spirit evident from the moment she emerged from her drug-induced coma and opened her eyes. Physiotherapist Johanna Newsom describes working with Sophie as 'a difficult privilege'.

Carolyn Martin
SOPHIE'S MOTHER

A lot of children are in hospital for a short time, and their parents might not feel comfortable about utilising the resources that are there, like walking up to the nurses station and saying 'I want you to page a play or music therapist for me'. I do that every time I walk in, it's just a habit. Some turn up, some don't, but you don't know if you don't ask. That's what they are there for and it just brings great joy and laughter. And the clown doctors — I could spot a clown doctor a mile off, and they would come and entertain Sophie. We made full use of those resources because we wanted hospital to be a happy place for Sophie.

On day three we realised there was this huge public interest in the accident. The outpouring of sympathy was enormous and we soon realised we had to keep the public informed. When you read the first bit of incorrect information in the media, you think, 'That's not right', and we wanted it to be right out of respect for Sophie. [Public relations officer] Debra Fowler worked with our friend, Trudy Wise, and with Ron and me to make public statements about Sophie's progress so the public were kept informed. Debra managed it beautifully, she let us know at all stages what was occurring and would say, 'This is what I've done', 'This is what I suggest we do'. She took control of that, so it was an area we didn't have to think about for some weeks, which gave us a breather. Then when the media wanted to work more closely with us, she worked extremely efficiently to make sure all of that ran very well. She still does a huge amount for us, because we still get packages of mail from Westmead Children's Hospital for Sophie.

Jan Donohoo

CHAPLAIN, THE CHILDREN'S HOSPITAL AT WESTMEAD

Part of an interfaith team, Jan Donohoo carries the trauma pager from time to time. That means she goes anywhere in the hospital where patients, their families or staff want her support — it's based on need, not denomination. Jan recalls the day that Sophie was brought in to Westmead.

What I remember first is responding to the trauma pager and going to the emergency department and being given just a few details of an accident at a preschool. Sophie had not yet arrived. I was directed to go out in the open waiting room and sit with a couple [Sophie's half-brother John and his wife Kate] who were very distressed. They and everyone else were watching the TV news coverage and they began frantically asking me details, but I didn't have any. I moved them out of the public gaze and sat with them until we were told [Sophie] had arrived and had been taken directly to intensive care. People were starting to gather in that waiting area — there just seemed to be people everywhere.

The distress and anxiety of all the people there was just awful. Nobody really knew whether [Sophie] would survive at all, and people were trying to make frantic phone calls ... it wasn't chaotic, but it was terrifying for everybody.

I got into the intensive care unit later that night, about nine or ten o'clock, and went from one family to the other just to let them know that I was there and that I would pray for them. I remember Carolyn grabbing hold of me and asking me to pray and I did. I didn't know what to pray and so I prayed that the best thing for Sophie would happen, and I didn't know if that meant she would live or die. I don't know that I've ever prayed that before, because usually I'm fairly confident to pray for healing. I remember saying — and I've always had this prayer for Sophie — 'You know what this family want, they want their little girl, so have mercy, please have mercy'. I've never cried about this [crying].

As the night progressed Carolyn became more and more incapable of movement and she went into profound shock. At one stage we thought she was in need of medical help. I got Carolyn into a wheelchair and wheeled her up to Westmead Hospital. It was just horrible to watch this woman so totally distressed. A few of her friends came and we got to Westmead and they put her into a bed in Emergency and assessed her. They just gave her some Panadol, and she went to sleep. She slept for a couple of hours and I went home at 5.30 a.m.

For the next ten days, Jan worked 10 to 16 hour days, succumbing to exhaustion on Boxing Day. During that time, Ron and Carolyn were confronted with the choice to let Sophie go.

They talked to me about that several times and although no one knew the future, Ron and Carolyn always wanted the best for their daughter. They saw some terrible things — it was very confronting at every level and I just tried to support them with whatever choices they made and kept calling out to God for mercy — also for skill and insight, care and compassion and good communication for everyone who dealt with this family. We prayed before every operation, every test, every procedure ... not only me, but all the chaplains.

I feel those prayers were answered. Sophie is regarded as a precious child. She has so many things to face that most children don't. What has grown out of it is a very strong awareness of the love that is stronger than death; what sacrifice means; and that, in the midst of terrible suffering and pain and distress and fear, God is real. People say, 'God must have done that so you'd learn'. I don't think He's a user. I don't think He'd cause the accident so Sophie could teach *us* things — that would be using her in the most despicable way. I think there has been mercy shown in the midst of a terrible situation.

I don't call it a miracle. I think technically, medically — absolutely outstanding. I think God gives people skill and perseverance and intelligence and dedication and ability and *all* those things. I just think it is God being merciful to that family, giving them what they wanted, with all the consequences. I think it is a miracle when anyone turns to God and calls out to Him.

I prayed that Sophie's family would be able to call out to God about everything, not just about Sophie's wellbeing, and that their understanding of Him would grow and they would be able to draw on Him in hard times. Not just for her healing, but for patience to hold them together when they were being pulled apart by circumstances; to keep Mitchell [Sophie's older brother] safe; that their friends wouldn't drop away. So I've prayed lots of things for the family — that they will be secure in God's care.

I wonder about Sophie often, about what she is going to have to deal with. The love poured onto this child is generous and a good thing to see, and yet this has had to make Ron and Carolyn ramrod-determined. I've got some questions for God about it all, but I don't think I'm going to get any real answers this side of eternity.

There's an African saying that steadies me:
God is good all the time,
All the time God is good.

Lisa Carnovale

PLAY THERAPIST, THE CHILDREN'S HOSPITAL AT WESTMEAD

In Sophie's time in hospital, she was surrounded by doctors, nurses, therapists, in a bed in a room in a public building, far from the familiarity of her own home. One of the ways of softening the medical harshness and helping her through the days was play therapy.

The play therapist's role is to help children cope in hospital, to try to normalise their environment as much as possible, especially when they go through trauma, as Sophie did. With something like that, it is important to keep things as normal as you can and try to get them to smile at the end of the day. In Sophie's situation you play a big part in rehabilitation — physio and things like that. Sometimes play therapists join in the physio sessions. Also we go into the burns baths and dressings and try to distract the children, so it is a form of pain management as well.

We do it mainly through distraction and relaxation. Sophie had a great imagination, so that made things easy for me. Distraction, relaxing, teaching her breathing techniques — because if a child can slow down their breathing, that automatically decreases the anxiety in the situation. Also forming a trusting relationship — the play therapist is one of the few people children meet in the hospital who is non-threatening. We don't do any medical things with the children, so we're a safe person to know.

I met Sophie in ICU. The first thing I saw was probably her eyes because she had bandages everywhere; the only part uncovered would have been her eyes. The first play session I had with Sophie was a short session, just reading some books to her. The second session was reading and singing some songs with felt pieces of Old MacDonald. She actually started to sing and that just blew me away; here she is bandaged up, could barely move at all except for her eyes. She'd turn her eyes to see me, and she'd start singing 'ee-i-ee-i-oh'. Those few little words, it made such a big impact.

Sophie just made it easy from day one to have a connection. There are some children you come across and it may take a few days to get them to trust you. With play therapy you look for a response in the child to know you have connected with them — even a slight smile. With Sophie you couldn't really see the smile too much but you can see in the eyes if a child is responding. Her eyes are quite expressive. The next time I took up switch toys, which have a button that is connected to a toy — little penguins that come down a ramp, for example. All it requires is a light touch to make it happen; it gets her to do something interactive, because she is playing such a passive role in her time in hospital. No matter what I took in she would go with it — that was something that stood out from the very beginning. Here she was bandaged everywhere, only a few weeks after the accident, and she's already responding.

In baths and burns dressings I learnt a lot from Sophie's mum as well. She would have her own distraction and imagination techniques. She would tell Sophie to imagine a bubble and to pick the colour of the bubble — it was usually purple or orange (Sophie's favourite colours) — and then she would tell her to blow the bubble away and use that as a breathing technique. Some parents are still dealing with their emotions in their child's baths and dressing times; I'm sure Carolyn was as well, but I found she was quite strong and really focused on how Sophie was coping.

There were days when she would be sick or she would have to go to theatre, the pain medication would knock her out. But if she was well enough, every day I would do a session, and the better she got the longer sessions would extend. I also went into her dressings every day, once she came down to the ward (from ICU) — that was the not so good part to it all. But her receptiveness and engagement made it easier. The nurse would come in and say, 'We are going to unwrap the bandages for the first time and we will be seeing this' (for example, her hands without her fingers). I would feel slightly anxious, as it was my first time seeing any child with amputations and burns as severe as Sophie. And then I thought, 'No, the parents are going in, if they can do it I can do it'. My focus would go straight back to Sophie again — how is Sophie feeling, what is she thinking, what is she saying? Sometimes she would make a comment about her feet that weren't there, and I would relay that sort of information to the doctors and the social workers and nurses. All this is important, because as much as coping with the pain it was also her learning her fingers weren't there, or her legs weren't there.

There were always jokes between us. I'd come in and say 'Okay, today we are going to do painting and sticking and Play-Doh', and she would always, no matter what I listed, come out with, 'And what else?' Or I'd have something extra for the end in a bag and she'd be saying, 'What's in your bag?' — not focusing on what I'm saying, but just knowing she is going to get some funny response out of it, too. Just special, one of a kind.

I looked forward to seeing her every day; it was a good experience. Saddening and hard to go through in one sense, but a real pleasure working with her. There would always be a laugh or a smile; I think she probably made me laugh more than I did her, even in the baths and dressings.

Sophie's own motivation and persistence in wanting to do things made it easier as well. I remember one of the first days when she came down to the wards, she was still quite bandaged up. I brought in some soft knitted balls for her to start moving her hands, and I just walked in being silly and put them on top of my head. Straight away she said, 'I can do it!' I'm thinking there was no way she could lift the ball to put it above her head, there was no way she could even move her arms at that stage, so I went up to her and I was trying to sit it on the top of her head. I've still got this great photo in my office, it's one of my favourites, and she was smiling, saying, 'I can do it, I can do it'. Just the grin on her face and the sense of accomplishment, that blew me away.

Cheri Templeton
PHYSIOTHERAPIST, THE CHILDREN'S HOSPITAL AT WESTMEAD

Burns physios get used to seeing their patients wince when the physio walks in the door. Their work involves pain and lots of hard work, but it is a crucial part of the healing process for burns patients. As scar tissue heals it contracts and gets tighter, so the physios position and move the limbs and joints to maintain the range of movement. Later in the process they help patients to learn the basics of sitting and walking again. For the physios, a determined patient such as Sophie is both a challenge and a blessing.

Sophie is a marvellous example of the impact of the courage and faith of a family on a child. In my 25 years' experience as a physio, I've found that in families that stick together, the children do well.

When you read some people's life story, you get a strong sense that they are meant to be here, they have a purpose. I'm not religious, but I believe that Sophie is meant to be a shining example to people. She's got a real role as an advocate for people with scars. In my work, I try to get people with scars wearing backless dresses, strapless tops — being more relaxed about it and comfortable with their skin.

I'm used to seeing the scars, but outsiders can be extremely cruel. Sophie is learning at an early age how to deal with the staring. People look at you for good reasons and bad reasons; look at celebrities like Princess Diana — they get stared at their whole lives. Sophie will have to learn how to handle that. It's important to speak up and tell people — 'I was in an accident', 'I got burned', 'A shark bit my hand' ... you have to meet them halfway. There will be times when she will be distressed by people's reactions when she is older, but I hope that she has the support networks in place now that will continue to support her through that.

For [Sophie's brother] Mitchell it has been very hard. With burns the whole family has the crisis, the whole family suffers. Parents in particular can find the staring and public response very hard; when people say, 'What's wrong with your child?' — or even, 'What did you do to her?' — they can feel accused.

Sophie has a determined strength to her. With her, 'no' means no — but there are ways of winning her over. As a physio working with burns patients, everyone hates you — you get used to it. I've heard it said that if your patient likes you, you're not doing your job! You have to do the hard stuff, the painful stuff, and it doesn't make for warm feelings. But Sophie — I remember once seeing her and she looked at me and this smile just started at the corners of her mouth and got bigger — that beautiful smile she has.

Johanna Newsom

PHYSIOTHERAPIST, THE CHILDREN'S HOSPITAL AT WESTMEAD

I first encountered Sophie in intensive care on the first day after the accident. I assessed the extent of her injuries — what areas were burned, or in Sophie's case what areas weren't. We were working to try and save as much movement at her joints as possible. Initially it involved a lot of positioning, splinting, moving her limbs around on her behalf while she was too unwell to do it herself. As scar tissue starts to heal, it contracts, it gets tighter. In any area of high movement such as across a joint, movement becomes restricted. Scar tissue will act like a thick band, so if you're burnt on the front of your elbow it will pull your elbow up into a bent position and you will have a lot of trouble straightening it out. We need to position the joint at each extremity so you can bend it as much as possible and so you can straighten it as much as possible, and actively move it through that full range of movement from fully bent to fully straight to make sure it's not stiffening up.

We didn't touch Sophie that first day. I went up with the other physio working in the burns unit at the time and had a look at her and worked on a bit of a plan as to how we might position her if she pulled through those first few days.

Between me and Michelle, the other physio who was in the burns unit at the time, we'd spend many, many hours every day with her, giving different exercises, applying splints and plasters. As she was getting better and starting to wake up more and being able to move more, we moved into the rehab side of physio — helping her learn to sit again, helping her to roll over, strengthening muscles, those sort of things.

We had the benefit of Cheri Templeton, the burns unit senior physio; she has over 20 years' experience in burns, so she has seen an awful lot in that area. There's nothing new about what you do with burns, it's standard physio: maintaining muscle length, maintaining movement, increasing strength, retraining function and movement. It's just a matter of applying it to the person in front of you.

Sophie was extremely motivated. She's a very determined young lady, almost to the point of stubbornness. There were times she was adamant that she was going to do something and that was just the end of the story! She presented a new challenge every day. Some days you'd walk in and she wouldn't have a bar of you, didn't want you to come near her, would scream the place down and you'd have to carry on regardless. Other days you'd come in and you'd think, 'Okay, she's got a sore here or she's going to need to have surgery here, how are we going to get around that today?'

Sophie was a fighter, she was never going to be one to lie back in bed and want you to do it for her. She was fiercely independent; she used to try to put her own splints on, or try to help with her plasters — anything like that, she'd want to have a part of it. When we got to the point where we were measuring her for pressure garments to help with her scar management she'd want to hold her own arm up and tell you where to put the tape, always wanting to help.

For the six months she was at Westmead, I would see her almost every day. It was really, really hard to go in there and do what we had to do. A lot of what we did hurt her, a lot of what we did was unpleasant, was painful. She didn't like it, and she didn't understand why it needed to be done. She was only two and a bit when she was burnt so she didn't understand what was going on. As time went on physio became a little less painful and more fun. Being able to take her in the pool or play in our gym, to encourage her to crawl or to sit by herself or to roll — it was easier to see the joy in Sophie then. It makes putting her and her family and friends through all that pain and trauma so much more worthwhile when you can see the end result.

She changed a lot in the time that she was in. Obviously she wasn't able to talk to us when she was first in, but her personality changed and she went from being quite shy to being quite boisterous and very well able to express what she wanted, what she needed and how she felt — there was no mistaking that.

Both her parents were very involved with her care and her physio. After Sophie was discharged we had them plastering her every night at home so that she didn't have to come into hospital every day, applying the splints and doing the stretches and exercises. Ron used to come in the pool with us. They were with Sophie every step of the way and I think that helped them to cope because they were doing as much as they could be doing, as well as being reassured that we were doing as much as we could. I would describe the Delezios as 'go get 'em' kind of people. If they thought something could be done for Sophie that wasn't necessarily being done they would ask why, and they would always listen to the answer.

It was probably one of the most difficult privileges working with Sophie. She was a challenge, a joy, a heartbreak — all sorts of things all at once.

Dr Adrienne Epps

MEDICAL DIRECTOR OF THE BRAIN INJURY REHABILITATION PROGRAM AND SENIOR STAFF SPECIALIST IN THE REHABILITATION DEPARTMENT, SYDNEY CHILDREN'S HOSPITAL

Sophie lost both of her lower limbs below the knee, and Dr Adrienne Epps was involved in her prosthetic management. As well as her role at Sydney Children's Hospital, she is on staff at The Children's Hospital at Westmead and works in the Limb Deficiency Clinic there.

It was a long time after the first accident until she was well enough for us to consider artificial legs — prostheses — for her. The Limb Clinic is a multidisciplinary team — we have a physio, OT [occupational therapist], social worker, prosthetists and medical and orthopaedic specialists. The team looked at what she was able to do at that time, what the potential was for her walking, and then made a collective decision about the prosthetic prescription and components that would be the most helpful for her to be able to get up and start standing and walking as part of her rehabilitation program.

Sophie had lost a lot of muscle and soft tissue as well as skin due to the burns, so it wasn't like dealing with an amputation where there was lots of good muscle and good skin to work around. She had a lot of scarring, very fragile skin, and one of her legs particularly was very thin because of all that loss of muscle and soft tissue. We had to consider what sort of interface was going to be best between the prosthesis and the residual limb, to try to minimise the friction and potential for skin breakdown. It was quite tricky; the prosthetist, David Hughes, had to work hard to provide little silicon liners that were going to fit adequately — initially to allow her to get up and stand and then to start walking. She progressed to the gel liners that she uses now and she does quite well, walking independently.

One of the amputations is through the tibia, the long bone in the lower leg, and it is not uncommon for growing children to get what we call boney overgrowth — a bone spur that can grow through the soft tissue and skin and cause pain and infection, requiring further surgery to treat. That is one of the potential things we have to look for. Because she is growing, her prostheses need to be replaced to accommodate changes in weight, body shape and longitudinal growth as well.

She has one hand that works quite well and she can write and do lots of things. The other hand has loss of fingers and I think there may be plans for the plastic surgeon to provide more movement of the wrist. She could be a candidate for prosthetic management of that hand; we usually find where some of the hand is still present, most people prefer not to have that enclosed in a prosthesis because you lose the ability to feel things and use the sensation, so she will probably never go down that route; she will use that hand to assist the other hand.

Managing Sophie from a prosthetic point of view has been very challenging. The community, public and media interest — that makes it more challenging to deal with. Everybody is in the spotlight. Sophie has been happy to be involved in the media exposure and doesn't seem to have found that particularly difficult. She really thrives in that situation and because she and her family allow their lives and experience to be experienced by others, there is an ownership there by other people.

The fact Sophie's face was spared means you can engage with her without seeing her with a burnt face. Eye contact and facial contact in communication is so important. Also she is the sort of girl who doesn't shy away from contact with people. She is delightful to work with; she has a really engaging personality. She is also very strong-willed. She still 'loses it' like other children when they have had enough and sometimes you've just got to back off and give her space and time to cool off.

She seems to be very motivated to get on and do things. Walking was something Sophie really wanted to do and getting used to prostheses was a process, because her skin had to get used to that extra trauma, if you like, of wearing legs. But she persisted with that. Having the prosthetic legs to get around and be like the other children was very important for her.

David Hughes

PROSTHETIST WHO MAKES SOPHIE'S ARTIFICIAL LIMBS

I first saw Sophie in July 2004 at The Children's Hospital at Westmead. By that stage she was nearly ready for prostheses so she had been through a lot up to that point. Sophie had so many complications. It wasn't just a leg issue, so many other things needed to be mended first — skin had to be good and muscle strength — those sorts of things. Just a healing process.

The first time I met Sophie was really to see how she was going and whether or not she was ready; mainly just to meet with Sophie and Ron and Carolyn. I think I cast her about two weeks after that visit for her first prostheses. That involves getting very messy with plaster bandage — basically wrapping the residual wounds with plaster bandages so you get a plaster mould of their leg. From that I make a positive mould by filling it up with plaster and then those positive moulds are used for the prosthetics. I make the sockets first — the sockets are the parts that go on the residual limb — then I make the rest after that. The type she has at the moment is different to the first pair she had. The first pair had steel knee joints, hinged joints that came up near her thigh and did up with Velcro. The idea of those was to take 70 per cent of her body weight through the thigh instead of her lower body. I wasn't sure at that stage whether or not she would ever go on to anything better than that because she was a big challenge. Just the shape of her residual limbs was a challenge. She'd lost muscle tissue and her left leg is very long and very skinny. So strength was one issue; I knew that that would improve. To a certain degree the skin integrity improves as well, but it is always going to be an issue. In some areas her skin was paper thin and there wasn't much movement. She had a good range of leg movement, but when you consider she has to tolerate the whole body weight somewhere on her limbs — at first it was around the thigh but the legs she is wearing now, she actually takes the weight around the residual limb, from the knee down.

Breakdown of skin has been a problem, but it is not too bad really. The current liners that she wears are made of polyurethane. It has very similar qualities to subcutaneous tissue, so it's got good cushioning. The liner is made slightly smaller than her residual limb; it has a little bit of stretch so it clings to the skin. Any friction occurs outside the liner — between the liner and socket — rather than on the actual skin itself. They had to be custom made for Sophie because she was an unusual size and shape.

The average prosthesis lasts 12 months, but when children have growth spurts they can grow out of them in six months, or even less in some cases. When that happens you can adjust them to a certain degree. In the case of a unilateral [one prosthetic leg], height is an issue, whereas a bilateral is not such a big issue because one leg is not going to be shorter than the other.

The technology has changed in the last ten to 15 years. In some countries they are attaching prosthetics to the bone instead of having a socket outside the skin, but they have had issues with infection. Whenever something inside the body comes outside, there is the risk of infection. Knee joints now can incorporate micro-processors, which allow the knee to respond instantly to information it receives about which part of the walking cycle you are in. There is a lot of development cosmetically too: in some countries they use a silicon finish that is extremely lifelike.

For Sophie's first pair I intended just to have a fitting here first and get her standing, but she was walking almost before I could slow her down. I think a lot of it is attitude; physically she did have obstacles, so her attitude was amazing. A couple of milestones stand out in my mind: when she first walked and when I took away the thigh prosthetics and gave her her current ones. I wasn't there to see her run; I would have loved to have been.

Whenever I think of Sophie she is always smiling. In my mental image, she's got that smile. I don't know if they capture that in newspapers and photographs, but if you ever meet Sophie she has that smile — and she is cheeky as well.

One Saturday, after I made Sophie's prosthetics, a car coming down the road here [outside his office in Lidcombe] lost control and went straight through the wall here. It was a Saturday afternoon; fortunately no one was here. Part of the brick wall was knocked out and flew across ... the car ended up in here. They have since built a steel fence, but it was an amazing coincidence.

Sandra Spalding
Social Worker, The Children's Hospital at Westmead

Sandra Spalding works in the burns unit at Westmead with patients, their families and extended families. Her work continues through to discharge and beyond, helping children make the transition back to school, deal with looking different, build up coping skills. She travels

the journey with the family right through until adolescence and early
adulthood, with new issues emerging at each stage of the patient's life.
She has been closely involved with Sophie and her family from the
night of Sophie's admission.

Having worked here for a long time, I'd seen worse than what I saw that night, so it wasn't so much the visual — although that was distressing — it was my awareness of what might be going on for the family that was incredibly difficult. My heart went out to them. It was a really difficult night for them, and the next few days continued to be incredibly difficult as Ron and Carolyn struggled with feelings of hope and despair and incredible grief. There was never any respite from anxiety, because there was improvement, then deterioration, then improvement, deterioration and so on in Sophie's condition.

There can't be anything worse than losing or anticipating the loss of a child. The constant fear is incredibly painful and draining. Emotions are all over the place — what is the new day going to bring, what challenges, what medical crisis which could mean the end of her life. As parents you don't know what to prepare yourself for, so you are living on high emotion the whole time.

My job was to help Ron and Carolyn contain some of those feelings of being out of control as they gathered medical information — much of which was completely foreign to them — and slowly began to develop some awareness of medical procedures, of what was going on, what was to be expected.

I worked with Mitchell a lot during that first admission, on his own as well as with his parents. The work with Mitchell is ongoing because siblings are often significantly affected, and sometimes they can become casualties in their own right. They can become really disturbed and it can impact on their lives to a great degree. Quite often around adolescence a lot of issues come up about, 'I wish I had been burned; you never loved me quite as much'. All of this can be simmering there without it being recognised, so we try to pre-empt it — so it doesn't get to that crisis point.

At a professional level you are meant to keep a distance, and there is a very clear understanding with Sophie as to what my role is and what we do when we are together. But because of the involvement we've had she's become very special to me and I care very deeply about what happens to her in the future and on a day-to-day basis. I can't prevent difficult times but I hope I will be able to be there for her. I have experienced profoundly poignant, moving moments with Sophie, some very difficult times when awareness of events had to be faced by her. Those were times when — I can get emotional about it now [pause]. Just watching her and her pain is very difficult; obviously she didn't know how I was feeling. Just observing her, and seeing memories coming to mind for her of the events of that day, and the way she coped with it and struggled with it at first, then rose above it.

Sophie has a wonderful, exuberant and outgoing personality — quite poignantly described by Carolyn in the very early days, before I was able to communicate with Sophie. Carolyn said that Sophie would run into her parents' room in the morning and jump onto the bed and say, 'I happy today!' I must admit that I wondered then whether Carolyn would ever hear those words again from Sophie. Listening to stories about Sophie before the accident were heartbreaking, because none of us could know whether she would survive or not. I remember telling Carolyn then that I hoped to have the opportunity of getting to know Sophie.

And of course she did survive, and then she had many psychological hurdles to face. One of these was returning to the Roundhouse for the first time. Carolyn, Sophie and I went into the building, and after some awkward greetings and welcomes Sophie became quiet with her eyes fixed in the direction of the spot where the car entered the building. I watched her as memories flooded back — I tried to 'read' her expressions and the degree of trauma she was experiencing. She remained contained and was able to have her attention redirected to meeting the children. She wanted to paint me a picture — joyous swirls of purple, one of her favourite colours, as though she wanted to express her joy at being back — an 'I happy today' experience!

She amazed me in lots of ways. I am used to working with children so I know how to interpret the kind of information they are giving; they communicate with me through play, you get to know them. I know Sophie quite well and can tell quite quickly when things are not going so well for her. Sophie communicates through expression, and her behaviour. I know when there is something important that is going to be told today. Some of the ways that she lets you know what is going on with her are quite incredible — very deep, very meaningful things, very painful things that she expresses in ways that are unique to her. It is only when you get to know Sophie that you know when to ask the right questions to make the connection between what you are seeing and what it really is. If you ask the right questions you generally get the answers quickly and accurately. I've got toy bears with expressions depicting emotions; when you talk with a child about life experiences — at school, in a park, in public places, at home — they can use the bears to illustrate their emotional response and let me know how they feel about the experience; they identify it through the bear. Quite often Sophie will walk in and pick up one of the bears and hold it, and I know that is the sign of what the feeling is. She does it quite spontaneously sometimes.

I've got many examples of burns survivors who were burned as young children, who are now young adults. Many of them are studying or working and some are married with children. You look at them and say how incredibly amazing their achievements are — and it is amazing, but when you know them and you talk with them over the years you find that there can be an inherent hurt, a sense of regret or loss that they carry associated with their burn injuries. In public situations those with visual burns are constantly noticed, but what people don't see is the pain they may be carrying inside. The patients I've worked with who were burned when they were very young and don't have an awareness of a different 'self' say, 'I think it is easier for me because I never knew myself before burns'. Those who are burned when they are older may be developing an increasingly mature sense of body image and consequent self-esteem, and suddenly that is shattered.

It remains to be seen how Sophie transitions the different developmental stages. The way Sophie is now is really a reflection of the hard work that Ron and Carolyn have put in. That doesn't mean to say they don't have their own periods of pain; there is the constant reminder of Sophie's injuries, but for the most part they get in and do what needs to be done. I think Carolyn and Ron will identify when Sophie needs to be withdrawn from the public spotlight, when it is not what she is wanting. Sophie is a determined little girl, with strong opinions about things; I have no doubt she will make her decision clear. She is quite bossy, you know; she will give me directions and sometimes she tries to avoid my questioning or the angle I want to take with her. She'll dig her heels in and I've got to then negotiate with her as to how much time she will give me working with her on that issue, so she can be in control.

She's gorgeous and an absolute delight to work with; I look forward to seeing her — I never quite know where the journey is going to take us.

Debra Fowler

PUBLIC RELATIONS OFFICER,
THE CHILDREN'S HOSPITAL AT WESTMEAD

The accident at the Roundhouse unleashed a torrent of phone calls, letters and visits from the media and from the public. Debra Fowler managed the media associated with Sophie at the time of the accident, and still deals with the Delezio family.

The response was unprecedented. We were inundated with media calls, all day every day. Burns children can be critical for a very long time and so that status doesn't change, but the media would still ring every day. And it wouldn't just be one journalist from each program phoning — sometimes it would be several journalists from one program phoning. There was a lot of pressure for journalists to get an exclusive on the story, which we couldn't provide until much later in the piece. The response from the public was amazing: toys, cards, flowers just streamed into the hospital constantly. They were sending the hospital money; they were sending the families money. By request of the families, we set up a trust or a fund for monies to benefit burns children, but then anything that came specifically for the families we gave directly to them. There were letters coming from overseas, donations coming from overseas; it wasn't just nationwide, it was an international story.

To protect the privacy of Sophie's family, I filtered that to ensure we didn't have anyone accessing the family who shouldn't have. Including media — in one instance a newspaper journalist was found sitting outside the operating theatre speaking to another patient's family. Our first priority is to protect the family from too much stress being added to what they are already going through. And to make sure there is a balance — providing the media with as much as you can give them, but not having them accessing the family directly. This was such a high-profile case and so extraordinary; it was Christmas and it captured the heart of the nation because it was something that could have happened to any child, your child.

I remember getting a phone call from a journalist saying, 'We understand that Sophie has had her legs amputated', which I didn't know about at the time. I spoke to Carolyn on the Sunday and said that I was getting all these calls. They had a wonderful friend of the family, Trudy Wise, who had experience in PR, and she was putting statements together for the family to release. On the Monday we all had a meeting and said, 'Look, let's manage this together', so Trudy and I managed that side of things together. Trudy was doing the regular updates, and because she was friends with the family it was easier; she was making sure it was exactly what they wanted. Because it was so unprecedented, it was a huge learning experience for everyone involved.

It was such an incredibly stressful time for Sophie's parents each and every day. You don't know if your child is going to survive, what is going to happen next. It is an extraordinary thing to be thrust into that limelight when you are just an average family one day and then headline news the next, and everyone is interested in what is going on and how your child is — not just while you are in hospital but also still today. It was three years in December and people are still interested. When you say 'Sophie' everyone knows who you are referring to.

I think there will always be a media interest in Sophie because she is such an extraordinary child in the way she's dealt with it. She is a particularly strong-willed child and that will serve her very well. She's had to learn to walk again, she has prosthetic limbs, both feet were amputated, she's had to learn a whole new way of getting by. I'm sure she has bad days but I've only ever seen her doing the very best she can and I think that is admirable for a child so young.

Sophie seems to cope with being in the spotlight pretty well. I think if Sophie didn't want to be photographed, she'd say so, because she is a child who speaks her mind. I remember that when we were at Disney on Ice, all the children were having their photo taken with the princess, and she didn't want a photo.

Everyone respected that; it was just me taking a photo for her, not for any media, but she didn't want a photo. I also think exposing Sophie to the public will help Sophie be accepted longer term because people are used to seeing her. People can be amazingly cruel when someone is different. I know Ron works very hard to break down those barriers.

There are many Sophies here at Westmead, they just don't necessarily have that high profile. A lot of children with chronic illness are in here from the time they are born; other children have been involved in serious car accidents or serious burns, or brain tumours, or liver transplants. Children who are brave and courageous and inspirational. It is just that other people don't get a glimpse into those children's lives the way that they do with Sophie.

I remember going up with Santa to intensive care on Christmas Day the first Christmas they were here, which was only ten days after the accident had happened. Sophie opened her eyes; we felt she saw Santa, whether she acknowledged him or not, but she opened her eyes. Santa was very upset at the time, because everyone knew about Sophie. I remember Santa coming back to the office and having a good cry before he was ready to go and visit any other children. I make sure intensive care is my last stop now, because it can be quite distressing. That was certainly a tough day.

I was writing a media release for when Sophie went home and I remember asking what it was that she was looking forward to the most, and she said, 'To lie on the grass and look at the moon and the stars with Mummy and Daddy'. And that is exactly what I put in, because that is what she wanted.

Lyn South

Some say the lifeblood of The Children's Hospital at Westmead is its volunteers. Quietly, they are everywhere: getting a coffee for a weary parent, sitting with a sick child, running a trash and treasure stall to raise funds for the hospital. Ward grannies such as Lyn South are volunteers assigned to give a special level of support to critically ill children and their families.

I would be with Sophie about five hours a day, two or three days a week, to give her parents a break, so that they could have time with their son or go and do shopping or have a sleep or any of those kinds of things. I think I started at the end of January; she was still in intensive care, totally bandaged — a very sick little girl. I was with her until she went home.

I had been with another little girl who had been burned a few years earlier and it doesn't concern me at all. I have a skin condition where I blister, known as EB [Epidermolysis Bullosa], and I have seen children bandaged all over their bodies due to genetic skin conditions so I can deal with that, I don't find it distressing. Some ward grandparents can't deal with children who are burnt — they find it too distressing.

When I first started there her mum said, 'I think this might be difficult for you'. I said, 'No, it's fine'. But I was never there when she had her dressings changed and those major things. I tried to be the comfort person — whenever they had to do something unpleasant I would step back so I could go and comfort her afterwards. She didn't have her dressings changed every day; when I knew it was happening I'd say to her, 'Now, when I come in next week what would you like?' and she'd say 'A cheeseburger, fries, chocolate shake and a toy'. So on my way to the hospital I'd call in at McDonald's; sometimes they'd say, 'We haven't got toys this week, we're not doing the special meals', and I'd say, 'Look, I've got to have a toy, it's more important than the food'. So in the end they got to know me and they would always have something there ready. I would get there and she would be having the dressings put on after the bath or whatever, and I'd feed her McDonald's or a chocolate Freddo or buy her a chocolate milkshake.

When she was asleep or unconscious I'd tell her stories about her family — you know, 'When you go home, Mum's going to take you shopping. Now, what do we put on the shopping list? Strawberries, yoghurt — you're going to make out the list and you'll go down and get in the car and Mum will say have you got your seatbelt on and you'll go to the shopping centre.' When she was awake we'd make stories up like that, talking about when she got home, what they would do. We talked about everything — she's a great chatterer.

She used to love colours like purple and orange; I'd have to scout around and find purple and orange nail polish and I'd paint her fingernails all colours. When the fingers were removed on the other hand she'd put that out; it was all bandaged, and she'd say, 'Paint my fingers on my other hand as well'. At first my eyes filled up because she wasn't realising she didn't have fingers on that hand [pause], so I'd just paint the bandages. I'd do it with the feet too, and I'd always be looking for a bracelet or a hair band or fairy dresses for her.

Her personality, the way she coped — she was just unbelievable. Sometimes she'd just say, 'I don't like that' and her mum would say, 'Well, we've got to do it' and she would accept it. Sometimes she would cry and be upset, but overall she was bright and smiley, despite having the most horrible things done to her. She looks at you with those eyes and she's just beautiful — she's the most gorgeous thing.

The low points were when she'd get an infection or something and be back in intensive care and struggling again. You'd be going along and she'd be coping really well and having a bit of physio; I might go in two days later and she'd be back in intensive care because of some sort of chest infection or skin infection. She'd be back to square one almost and then she'd bounce back again.

I hope I made her happy on some days and kept her busy. Probably I contributed as much to Carolyn and Ron, helping them. Also Mitchell; he would say to me some days, 'Are you going to be here all day with Sophie, Lyn?' because he knew he'd have his parents to himself and that was important for him. She was always pleased to see me and when I ring her now she's happy to have a chat; I think we have a good relationship and I just hope I made things easier for her.

Joyce Duncan

VOLUNTEER, THE CHILDREN'S HOSPITAL AT WESTMEAD

Next year will be my twenty-fifth year as a volunteer at the hospital. With Jill and Marge I run a trash and treasure stall on level one, near Clubbe Ward [the burns unit]. When Sophie first started to come out of the ward and go out into the gardens, she always passed the trash and treasure table. After a little while when she realised we had different things on the table that caught her eye, she'd say, 'Joyce, what treasures have you got for me today?' She was a very polite little girl, she always said thank you and was very selective in what she bought, she didn't just buy anything. Carolyn said that even when she was going to kindy, she was very selective in what she wore and what she took and she always took a bag with lots of treasures in it. So I think from early on in her life she liked to have things of her own. Then of course when she came into the hospital it was important to her to be able to continue on with her life as at home. I think she gained confidence in coming to talk to us and hopefully we were able to play an important role in her recovery.

I am starting to become very involved in raising funds for Day of Difference because what Carolyn and Ron are doing is very important. Sophie and Carolyn came out to my garage sale. I said to Carolyn, 'Take Sophie into the lounge room and we'll have a cold drink and a cup of tea'. Soph is a bright little girl and she really has no inhibitions. She looked at me and looked at all the girls — and these ladies are in their seventies and eighties — and said, 'I'm going to put on a concert for you ladies, so I want you all to sit down and keep quiet, and do as I ask you to do. First of all I want you to clap your hands' — and then she says, 'I want you to stand and wriggle and shake'. Here she is on the floor wriggling and shaking, and she says, 'Come on everybody, stand up and do the things'. She's got a lot of personality and a terrific tenacity, which I found amazing in a little girl of that age.

One day I remember Sophie said, 'I had a bad day at school today, Joyce', and I said, 'Oh, didn't you do your work properly?' She said, 'No, they weren't nice but I was bad to them too'. I asked her what happened, and she told me, 'They said I looked like a monster, and I said I looked like a beautiful monster and they looked like an ugly one'. They have explained to Sophie that she is a little bit different to other people, so she must understand that people will look at her.

Joan Cottrell
Volunteer, The Children's Hospital at Westmead

Joan Cottrell has a special place in Sophie's life: she helps make the specially adapted clothes that Sophie needs. Even now Sophie needs special T-shirts after each operation she has, so Carolyn will ring Joan and ask her to help.

I was here the day of the accident when Sophie was brought in. We didn't have any connection with her then because she was so ill. Then Carolyn wanted a fairy dress made for her — she wanted to be a fairy — so that was the start of my association with Sophie. I do a lot of sewing for fundraising for the shop and different departments for the hospital.

We had to make her clothes in two halves and Velcro them together because she couldn't move her arms. When [the physios] were trying to get her to lift her arms, I thought I'd make her butterfly wings and that might make her lift her arms up. They were organza tulle that floated up and she thought that was lovely. I saw her going in and out of the front door waving and I thought, 'Oh, we've achieved it'.

One morning I was asked to go down to see Carolyn regarding some clothes. Sophie was in the dressing room and had just had her dressings taken off. At that stage she was in body suits, so the physios were just about to put her body suit on and she said 'Mum, show Joan what we bought'. Well, Carolyn produced this tiny little cotton bra and Sophie said, 'I think I'll wear it today'. The physios were trying to get her body suit on and she sang out, 'No, the bra goes on first'. She was adamant; she must have been watching Carolyn get dressed. I left after a while because I couldn't stand watching to see who was going to win; there were three nurses and the physio trying to get the body suit on. Those sort of things happened all the time, she showed that determination.

Carolyn and Ron were telling me, Sophie doesn't think there is anything wrong with her. She said, 'Mum, so and so said she is sorry for me today, why is she sorry?' You know, she just doesn't think there is anything wrong with her.

She's always been an inspiration to me; just recently I had to go into hospital myself, and Sophie sent me photos that she had taken for me because I was going into hospital. There was one of her in her first school uniform and I took it into hospital in a frame and put it alongside my bed. The doctor didn't know whether I was going to come through this op; I looked at the photo and thought, 'Okay Sophie, you can do it, I can do it' and it gave me the inspiration and courage to face that op. I didn't worry about it afterwards and I came through it.

6

A second blow

Sophie's survival after the accident at the Roundhouse seemed a miracle to many. Her injuries were profound and lifelong, yet her motivation — some say stubbornness — seemed to carry her through. With abundant love and support, Sophie was going to Balgowlah Heights Public School, enjoying friendships, and learning to walk on her prosthetic legs — her 'lucky legs', she called them. Then on 5 May 2006, two years and five months after that first accident, Sophie was hit by a car on a pedestrian crossing in Seaforth, near her family home. Again her life hung in the balance.

Ron Delezio and Carolyn Martin
SOPHIE'S PARENTS

Carolyn: The day before the second accident, we had met with Peter Hayward and we had put off an operation, to give Sophie two full clear terms at school with no medical intervention. It would have been her — and our — biggest gap from hospital. We've never had a breather — and in a sense it has probably made it easier. The second accident was almost a continuation. While it was shocking and traumatic and all of that, we didn't have the same first-time shock element to it, so we were able to approach it more calmly. Everyone clicked into the same routine, everyone did what they did before.

You know, it's funny, you think back and think how life could be different. That day was such a beautiful day, I said to Bec [Carolyn's goddaughter, who was pushing Sophie's stroller when it was hit], 'Do you feel comfortable about taking the pram and walking Sophie home from school? Because I can organise a taxi.' I would imagine she would carry enormous guilt, knowing that it wasn't her fault, but still knowing this terrible event occurred. One of the things we've never done is attach blame to anyone.

There are all these weird connections — little miracles that happen. Like Adelle [Pink] — her little girl Emily and Sophie swam together at Arranounbai [Sophie's preschool]. Of all the people to be passing after the accident, she was the perfect person to be there.

Ron: She had no idea who it was at first; then she locked her kids in the car and said, 'You stay there', and was cradling Sophie in her arms, telling her how much she loved her.

Rebecca Myhre
CAROLYN MARTIN'S GODDAUGHTER, WHO WAS PUSHING SOPHIE'S STROLLER WHEN IT WAS HIT

Rebecca is from New Zealand and has always been very close to Carolyn — she was flower girl at Ron and Carolyn's wedding and lived up the road from Carolyn's parents in New Zealand. She was staying with Sophie's family in May 2006, spending time with them before moving over to the UK.

I've always loved Caro to pieces. I'd gone over [to Australia] quite a few times; I went over when Sophie got out of the hospital with the first accident and helped out while Caro's mum was back in New Zealand. The summer after that, I went over and I nursed Sophie and stayed with them the whole summer, which was really cool.

The day of the accident, I was picking Soph up from school; because it was a nice day we were walking. I went out with the dog and picked her up from school and we had an awesome afternoon. There's a shop down from the school and they have little kid's size trolleys. I let Soph buy whatever she wanted — we had so much junk food! All the school kids were there and they were saying, 'Oh Sophie, Sophie' and she was waving at them like she was a princess or something. Then we wandered back and chilled out. We had our afternoon planned; we were going to play dollies and stuff. I'd never actually used the crossing because it was on the other side of the house. But because I had the pram I decided we were going to use the crossing, that would be safer.

We stopped at the crossing and I got Tara [Sophie's companion dog] to sit down; it is a really busy road, so when we were stopped a few cars whizzed past us. The first car stopped; I was looking to the left to make sure that the traffic coming from the other direction was going to stop as well. I started to walk across and — she got hit. I was probably only halfway across the first car but because the pram sticks out so far she got totally

127

caught by it. The pram was dragged further down the road and Sophie was dragged and thrown out of it.

I had a bit of a meltdown. I hate blood — even my own blood is pretty traumatic for me — and I had a big screaming meltdown on the side of the road. You hear about these people who do amazing things in accidents, and I just wasn't one of those people. I was on the side of the road in a complete state; I didn't know what to do. I was too scared to go up to her. Some guy came up to me and gave me a hug and I was saying, 'Is she alive, is she alive?' and he said, 'I'm so sorry, no'. Then a woman walked up to me and said, 'No, she's alive and she's crying; you should come over and talk to her', and I was saying, 'I've got to ring her mum'. My bag was up the street with the pram so I went over to where she was. I went, 'Soph' and I must have been yelling, because the woman was saying, 'Okay, she's trying to have some quiet time'. I tried to ring Caro and I couldn't get through to them and I was trying to talk to Soph. Then there were ambulances and loads of people everywhere. Caro rang me back and I told her what happened, through my sobs. I held the phone to Sophie's ear so Caro could talk to her. Soph couldn't talk, she was just whimpering, but she definitely calmed down when she was talking to her mum. Soph just held the phone there while I was shaking the whole time. Then I jumped in the ambulance with her. I went up to where the helicopter was and just kept in contact with Caro and Ron; there were loads of people working on Soph so I couldn't get near her. I was going to go in the ambulance with her to hospital but Ron wanted me to go back home so I could be with Mitchell.

I was on the phone saying, 'I'm so sorry'. Ron asked me what happened — he's like that, 'What went on, what's happened' sort of thing. But Caro was just saying, 'Stay with Sophie, Sophie needs you to be strong, just be with her, you need to be there for her'.

I had flashbacks for a long time. The biggest thing for me was I felt really guilty. I didn't see Caro or Ron for a while because they were at the hospital. By the time I talked to the counsellor I'd worked through quite a lot of it myself, just by talking to people. I'd spoken to the police too and they told me, 'It's not your fault'. The other big thing for me was to see Sophie and to see Caro and Ron. Once I'd done those things I actually felt more sane about the whole thing. But the night it happened I was on masses of adrenaline; I didn't sleep at all, totally wired. In the morning all my muscles ached from being clenched up.

We couldn't tell Mitchell about it, so Mitchell came home and was saying, 'Oh, what's wrong Beccy?' and I had to say, 'Nothing, nothing, had a bad day'. It wasn't my place to say it to him, it was for his parents to do. Later on that night Ron rang and told him. His cousins arrived [Carolyn's sister Ann-Louise and her two daughters had flown across from France to visit when the accident happened] and they were amazing; for two young girls they were so mature about it. That took my mind off things as well — I made them dinner and hung out with Mitchell and stuff.

I had to change my flight out of Sydney because I was running out of money, so I left when Sophie was still in a coma, which was really hard. I was thinking, 'Should I stay until she's recovered?' but people were saying it could be months before she came out of the coma. She actually came out of the coma the day before I was originally meant to leave. But then I talked to them when they got home. She was just the same, the same strong beautiful girl that I totally adore. I got really upset afterwards but it was a relief, so amazing that she came through.

That man who told me Sophie was dead, I guess when he first saw her she wasn't moving — she didn't move or anything straight away, so that's just what he thought. He was a good guy; I got him to take the pram and the dog back to the house when it happened and he brought over a bunch of flowers the next day.

When the accident happened the paramedics were saying it was a really good sign that she was conscious, it was a really good sign that she reacted to her mum and she opened her eyes. But you don't know for sure — at the hospital some of the nurses were saying, 'Oh my God, she looks terrible' when they'd seen her and I still hadn't seen her, so it was quite hard at times.

The publicity was pretty intense, especially initially — I found it quite invasive. Ron told me not to talk to any reporters but the morning after the accident I was outside and noticed a car hanging around. Half an hour later a guy came to the door and he asked to speak to Rebecca. He said he was from a newspaper, and I said, 'I'm not allowed to speak to the press'. He said, 'Okay, I just wanted to ask if you thought traffic lights on the crossing would make a difference'. I said, 'Yeah, clearly' — bearing in mind I had had no sleep all night and was running on massive adrenaline. I said a few sentences, which they made into an entire article. I guess that I was angry about being tricked into talking to that reporter but I was also thankful that the media never attacked my role in what happened.

I always loved the family; they were such an amazing family before the accident. They would say to me and my friends they didn't even know, 'Hey you guys, come and stay for three weeks'.

They're so loving. Caro's a complete inspiration to me, how she deals with all the stuff she does and still manages to have all this love and devotion. And Sophie's such a sweetie, she's the cutest little thing. She's so funny and really strong — she's amazing.

Adelle Pink
PASSER-BY AT SECOND ACCIDENT

In a remarkable coincidence, Adelle Pink was one of the first drivers to come along immediately after Sophie was hit. Adelle knew Sophie from Arranounbai School.

My daughter Emily has been attending Arranounbai since she was about 18 months old, because she has developmental delays. We met Sophie when she started swimming and there was an opportunity for the two girls to swim by themselves together. In the swimming pool Sophie is amazing. She comes to life and she's a very good swimmer. So that's how we met. I didn't meet Carolyn because the circumstances weren't that way, but I used to watch Emily in the pool with Sophie, so I knew Sophie.

The children were all home and I thought we'd go and get a DVD for the night. I don't usually do this, but I put everybody in the car and we drove down the street. I got to the end of the street and I heard a girl screaming. Immediately I thought, 'A girl's been beaten up', domestic violence or something like that. So I thought I'd stop and see what's going on; even if I can't approach, maybe I can be a deterrent. Then my 12-year-old — who's pretty sure he's psychic — said, 'It's

Sophie'. We couldn't see anything, we only heard this girl screaming. I said, 'What do you mean?' He didn't answer. I pulled up and got out of the car and I saw a child on the road. I told the children to stay in the car and I ran over. Someone had put a towel right up over her head; I ran around to her face and pulled back the towel and saw it was Sophie. I was surprised that there was nobody with her. I realise now that it had only happened that minute, split seconds before. So I knelt down behind her head and told her who I was, that I was Emily's mum, and lifted her head off the road and put the towel underneath so her face wasn't on the tar.

It's like you're in a time warp, a vacuum of time. You're only intent on that one space, right there, and the focus is 100 per cent on that person. Everything else goes away. There were people coming close, but anybody that was shouting, I'd say, [whisper] 'Don't shout, don't shout'. I felt compelled to protect her and comfort her. I'm such an overprotective mother that I would normally have been distracted with my kids in the car, and thinking about what's going on over there. But it was as if they were completely gone while I was with her, talking to her, stroking her head.

She was conscious, but I wanted her to go away from the immediate — you know how you can just drift away and you don't feel things or see things so intensely, your senses are dulled. I wanted to take her away from her immediate pain, so I talked to her about fairies and beautiful places and that sort of thing. It was as if I entered a different place; I didn't know half an hour had passed. I didn't know that I had pins and needles in my legs and feet from not budging, not moving away from that job.

As I sat with Sophie, I felt that she was coming and going, that she was shifting between life and death. Sometimes she was there, was present, and sometimes she was not. It was like an ebb and flow, and I wasn't sure what my job was — whether to keep her here, or let her go. I'm still not sure about that. I'm not a black and white person — if I was, it would be much easier, I guess. It was difficult, knowing what was the right thing to do. [Pauses, recovers.]

I don't want to go into graphic detail about it all. It was quite gruesome, what I saw — what had happened. But the ebb and flow of life, the question of whether Sophie was staying or going — that's the biggest thing that affected me.

When I got there, I thought Sophie was dead. Whoever put the towel over her head did a kind and thoughtful thing, to get something to cover her. It may have been that in covering her face, they simply pulled the towel up further than they meant to. But at the same time, there was a woman nearby who was screaming, 'She's dead!' So with those two things together, of course I thought that she was dead. But when I pulled back the towel, I thought immediately that she was alive.

It was difficult to know if I should help her stay or help her go. But I felt very connected with her — she just felt like my child. She was only a baby. I was drawing on everything I knew to help her. All of me. Anything I'd read, anything I'd felt. I had done Reiki ten years before the accident and I guess I was using that. I've had a couple of experiences where people have had very bad accidents. There was a man who had a building fall on him when he was demolishing it, and he was crushed. I knelt with him and he had his head on my lap until the ambulance came. I guess I drew on that. And all of the fairy stories I've ever read to Emily and the kids about beautiful things.

A friend of ours, John Maclean, is a wonderful man who is a paraplegic and does a lot of work with kids in wheelchairs. My husband had told him that I was at the accident, and John knows Ron through the charity work. We were at John's fortieth birthday party; John came over to me and started talking about Sophie. At the time I was still seeing the trauma counsellor and it was very hard in those circumstances to be confronted with that. I'm much better now, but it's taken a long time to get better, to feel safe and not anxious all the time. Anyway, John sweetly rang Ron and said, 'Maybe it's a good idea if Adelle sees Sophie again as she is now'. So I walked up the street and visited them.

It was hard not to be emotional — that was what I was most anxious about, not being emotional in front of Sophie, because I didn't want to burden her. It was so wonderful to see her and touch her and tell her that I loved her. Sophie was just being her little self — her big self actually. I feel like I'm in the presence of royalty when I'm with her. Because of the stunning beauty of her face — and she is absolutely beautiful when you see her up close — for me, the injuries disappear. When my daughter's with Sophie she notices things like she's got a Band-Aid on her hand. My daughter has never said a word about the major injuries that Sophie had, she doesn't see them. She does see other differences in other people, but she just doesn't seem to see it in Sophie. She'll hold her hand, the hand that doesn't have the fingers, as she did one day when they were swimming together. They came out of the pool together and Emily took hold of Sophie's hand when Sophie was in the wheelchair. She was swinging her arm and singing and didn't notice. It took my breath away, that she could overcome that. It gives me hope.

Emily and Sophie are friends, so Emily goes up to Sophie's place every so often — especially in summer, to go for a swim. They do swimming lessons together as well. The strange thing about it is that this incident is separate from how I see Sophie. I'm fine to see her, give her a cuddle, talk to Carolyn. This event is separate to that relationship. It's like it's its own little story: the Sophie that day was not the Sophie who goes to school and plays with friends and goes swimming. In that moment she was — somebody else, something else. For me, anyway.

About a year after the accident something happened — a change in me, a shift. One day I drove up the street where the accident happened and the charge that I used to feel was gone — almost gone. It's still there; I don't think I'd ever in my life drive up that street without being aware of it. But the terrible pain of it seems to have gone.

My feeling about Sophie is that she is a great spirit, come to do a very big job for humanity. I feel it was an honour to be at her side to do anything I could — to give the love to her to stay here and keep doing the job she's chosen to do.

Dr Michael Novy
SPECIALIST IN EMERGENCY MEDICINE WITH CAREFLIGHT

The NRMA CareFlight helicopter crew sent to Seaforth to treat Sophie consisted of four members — a pilot, air crewman, doctor and paramedic. CareFlight employs its own specialist doctors who are trained in critical care medicine. Michael Novy was the doctor on the team that treated Sophie.

I was part of the team on the Friday afternoon of Sophie's accident, along with the paramedics and the pilot. We were at our base at Westmead when we were informed of a child who was in cardiac arrest after being hit by a car, so we responded at speed. We got there quickly and met up with the ambulances at Seaforth Oval. Myself and the paramedic started to resuscitate the child; it was only at that point we realised that this child had extensive burns all over her body and had undergone some amputations to her lower limbs and we thought, 'This is Sophie Delezio'. It was a shock — here was someone who had gone through so much trauma at such a young age, and so much rehabilitation to get to where she was, only to find her in the back of an ambulance clinging onto life. But you have to exclude the emotional effect that it has on you at the time; you solely focus on the resuscitation of the child.

Sophie was critical, she had obviously lost blood; she was conscious, but her airway wasn't protected, she had a lot of blood in her oropharynx [the area of the throat at the back of the mouth], and was very shut down. Our major concern initially was to try to stabilise her airway so as to gain some IV access, and then to make it safe to transport her. The ambulance officers made the call to wait for medical support to come — her injuries were so critical, she would not have survived an ambulance drive to the hospital at that time of day.

It takes about three minutes to get airborne and then seven minutes to fly from Westmead to Seaforth, so we were on the scene about 15 minutes after being notified of the accident. This happened in peak-hour traffic on Friday afternoon; to get her to a major trauma hospital in an ambulance would have taken a good 30 minutes. So the decision we made was to stay there and treat her to the best of our ability to get her stable and then get her to hospital.

We had the option of flying Sophie to Sydney Children's Hospital or to Westmead. The flying distances were relatively similar, but the transit from the helipad is far quicker and far easier at Sydney Children's at Randwick than Westmead. That was our main determining factor; it was less about taking Sophie back to where she had been previously treated, it was more about doing the best thing for the person we had in front of us. We decided as a team that [Randwick] was quicker, and getting her there would allow us to treat her between the helipad and the emergency department.

Sophie's previous injuries compounded the difficulty of gaining intravenous access. She didn't have all of her limbs and her burns were so extensive. But through the skills of the ambulance officers on the scene, we were able to gain intravenous access pretty quickly and were able to improve her outcome.

The good thing is Sophie didn't have any brain injury as such and it was because of the way in which we resuscitated her on the scene and intubated her and decompressed the problems she had on her chest, which thankfully allowed her to have a positive outcome.

Just two days ago I dealt with a seven-year-old kid hit by a car, very similar injuries, in fact more than Sophie. This can happen to anyone, any child, any family. Ideally we would like to live in a world where no one gets hurt, but that doesn't happen. How many other children don't survive similar injuries, don't survive similar traumas, if they don't have the family and the support that Sophie has? So tangled with Sophie's misfortune there is an incredible amount of support. Do you call it luck? It is fate she has survived these two terrible incidents. In the job I do, you realise how precious life is, how fragile life is. The kids we are given so that we can enjoy life and enjoy our family can be taken away from us at any time. So you realise not ever to go to bed upset with people; enjoy every day for what it is because you don't know when it might be taken away from you.

We tend to do our job and move on. After Sophie I went overseas for my first holiday in a long time. I came back and to see her out of the intensive care unit and interacting with her family — there are not many times there is a tear brought to my eye, but there certainly was then.

Cameron Edgar
AMBULANCE SERVICE NEW SOUTH WALES PARAMEDIC

I am part of the Ambulance Service helicopter crew that responded to Sophie. When we arrived she was in the back of an ambulance on a stretcher; when we opened the side door and spoke to the ambulance crew who was dealing with the patient we realised it was Sophie. Prior to that we had no idea who it was; the only report was that it was a child pedestrian who had been hit by a car and was critically injured. A doctor from the helicopter and myself jumped in and worked in with the crew that had already commenced treatment.

I don't think I'd be talking out of school when I say for pretty much all of us in the ambulance, there was a bit of a gasp when we realised who it was. For us as paramedics it is horrible to deal with injured people at all, let alone kids, let alone someone like Sophie who has already been through something. It took us all aback a little bit, but at the end of the day you put to one side who the patient is and you look at the specific clinical conditions and deal with them.

The first things we need to do in that situation are to find out what injuries have occurred and what the mechanism of the injury has been. [Being told she was] hit by a car gives us a little bit of information, but we need to try and get as much information as possible. We had heard reports she was still in her stroller when she was hit by the car, we'd heard she had been thrown some distance after being hit — all those sorts of things help paint a picture of the level and type of injuries that have been sustained. The other thing we need to do is confirm that information by looking at Sophie and assessing the patient clinically, and work with the crew that has already made an initial assessment and commenced a level of treatment, so we are not doubling up on what has already been done, but adding to what has taken place. That is very much our role as a helicopter medical crew, to make sure we supplement and support the care that has already been delivered by the road ambulances.

I would probably say Sophie is one of the most clinically complicated patients I've had to deal with from a trauma perspective. Particularly because a lot of the indications and the benchmarks to assess someone who has been hit by a car or who has significant head injuries are things such as body structures and the shape of someone's head. With Sophie those sorts of indications were very difficult because she had some deformities and we had to try to figure out whether they were new or pre-existing. I specifically remember feeling all of her head to feel the shape of it, and thinking, 'This is not the normal shape of the head'. We have to make almost split-second decisions as to whether an injury is new or old. With a burns patient it is even more difficult; you have thick burn scars on the skin which makes it more difficult to look for veins when you want to put a drip in or assess pulses. So she was a very difficult little girl for us to look after. If we can't get an IV drip in then we look at other options such as an intraosseous infusion, which is basically a needle that goes into the bone in her leg. We can't put that in beyond anywhere where there may be a break in the bone. Sophie was so difficult to try to get a cannula [tube] in, so we looked at putting an intraosseous infusion in, and one of the areas we were considering was in the area where we thought she had a broken leg. Down the track relatives were able to pass on that, in fact, that was the normal shape of her leg after her initial accident. All that information eventually gets to us, but we've got to make the best decision possible with any information immediately to hand.

When we get in the back of the ambulance, we work with the paramedics who are already treating the patient. We anaesthetised Sophie, one of the paramedics on the road ambulance got a cannula in her arm and then we gave her additional drugs — a general anaesthetic — which are beyond normal ambulance protocol. Once we did that we intubated her, which means passing a tube into her windpipe to breathe for her. The whole idea of that is to put her into a state of suspended animation: to slow everything down and manage all her injuries as best we can, try and take the load off her by doing the breathing for her. It just allows her to be controlled from our perspective so we can do additional procedures. We believed she had collapsed lungs and we had to deal with those by putting needles in some areas. In the back of the helicopter we have very limited room to work, so we do what we can prior to taking off. Sophie was a very unstable patient at the time, one of the sickest I've seen in my 13 years as a paramedic. We stabilised her to a certain degree; then we were going to move her, and then something else happened, so we dealt with that; then we decided we were going to lift her up onto the helicopter and then something else happened, so we had to deal with that. We knew we had a very short trip to hospital; it was exactly five minutes from when we lifted off at the scene of the accident to the time we touched down on the helicopter pad at Sydney Children's Hospital; whatever we did, she ultimately needed to be in hospital very quickly.

There was some very brief discussion of going to Westmead; at the end of the day Sydney Children's Hospital was the closest. When you are dealing with a critically ill patient the history of the patient is important, but getting them to a facility to deal with their immediate problems is the most important thing. Once they are stabilised then the history can be dealt with, either by transferring the patient or getting records brought over to the hospital they are in. Lots of options are put on the table and you make a split-second decision. We also discussed road transport to Royal North Shore Hospital, but we look at things like time of day and the ability for us to get her to the right type of hospital — any adult trauma centre would be able to deal with a child, but at the end of the day we try to do what is best practice. We had the ability to get her further away in a very fast time period, so that is why that decision was made.

We made sure early on in the piece that the hospital was alerted to the fact we were coming in and we would give them more information just prior to us leaving. Giving them that heads-up in advance makes a great deal of difference for us and them. As soon as we take off I get on the helicopter radio and tell the ambulance service operations centre some important details: what our ETA at the hospital is, what we've got, what the mechanisms of the injuries were. We also highlighted the fact this patient had previous medical history; we don't give patient details over the radio in terms of names and so forth. All that information allows the hospital time to prepare for our arrival and when we got there, they were well prepared and worked very well with us. They almost seamlessly moved Sophie from our stretcher to their bed whilst continuing treatment.

A couple of weeks afterwards the hospital invited all the ambulance officers involved in the case to a clinical debrief of the case — what the hospital saw and how they dealt with it, and what we saw and how we dealt with it. That was very important for all of us to see how things went, how we can do what we do as best as possible in the future, but also to get an understanding of what the hospital does and for them to get an understanding about the environments we work in.

At the time of Sophie's accident I had a daughter who was two and a half. It was the first major child trauma case I've done since having a child and that makes a significant difference when you go home at night. The first thing I did that night was go home and go into her bedroom while she was asleep and just stare at her for a while. It makes a big difference, it certainly does.

Aram Kraefft

SENIOR CONSTABLE, METROPOLITAN CRASH INVESTIGATION UNIT

Aram was responsible for overseeing the police investigation of Sophie's second accident. At the time of this interview the case was still subject to ongoing court proceedings.

It started off as a normal day. I was on from two o'clock in the afternoon. I'd been doing a couple of other errands and I was on the way back to the office when I got the call from our referral officer, who told me that Sophie had been involved in a collision. At first I didn't believe it — I think most people didn't. It wasn't until then that I heard the commercial radio broadcast saying that the road had been closed. So I got back to the office in Parramatta and kitted up with all my gear. I arrived out at the scene around quarter past six in the evening and started my investigation.

When I got there the scene was quite well preserved already. I spoke with local police; they told me what they knew about the collision so far. I opened up the crime scene, in the sense that I widened it out to have a wider cordon. I had to be conscious that traffic still had to get through from time to time. Then my main priority was preserving the evidence, finding the evidence and retrieving any evidence that had been removed.

There's a whole science to what I do. First of all I look at the roadway physical evidence, the vehicles involved, the debris or any indicia [physical indications] at the scene that may relate to the impact. Let's say it's tyre marks — are they impact, pre-impact or post-impact type marks? Then it's a matter of distinguishing the characteristics of those tyre marks; I've got to correctly identify how they were caused. It's not just a skid mark on the road, there are many different types of tyre marks and many different ways they are caused: whether a vehicle was accelerating, spinning wheels or braking harshly, whether it's spinning around itself, whether it's through critical speed. Then you look for the areas of initial impact and what's called maximum engagement, which is where vehicles or vehicles and objects thrust most of their momentum on each other. If it's a vehicle-to-vehicle contact you might have gouge marks on the road — road scars. Then there's follow-on scrape marks after impact, and there's debris spray. Debris may include vehicle components or engine fluids, and they tell a whole story about impact zones, principal directions of force and all that sort of stuff. Debris can also include organic matter. In Sophie's case the collision debris included some of the vehicle, such as the plastic surrounding the front numberplate — Sophie's pram was directly in front of the car, it's not as if it was a glancing blow. There was part of her uniform that had been cut off by the ambos and had been left behind. There's debris from the pram itself and organic matter. There was blood on the road, streaks and blood trails, and in the area where Sophie had come to rest on the road there was a bit of blood pooling. At first it is a bit freaky to see that, you think, 'That's a person's blood' —

in particular Sophie's blood — but to me, it's a piece of evidence. You think of it clinically and get on with what you've got to do. It's just a piece of physical evidence, the same as the vehicle, the same as tyre marks, the same as the roadway structure itself.

Of course there's the vehicle to look at too: there was very clear contact damage, imprint marks, on the car, which matched up to the framework of the pram. I had to work out exactly where the pram was in relation to the car when the car hit the pram. We also mechanically examine the car to make sure there are no component failures or defects — steering, suspension, acceleration and all of that.

Towards the end of the scene investigation, I arranged for the offending driver, John Sharman, to be transported to Manly Police Station upon his discharge from Manly Hospital, where I arranged for my colleague to formally interview him. By the time I finished at the scene and got to Manly Police Station, the offender had been interviewed and was waiting in the custody area. I spoke with Sharman for some time, advising him of the evidence at hand, and the pending offences he might be guilty of. After our conversation, I went to the muster room and prepared the event report, facts sheets and the court attendance notices. Once these notices were issued, I prepared a situation report for the appropriate police.

I got to the scene at quarter past six in the evening and I didn't leave there until 10.45, so I spent a good four and a half hours there. Relatively speaking this was a very simple scene. I've had some complex scenes where you've got two or more vehicles involved, there's road scars, there's oil, there's damage, there's different tyre marks, there's all that sort of stuff to capture. So it wasn't a complex scene as such; it wasn't a high-speed collision, there was no evidence of excessive speed.

I've attended over 300 fatal and serious injury collisions since I've been in the crash unit. It was upsetting to hear that it was Sophie who was involved in this, but I just had to kick into work mode, I had a job to do. I had to set the priorities, I had to make sure all of the evidence was firstly going to be interpreted properly, and secondly captured and recorded, because I knew that whatever I was doing at the scene was vital for any evidence that was going to be brought out in the court process, down the track. I completely switch off emotionally and get on with the job. I have become — not cold, but almost robot-like; I've got my set pattern and I kick into that. I'm still human, I still do get emotional at times, but not at the scene. I'll have a debriefing with my colleagues later on, we'll have a talk about it. I can certainly empathise with a lot of the situations that I investigate. I have two young boys who are eight and ten years old, and I could appreciate the anguish the Delezio family had to go through. I was also conscious of the fact that Mr Sharman deserved due empathy and respect. All this aside, I concentrated on switching off emotionally, and dealt with the task at hand.

I've got many investigations happening at one time so I've always got a fairly firm attitude that whatever collision I investigate, I will do it as thoroughly as it needs. I don't care who's involved, whether it's well-known people like the Delezios or someone who isn't high profile at all. To the public they're unknown, but they deserve just as much integrity and just as much thoroughness in my investigation as anyone else would — they're all people. I had to drop everything and work on this one, but I was very conscious not to let that interfere with all the other investigations I've got going.

I contacted Sophie's family the next day. Initially it was to introduce myself and let them know what my role was; I also needed to get updated information from the doctors on Sophie's condition and how she was going. From there on I spoke with Ron and his solicitor, Rod Smith, a fair bit, and just kept them apprised of the progress of the investigation — and of course, the court case as well.

Sophie's parents are absolutely remarkable in their emotional strength, how they could be so focused on their daughter and so composed to the media. Naturally they would have been extremely distraught by Sophie being involved in the second collision and the injuries she suffered. My hat really does go off to Ron and Carolyn for their strength. It shows how much they are supporting Sophie, and that rebounds on Sophie — she knows that she is getting that support, and that has encouraged her as well. They displayed a lot of emotion, of course, but also a lot of courage right from the start. Their attitude was, 'Let's get Sophie better, let's think positive, let's work towards that'. They almost set about a program: 'Sophie *will* get better, Sophie *will* move on'.

Sophie's a beautiful little girl, she really is. She is very strong-willed. Just look at her rate of recovery — she suffered some horrific injuries, and she's got the neurological injuries now. She's got an incredibly positive outlook for what she's been through. She had all these medical procedures to go through but she just took it all in her stride. When I saw her in hospital she was playing with crayons, and it was like talking to a child who was growing up normally with nothing traumatic that had happened to them. She's got a good sense of humour and she's a very cheeky little girl. I was mucking around in the hospital ward and being a little bit silly, as you do with young kids. She said, 'Oh, you're funny' and I said, 'Am I funny or am I silly?' and she said, 'You're funny-silly', and started giggling and laughing her head off. She thought it was absolutely hilarious because I was dancing around doing silly things, and we had an absolute ball. She just smiles so quickly and easily. She's absolutely a little treasure; she's a little angel.

Sophie's second accident sent shock waves around the nation. There can't be many people who didn't react with disbelief at the news. For the people who had worked so hard to help, support and heal Sophie after her first accident, the impact was particularly shattering.

Dr Peter Hayward

PLASTIC SURGEON, THE CHILDREN'S HOSPITAL AT WESTMEAD

I actually started shaking, which I wouldn't want to admit much, because surgeons are supposed to be a bit tough. The thing that is not well known is she came close to dying and the people who saved her there are very similar to the people who saved her the first time. The reason Sophie isn't dead is because people resussed her up on the football field. She arrested up there — cardiac arrest. The guys in the helicopter saved her life, full stop.

The hospital did a great job keeping her alive, but she'd be history if it wasn't for those people.

Sandra Spalding
SOCIAL WORKER, THE CHILDREN'S HOSPITAL AT WESTMEAD

We were here at a meeting at the hospital, and the call came through to Cheri [Templeton] the physiotherapist. It was shattering; I felt like I'd been hit with a sledgehammer. I remember that evening well. It just doesn't seem fair, it just seems so wrong. It is like, 'What is the universe doing, this is not okay!' But that is life, and life is not always fair.

Jan Donohoo
CHAPLAIN, THE CHILDREN'S HOSPITAL AT WESTMEAD

I was at home and I felt physically sick. I heard it on the news, and I used to live around the corner in Seaforth so I knew exactly where it was. It was just awful. We live in a world full of beauty and wonder — and I don't mean just geographically, I mean people — and terrible things happen. People in Africa, South-East Asia and the Middle East have no expectation like we do in the West that everything is going to be okay. We are so individualistic and think we can achieve everything. I can't rationalise what happened to Sophie the second time. It was just a terrible tragedy and it seemed so unfair. I think it is a category mistake to talk about fairness but that's how we judge things — why should this happen to a little child? Does it mean that God doesn't care? No, that's not what it means, because God *does* care, and this family knows that. Why didn't He intervene? I don't know. Theologically, He *has* intervened. For me, the only way it makes any sense is, His own Son suffered and died. That's how He's intervened and it will not be like this forever, it cannot be. A lot of people don't accept that and I understand.

Lisa Carnovale
PLAY THERAPIST, THE CHILDREN'S HOSPITAL AT WESTMEAD

Sophie was one of the first children I worked with who had such full-on, long-term, huge injuries. You try not to get too close, but some kids just draw you in, and she did. When she had the second accident, I was in the car and it was on the radio. I had to stop — I couldn't drive home. I wanted to cry, the first thing that came to my head was, 'She can't go through all this pain again'. I'd seen all the pain she'd gone through; I guess you think you are fine with it, but something like that happens again and it brings it all back.

Johanna Newsom
PHYSIOTHERAPIST, THE CHILDREN'S HOSPITAL AT WESTMEAD

I was told about the second accident face to face by someone who was involved in burns circles. I was told at the end of my work day and I ended up staying at the hospital to watch the news on the TV at the hospital to find out more about what was going on. You couldn't believe that it had happened to anyone, but not to Sophie again. The worst thing was that we just didn't know what was going on. Rightly or wrongly our hospital feels a sense of ownership over Sophie; she's our little girl, she was with us for six months, and we just didn't know anything. It was heartbreaking and it was horrible. All the different news reports you heard for that first 24 hours were so conflicting; some would tell you she was okay, that she was sitting up talking, and the next would tell you that she was two heartbeats away from being dead.

Dr Jonathan Gillis
INTENSIVE CARE SPECIALIST,
THE CHILDREN'S HOSPITAL AT WESTMEAD

I was on duty in intensive care when I heard about Sophie's second accident. It was hard to believe, it was devastating. She could have gone to either intensive care unit; we expected her to come to ours and we found she had been airlifted to the other for logistical reasons. Part of me was unhappy she wasn't coming; part of me was emotionally relieved we didn't have to go through that. We would have liked her to come because it would have seemed more complete. Both intensive care units look after the sickest children in New South Wales so she would have got as good care, that wasn't the point — it was emotional.

Dr David Murrell

ANAESTHETIST, THE CHILDREN'S HOSPITAL AT WESTMEAD

I'm very glad she went to Sydney Children's Hospital; I think it would have been very hard seeing her that night. However hard you push, that emotional response when it is someone you know, it is very hard. I think it was better that she was being looked after by other people who could maintain a little distance. The thought of going right back to losing Sophie would have been absolutely horrendous. If Sophie wasn't going to make it, that would have been too much to bear and I don't think we could have supported Ron and Carolyn through that either; I wouldn't have had the strength to do that.

Craig Davis

PRINCIPAL OF BALGOWLAH HEIGHTS PUBLIC SCHOOL

Her second accident hit so hard because she progressed so quickly at school, she was going from strength to strength, and that just seemed like another blow she didn't need. I guess it knocked everybody around because she had come so far in such a short time.

We were getting media ringing us assuming the accident had happened outside the school and saying, 'You must know about it'. I said, 'Look, we saw her leave that afternoon' — I knew there was no way in the world that it had happened here. We called the staff over the weekend and said, 'This is what we know', so they were ready to support the children when we came back to school on the Monday.

Garry Smith

PRINCIPAL OF ARRANOUNBAI SCHOOL
(WHERE SOPHIE ATTENDED PRESCHOOL)

There were a lot of people here very affected — disbelieving, upset, wanting to know every ten minutes what was the update. We looked to each other for support, rather than looking outside for support. Most of us just needed to talk it out really, just sit and have a coffee and marvel at the bad luck that one little resilient girl can put up with.

Karni Liddell

PARALYMPIC SWIMMER, MOTIVATIONAL SPEAKER AND
MEDIA PERSONALITY

On the day of the second accident, I was at a spinal injury function in Brisbane with Alan Jones as the MC. I went out to a pub for a couple of drinks and my phone kept ringing. Susie Eleman, who is a great friend of mine — she is also a media personality — called me and said, 'It looks like Sophie has been hit by a car'. It was so loud in the pub, I just kept on saying, 'No, no way, it must be a mistake, it doesn't make any sense'. I was thinking, 'How could she be hit by a car, she's hardly ever outside' — with her skin and everything, she really can't go outside a lot. So I ran outside; I was bawling by this stage. I was trying to get a cab, I couldn't push my wheelchair, I was devastated.

I flew down to Sydney; the first thing the guy who helped me off the plane said to me was, 'I'm just so upset about that little girl, Sophie Delezio, do you know who she is?' He was saying, 'Maybe someone is trying to tell her something, maybe she is not supposed to be here'. My heart just broke and I wanted to abuse him, but I couldn't talk. Sophie has survived two accidents, so she has shown us that she has more fight and spirit than most of us, she is definitely supposed to be here with us! When I got to the hospital and saw Carolyn I felt sick when I saw her, but as usual Carolyn was upbeat and positive. I was really trying to hold it together and I sat above the bed and talked to Sophie. She was obviously unconscious, and she opened her eyes for the first time and she looked at Carolyn. A few tears came out of her eyes and everybody ran over to put her back under.

7
Two steps ahead

A ripply 'canopy' over the entrance to Sydney Children's Hospital echoes the waves at nearby Coogee Beach. In the foyer, bright painted butterflies dance and flutter overhead.

Sophie was admitted with a brain injury, punctured lungs, nine broken ribs, a broken jaw, a broken collarbone and fractures in her spine. Ironically, Sophie and her family benefited from the fact that they had been through a serious injury before; they knew what it was like to be in hospital, how the system works. Sophie surprised her doctors and therapists at Sydney Children's Hospital — as paediatrician Dr Jonny says, 'She was always two steps ahead of where I thought she'd be'.

Ron Delezio and Carolyn Martin
Sophie's parents

Carolyn: One of the wonderful things that happened is that the two hospitals worked so well together in joint care. Jonny Taitz wasn't on duty that night, but he came in immediately and walked with us from Emergency to have the CAT scan and took us up to intensive care — he just babysat us a little. Peter

Hayward came over from Penrith and John Harvey [head of the Westmead burns unit] came over from Westmead; we had a team. Peter Hayward didn't have to be at Sophie's bedside every night; John Harvey didn't have to be there; the CEO of Westmead didn't have to be there. But they all rallied and gave us a great deal of support. Each of them, particularly Peter Hayward and John Harvey, were in heavy discussions with the intensivist working with Sophie, and they were able to relay the information to us in language we understood, so we weren't having to deal with new doctors.

Ron: The second accident was a completely different injury. Even though Sophie was in a coma and very sick, we'd had the experience with something a lot worse before so we were much calmer about it. It was easier — if we can say that.

Carolyn: She was still acutely unwell, but for maybe four months in Westmead we didn't really know if Sophie was going to survive, whereas we knew by day five at Randwick that she would survive. Every day we were getting more positive signs, though it was still very serious. As Peter Hayward said, 'The miracle in this one is Sophie surviving the lung injury'.

Once we were through those first few days I would coordinate these teams of people to come, the music therapists and play therapists. They enjoyed having Sophie as their patient because she was so receptive. One day we'd gone back in for more surgery and I'd rallied the troops. We were in a day-stay ward and there were kids who had just been sedated for theatre, so we moved down into the playroom and we were having a little music session singing Hi–5 songs. Then another child came in with her parents, then another child — there ended up being six children in there with their parents, all having a music session and singing songs. There was music and joy and singing and laughter coming out of this playroom in a hospital environment, and I thought it was wonderful for Sophie to be the catalyst for that.

Dr Matthew O'Meara

DIRECTOR OF EMERGENCY, SYDNEY CHILDREN'S HOSPITAL

Dr Arjun Rao

PAEDIATRIC EMERGENCY FELLOW, SYDNEY CHILDREN'S HOSPITAL

Like everyone, the staff at Sydney Children's Hospital in Randwick were stunned by the news that Sophie had been hurt again. But they had to set emotions aside to give Sophie the best possible treatment. Dr Arjun Rao was the team leader in Emergency when Sophie was brought in.

Arjun: We have a dedicated phone in Emergency that the Ambulance Service rings through on. It has a different ring, so as soon as it rings the whole department knows — we call it the bat phone. So everyone knew the details — it was a five-year-old girl involved in a car accident, we had some idea of the serious injuries.

Matthew: We've got equipment for everyone from a prem baby up to a 120 kg adolescent, so that gives us time to get equipment ready. Also to get an idea of people we need to call; if it is an all-hospital response, we pull in people from all around the hospital.

Arjun: We put out a medical emergency or a trauma call — in this case it was a trauma call. We've got staff in Emergency as well, but we have to manage how many of those doctors we can take into the room with us, bearing in mind there is still a busy emergency department to run, with other sick children.

Matthew: We often have three doctors and three nurses in Emergency plus intensive care doctor plus ward registrar and resident, plus anaesthetic registrar, hospital coordinator, radiographer, porter — social work of course is part of it. I'll show you the size of the room, it's not very big . . .

When any child comes in, they would come into the resus room. We transfer the children onto our resus bed and we receive a handover from the staff involved in pre-hospital care, who tell us a bit more about what's happened, what injuries they have assessed and what management they've instituted. It is really important the room is quiet because there are lots of people there; we are all listening so we know where we are at, where we are starting from. It is unusual in Sophie's case that she was brought straight from the accident scene to a children's hospital. Most people who are injured get treated on the scene by an ambulance crew, paramedics who are very good at managing life-threatening problems, and take them to a big hospital. But there is a trial going on at the moment, sponsored by the NRMA [National Roads and Motorists' Association], called the HIRT [Head Injury Retrieval Trial] trial for head-injured patients. They are trying to see if rapid retrieval with a doctor to the place where they are going to continue their care improves the outcome of people with head injuries. Because Sophie had a head injury, the team listening to the airwaves about all the ambulance cases thought, 'This sounds like it could be one for us'. The doctors can do even more than the paramedics — they can use drugs to put her to sleep, to help her breathing. So instead of going by road to the major trauma centre, which would have been North Shore, not only have they got their medical and paramedic expertise in the helicopter, they also have that vehicle to move them to one of the kids' hospitals.

Arjun: The helicopter lands at the helipad, just under 100 metres away, on this level. So she got straight here rather than going to one hospital and then another one later — particularly important for kids who need urgent operations.

Matthew: Sophie got really good care from the scene on; she didn't need a major operation. Most kids with injuries don't, most need good care: getting their airway right, getting their breathing right, getting their circulation right, giving them fluid and blood. Most of it is really good paediatric nursing and medical care, and that is what she got.

Arjun: We start with A,B,C [airway, breathing, circulation] — and then neurological status, what the level of responsiveness is like, what we think the injuries have been, and looking at pupils. Then we progress to what we call a secondary survey, where we'd look for other injuries. We roll the child and look at the back and we either address things as we find them or note them as something that needs to be addressed later, but keeping in mind all along the main things are airway, breathing, circulation.

Matthew: The problems with airway, breathing and circulation are the things that will kill you. What we try to do is fix the problems rapidly to keep the child alive. Even though it might be obvious they've injured their legs or have a big cut on their head, there are things that might be more important than the obvious ones. We have a very structured way of dealing with it. The kids who are conscious and awake we obviously have to deal with differently; one person talks to the child and explains what's going on. In Sophie's case she was anaesthetised so she wasn't aware of what was going on. She was not aware of the helicopter trip, coming across to Emergency.

We knew it was Sophie coming in. It didn't really change anything, because it's a standard approach. The main thing that was different with Sophie was all the media reaction. The job at hand is looking after a child who has been injured; you've got 30 or 40 other people in the emergency department who are also your responsibility, and the media is just a distraction. It is an enormous event in any family's life for their child to be injured. We want to be getting on with the job, but we don't want to intrude on Sophie or any other child who is critically injured, or the other people in the department. They are here because people are sick. It's not like *ER*. There isn't the shouting, there isn't the romance. On the telly things happen perfectly and people shout out a bunch of acronyms and things get done straight away. But sometimes it is quite difficult to get things done.

When things are stable, the parents come in. We talk to them, explain what is going on, let them see their child. We try to involve them as early as possible. If there are lots of things to be done and there isn't much room, sometimes that needs to be a few minutes later than we would ideally like, but that's all part of it. In Sophie's case, there was a lot to do; we got them in at the earliest stage we could, which was once we'd really stabilised everything and there was physically room around the bed to come in and hold her hand.

Dr Jonny Taitz

PAEDIATRICIAN AND CLINICAL OPERATIONS ASSISTANT DIRECTOR, SYDNEY CHILDREN'S HOSPITAL

'Dr Jonny' was Sophie's paediatrician and had been caring for her since the first accident. When Sophie's second accident happened he was working at Sydney Children's Hospital (he was previously at Royal North Shore Hospital).

I actually wasn't at work that day; I'd gone to a meeting in the city and I was on my way home when I got a call from Paul Francis, who is the chairman of the Humpty Dumpty Foundation [a children's charity] and a good friend of the Delezios. He told me that Sophie had been knocked down. My first response was shock — I couldn't believe it, I thought he was kidding. I said, 'Are they certain they have the right Sophie Delezio?' — it couldn't possibly happen to the same girl twice. She was finally getting better, she had a six-month surgery-free period, and this happened.

Our first call from the helicopter was that she wasn't breathing, she had a very low level of consciousness and her pupils were not equal in size, which is very serious as it implies serious brain injury. The heroes of the day were definitely the CareFlight team. They responded to her injuries and stabilised her. She was quite distressed and in a lot of pain. She had a severe head injury and she wasn't making a lot of sense. They correctly decided to anaesthetise her and get her to the Children's Hospital. Most of the doctors in the team were at Westmead but Randwick is closer, which is the key.

She got here at about quarter to six on the Friday evening. Again I was faced with the very real prospect that Sophie might die, and having to tell Ron and Carolyn that I thought this was a likely scenario. We then went from there to the CT scanner and I had to sit with the parents while they phoned Mitch again, the second time, and said, 'Your sister has been badly injured'. I always think of Mitch — he's done it pretty tough. He's a sensitive little guy and having seen his sister involved in two serious accidents and the loss of his parents for protracted periods of time is not ideal for a growing boy. People sometimes lose sight of that.

So we were there in the scanner and fortunately the first scans were much better than we thought — didn't show any serious bleeding, didn't require any surgery that night, just stabilising in ICU because of her injuries, which were many broken ribs, bruised lung, bleeding and a broken collarbone. She remained on a breathing machine because with all those ribs broken you can't breathe properly. We had a lot of problems with her bleeding that night; we used a new drug called Nova 7, and that stopped the bleeding. That turned things around. She spent a considerable period in ICU — about ten days. We were very worried about infection because she had all the tubes and lines. Drips were a major difficulty — because of her severe burns it is impossible to put in a line, so we had to get a senior paediatric anaesthetist involved to help us with venous access.

We had a lot of discussions about whether she should be transferred to Westmead where everyone knew her, or stay on at Sydney Children's Hospital, Randwick. Ron and Carolyn were quite determined for her to stay at Randwick and we supported that decision. We were conscious our colleagues at Westmead would be feeling desperately uncomfortable about a long-term patient of theirs being treated at another hospital. We always try to do the right thing by any family with any injured kid, and Sophie is no different to any other child in terms of that philosophy. So she stayed on at Randwick for a further three to four weeks.

It was a gradual process, one day at a time. Each day she would improve, mostly; some days there would be setbacks. Our biggest problem was pain relief, and her feeding — in fact I broke one of my rules, I actually recommended Ron go to McDonald's to get some hot chips. We don't normally do that for kids in hospital because of the nutritional content, but I was so keen for her to start eating. I was so desperate I rang the good folks at McDonald's and they brought in some burgers and chips and milkshakes. Sophie had some and the parents and staff enjoyed the rest, so that wasn't too bad for morale.

There were a lot of problems with the injury to the back of her head; the skin graft was initially unsuccessful so we had to regraft it a second time. The plastic surgeons used a specialised system called the VAC system [vacuum-assisted closure therapy, in which a pump is used to help the wound to heal and reduce infection].

Gradually each day Sophie would become more animated; she was surrounded by pictures and cards and gifts. Sophie has become something of an icon in Australia and beyond. She represents the fighter in all of us — someone who can overcome horrific injuries and get on with her life without feeling sorry for herself.

We were flooded with gifts for Sophie; the postie was doing two extra rounds just to deliver gifts and cards to Sophie. We had a candlelight vigil outside where kids came and wrote cards — even those who had never met Sophie could identify with her situation. I have never encountered such an outpouring of support. The media were camped outside for days when the story broke. I think the Delezios got up to 16,000 emails. People were following the story from the UK, the States — even one of my colleagues from South Africa saw something about this case.

Sophie is unfortunately one of many motor vehicle accident victims we see at this hospital and at Westmead. Some will die. We try to say we have plenty of children like Sophie. Sophie just happens to be the most well known. We want to stress that we look after all children — that is a very important message. I would like to think we treat everyone as equally as possible.

I think it is also important that people appreciate the teams that have gone into saving Sophie. I might be one of the most recognised of the team but it really is a team effort at our hospital. We are all deeply committed to improving the lives of all children in New South Wales and beyond. I don't take any credit for anything personally, apart from telling Ron and Carolyn that their daughter might die — twice, and I'm glad I've been wrong twice. I don't mind being wrong on these occasions.

Doctors don't like to use the word 'miracle' a lot. Sophie's survival from her first accident *was* miraculous, though. I didn't expect her to survive — I didn't give her a chance at all, given the horrific nature of her injuries. But behind every miracle is a team of hardworking professionals: doctors at the children's hospitals, the burns surgeons, the ICU nurses, their dogged determination, the work that these professionals do is what allows miracles to happen.

Sophie is tenacious, independent, strong-willed, determined, a fighter, a true blue Aussie. A joker, determined beyond belief. She is someone who is deeply loved by her family and the staff at both hospitals; someone who lights up a room immediately, despite her injuries. But she's also a kid just trying to get on with her life. Sophie goes to school and she does her homework and she has a dog and a brother and parents and grandparents and friends. She just happens to be in hospital a lot of the time, so we try to make things as normal as possible. She has special needs and will for a long time, but she is just a little girl trying to get on with things, and she needs to play with her mates and do the things that children of her age do.

I know Sophie has started asking questions about the accident and wanted to review the site and who was with her, which is good and we encourage that. But children have a very concrete way of thinking; when she is a teenager she will become more reflective and abstract. She will question this very deeply and this will affect her and we shouldn't lose sight of that. Issues of sexuality, puberty, of partnerships — those are all going to have major bearings on her.

Sophie always surprised me; she was always two steps ahead of where I thought she'd be, given the severity of her injuries. One day she waited for me and got up and walked — we weren't expecting her to do it. When she left hospital we planned for her to come out in a wheelchair. I turned around and much to my shock she was walking out on her prostheses, which she had only been doing for a day. She was determined to walk out of the hospital. That was an amazing moment for all the staff — that is what it is all about for us.

Anne Hardwicke

NURSE MANAGER FOR INTENSIVE CARE UNIT,
SYDNEY CHILDREN'S HOSPITAL

Sophie came in after I had left on Friday afternoon. As I got home I remember seeing the chopper come in, as our house overlooks the city.

When a patient first arrives there is a flurry of activity. I guess intensive care staff and to a degree emergency staff like that adrenaline buzz, that's what makes them work well — it's difficult for others to understand, but they enjoy the high intensity, the urgency of things. That's when people pull together and function really well.

It was perversely fortuitous that the family had had a significant ICU experience before, so they were already very conscious of some of the key things that protect a critically ill child, such as hand-washing, and the way systems work in an ICU. The family imparted that quite early on — 'Don't worry about us too much, we know what we need to do to protect Sophie'. But they were just distraught, so emotional and psychological support for them was offered by nursing staff, medical staff and social workers. Many other staff unwittingly also contributed to this support, including clerical and domestic staff.

Sophie was a little different because she is a very high-profile girl. Everybody in Australia is familiar with Sophie's progress, so naturally this rocked the nation. You know, no child should experience anything like this in a lifetime, but every child is precious and every child deserves the best care. So to all intents and purposes, she was another ICU patient. But because of her high profile, people were very conscious of media being present and very conscious of the family's privacy. In ICU we have a video intercom system, so we can curb activity to a degree. Because of Sophie's profile, the nation wanted to know, so we were asked for frequent reports.

Some people in ICU have deep spiritual beliefs, some have a genuine belief in what they do clinically — everybody is different. There are also different levels of maturity across the group of people caring for a child such as Sophie. A new graduate nurse coming out of university hasn't got the life experience to build on, or the professional maturity. There are lots of avenues to glean support from. But whilst those support mechanisms are there, grief is part of it, and you can't teach someone how to deal with grief — it is a very individual emotion.

Sophie was in ICU about two weeks; she was on the breathing machine for 12 days. As children's conditions improve we start to wean them off medications that support the body's systems, we start to wean down the support of the machines. She was very heavily sedated and she was artificially comatosed in the early days to allow us to deal with the body system's needs. When things improve, you start to see pumps diminish, dials turned down, you see trends across the chart smooth out, you don't see the peaks and troughs as much. With any child in intensive care there is always fear — the child is there for a reason, they have had a significant injury or surgery that requires close monitoring. They are susceptible to change at any given time, but there does come a time where people relax, take things a little bit more in their stride.

The parents are kept up to date with any changes; we do encourage them to take a rest but they are there pretty much 24 hours a day. The night after Sophie was admitted, we had another significant patient admission; it was the family's first experience of intensive care. I remember talking to the mum and dad, and the dad had said Ron had taken them under his wing and sat with them till three or four in the morning. The penny suddenly dropped as to who he was talking to — Sophie's dad. He said Ron was just wonderful, he offered so much support. That was fantastic, that they were using their experience constructively to help support other families. Unless anybody has been there in their life they can't understand. You cannot put yourself in that person's position.

In the very brief period that Sophie was with us without any of the breathing support, she made her personality known. She clearly is a very strong little personality with a good sense of humour, and she certainly made her mark on people in that short period of time.

We will keep hearing about Sophie, and that's good because people can look at it in context — she is out there living a normal life with a great loving family, which often we don't get to follow.

You often see children leaving who are orphans or have lost one parent or all of their family, so it is good to see she is progressing and leading a normal life. I think she's got that inner strength that she will draw on throughout her life — and the care and support of her family. They will be with her every step of the way.

Anita Mudge
PHYSIOTHERAPIST, SYDNEY CHILDREN'S HOSPITAL

Skye Waddingham
OCCUPATIONAL THERAPIST, SYDNEY CHILDREN'S HOSPITAL

Anna Young
OCCUPATIONAL THERAPIST, SYDNEY CHILDREN'S HOSPITAL

A team of therapists was assigned to work with Sophie, regaining the physical condition she had achieved before the second accident. Occupational therapists were called in to look at Sophie's positioning when she was still in an induced coma; because of her many injuries it was hard to get her in a good position. They also needed to find a way to lie Sophie on her side, to relieve the pressure on the back of her head. Anita Mudge recalls seeing Sophie in ICU on the second day after she was admitted.

Anita: The first time I saw her in ICU she was just lying there with drips in and I was shocked. I thought, 'Oh, that is such a damaged child'. And then within five minutes of meeting her, you forget about it. My other impression was how a really strong family unit can affect a child's ability to cope.

Skye: What was quite different throughout all of Sophie's stay was that her family had lived through the ICU experience before. It is a very different environment and it is quite intimidating — lots of machines and lots of unfamiliar medical practices, and your child is in a critical condition. But Sophie's family were very proactive from the word go.

Anita: They had already worked out strategies for the best way to get Sophie to do things. For example, she had been off her feet for three weeks or so before we got the prostheses back on her legs, so she had developed quite a lot of stump sensitivity. First you have to put a stump liner on and then something like a sock that goes over the stump liner, then the prosthesis. Her mum had a really good way of gradually doing it one at a time and invented different reasons to put it on: 'Let's just do this and then we can go to the fairy garden'. If it didn't work the first time, she'd put the stump liner on and the sock on and leave that for a while and then a bit later go for the next step — she'd obviously worked out the best way for Sophie.

Skye: There had been so many people involved, and we were a whole new team coming in. She had had the Westmead therapists and community therapists as well, so she'd dealt with three OTs and however many physios — and then they were admitted here. She had a lot of existing things in place, like wearing splints on her arms to maintain range of motion. The family gave us the history behind all of those services, and we also made contact with the therapists at Westmead to find out more.

Anita: They'd made such huge gains before this last accident with her movement and range. Then she was in the induced coma here for so long, so the ICU phase was all about positioning, education, maintaining range of motion, comfort and looking at pressure issues and skin integrity.

Skye: As Sophie started to wake up we also tried to look at the overall environment of intensive care: because she had a head injury, we were trying to cut down on the amount of stimulation in her environment. We tried to limit the amount of people and visitors at one time. That was quite tricky because Sophie had a lot of people who were very interested in how she was recovering, lots of medical teams and therapy teams.

In ICU we began trying to get Sophie to start sitting up. We talked to the family about what were some of Sophie's favourite toys, and used those toys to encourage her to sit up, engage with us and I guess trust us because she had met so many people.

Anita: She definitely didn't want to engage much without her mum being there. I remember the first time I met her, she'd come out of ICU and moved to the ward. Her mum had gone out to take a phone call and there were a few of us around the bed; she kept looking at me, very hesitant. She kind of waved me over and said, 'Please get my mum, I need to go to the toilet'. I said, 'Well, we can help', but she said, 'No, get my mum'. She knew her mum knew the right way to help her. She had so many pressure sores, she had a central line [an intravenous tube near the heart] in for a while. And a clavicle fracture. Probably she had quite a few experiences along the way of people moving her uncomfortably.

Anna: Sophie's parents are very strong people, particularly Carolyn. Ron always says that he is more emotional than Carolyn in many ways, or shows his emotions more, and I definitely noticed that. The other thing I noticed was how beautifully Ron and Carolyn interacted with Sophie. One time when she was in the drug-induced coma and we rolled her, Ron was holding her hand and Carolyn was assisting with the roll. We were looking at the skin integrity on her back, and Carolyn was saying, 'Oh you just look so beautiful Soph, you just look beautiful', and it was so strong, such a beautiful way of interacting with her.

Anita: I remember Sophie made this crazy hat for Ron. I think it was his birthday, and he had to wear it around the ward while she went out to prepare a birthday party for him; if he tried to go out he had to wear the hat. She could be quite directive at times. We would institute a game or an activity so that she would do what we wanted her to do; for example, standing up so she could put something up high or standing up so she could throw a ball in the basket — just a way to get her up and out of the chair to strengthen her legs. She'd quickly work out that's why you were doing it, so you had to have a few things up your sleeve. That's why it was great to have play and recreation in some of our therapy sessions. We were trying to pull in all these resources, because she's clever, she's lived through the hospital experience. She's had so many people try the same tricks before.

Before Sophie came into hospital, she was walking with her prostheses, she was going to school, doing stairs — and the physios had worked very hard with all of that. One of the main goals in physio was to get her walking as soon as possible. If you try to get her to do some exercises to strengthen her quads, say in bed, it works for one or two goes and then she loses interest very quickly. So getting her up and going was the only real way.

Lying in bed in ICU for three weeks, Sophie was limited to one or two positions because of everything else going on. So there was a lot of work with the nursing staff and family regarding positioning. Sophie did really well with that. By the time she came out into the ward she had restored just about all the range she previously had in her legs and was only missing about five degrees in her right hand and shoulder. They must have been really good in ICU about her positioning and her stretches. Also Sophie herself — once she could start doing it, she did. You find that with children a lot — once they are able to, they will move. She was always moving around in bed, lifting her bottom up, so she gave herself quite a lot of stretching and mobility work without meaning to.

Anna: Her tolerance to pain must be much higher than the majority of people. I remember Dr Jonny Taitz said everyone was with her and looking a bit down, and she was saying, 'What's wrong everyone? It's not that bad, they're only broken bones!'

Anita: Ironically the things that seemed to bother her the most were the secondary effects of being in hospital rather than the fractures. I was looking back at her notes — I forgot completely that she had a jaw fracture; it didn't stop her talking! The arm didn't seem to bother her so much, it was more the daily dressings she needed on the pressure areas that really caused her a lot of grief. And not wearing the prostheses, she got a lot of stump sensitivity. Probably the biggest challenge from my side of things was getting them back on. At the start her parents would put them on when she was in bed or when she was in her chair, just so she could spend time with the pressure on the stumps. That gradually got better and better. I remember her mum saying she walked in the cafeteria to give something to someone and that seemed to be another milestone, because not long after that she started asking to have her legs on.

Anna: Working in a children's hospital people always say, 'Oh, it must be so difficult working there'. Actually the opposite is true. Every day you walk away from work thinking, 'What have I really got to complain about — look how these kids just get on with it and don't think about the disability or illness and how their life has been affected'. It really makes you think about how you are as an adult and what we think we can achieve. Sophie is just one of many inspiring children we are fortunate enough to work with. They surprise me in such a good way.

Lauren Wood

DIETITIAN, SYDNEY CHILDREN'S HOSPITAL

Sophie's anaesthetist at Westmead, David Murrell, commented that, 'Nutrition is terribly important after burns; you could say the dietitian played as much part as we did [in Sophie's care]'. It had been a battle to get Sophie's weight up after the first accident; Lauren Wood had the difficult task of helping her to regain the ground she had lost.

The first time I met Sophie was after she was transferred to the ward. When I first met her she was in a wheelchair kicking a balloon looking very gorgeous and was straight away, 'Hi, who are you?', which I thought was cute. There were so many people in here all the time, I felt as though I was invading her privacy — but she made me feel comfortable in about five seconds.

Burns patients generally have higher nutritional requirements. They cannot regulate their body temperature as well as a person with normal skin; also grafts require more protein because your skin is growing and repairing at a faster rate turning over a lot more skin cells. Sophie's protein requirements were probably a little bit more than what she was getting at first, but that was something we concentrated on a lot. We got Sophie to about 50 per cent of her energy requirements initially because she wasn't tolerating her tube feeds. Patients often experience vomiting, nausea, diarrhoea. Sophie's main challenges were nausea and vomiting. You have to weigh up getting adequate nutrition and underfeeding and what the consequences of each are. With Sophie the consequences of underfeeding were she wouldn't have enough dietary protein to start the grafts going and so she would have to break down existing muscle tissue instead. Also how difficult it had been for her parents to get the weight back on previously — Carolyn and Ron were adamant that they didn't want her to lose weight as much as we could prevent it. She'd just had her legs moulded, and weight loss was going to affect how they fitted. They were very conscious of the importance of nutrition from day one. They requested to see a dietitian when they were in ICU; they had the whole picture in sync before I walked in to the room.

Sophie was on a lot of medication that decreases your appetite, there were a lot of other things going on in her room, big things happening in her life — food was a very low priority. She needed reminding to eat constantly. Also she had taste changes — certain medications can change your taste. We use a lot of dairy foods to get protein and fat into children of her medical background; Sophie doesn't like dairy, and her dislike for dairy was accentuated after the accident. We have managed to work around that but it made things a lot more difficult. I remember her favourite food being two-minute noodles. I was quite excited because they have carbohydrates, and I was thinking what I could add into it to make it a bit more valuable in terms of nutrition. Then Carolyn said that she just takes the soup from around the noodles and none of the noodles!

A couple of days before she went home I was saying to her, 'What do you feel like tonight for dinner?' She said, 'Mummy and I are getting McDonald's,' and went on to tell me what they order — 'Mummy has a hamburger meal and I have her toy and I eat as much as I can of my meal'. I suppose for Carolyn and Ron it was quite normal for a dietitian to be recommending McDonald's because it had been said before. Weight gain was our goal, so whether we did that through dairy or McDonald's, I really didn't mind. It was fat equals weight gain equals Sophie is going to be a more robust person to fit into the legs she was fitted for. I remember mentioning it in the case conference in front of a lot of teachers and people who hadn't considered that point of view; I hope I brought them onto my side by the end of it. To hear a dietitian recommending chips and chocolates and extra bits of cake, not just one or the other ... I remember getting a 'what's going on here' look!

With Sophie you can't use takeaway food as a reward, because we want that to be a more regular thing than just a reward. It becomes more a matter of, 'What can we offer a child who is getting presents by the billions that is going to motivate her to eat a little more than she has the appetite for?' It was basically lots of encouragement. It worked to an extent, but all the medications were affecting her appetite. I was there about 5.30 one afternoon and I started talking to Sophie about dinner. She was whispering to me, 'I want to make a picnic for Dad', and I said, 'Great, let's do it'. Ron could hear every word but we were pretending we were telling secrets. And I said, 'What about fairy bread?' — I can get lots of butter onto fairy bread — and she said, 'Yeah, and Maccas, we'll put that on the tray and that will be a dinner party'. I said, 'That would be fantastic, you would be a great waitress, you're on wheels — you could do it at 100 miles an hour!' Later Carolyn told me Sophie didn't want a bar of it, she just wanted to do the cooking. Ron and Carolyn had to eat it because they felt so guilty wasting all this food beautifully prepared by Sophie.

Sophie is the most charming child. Without fail, every time I came in she said, 'Guess what I had for lunch today?', and I got the impression that that was because she knew I was going to ask about food, not that she would have said that to anyone who walked in. That was really charming and really cute, that she knew that was what she was meant to speak to me about. Very well adjusted to lots of different faces coming in and able to say hello and have things to say, no matter who walked in and out. Had a smile on her face and those gorgeous eyes always looking at you, sussing out what you are doing.

Michelle Driver

PLAY THERAPIST, SYDNEY CHILDREN'S HOSPITAL

Fiona Lamb

REGISTERED MUSIC THERAPIST, SYDNEY CHILDREN'S HOSPITAL

Michelle: I was working with a patient in the intensive care unit. Sophie was in her room, diagonally across. I was aware that she was starting to wake up that day — they were weaning her off the sedation. I was on the floor with the other child, doing some drumming work and general play. Sophie's nurse noticed that Sophie kept watching and smiling, so she called out to the patient and they were waving at each other. When I left I stuck my head in and said hello and who I was and I asked her if she would like me to come back the following day. I didn't offer to see her then and there because she had just woken up, she needed time. So the following day I went back and I took the music therapist with me — not Fiona, Verena, another music therapist who works with us. Sophie's mum and Mitchell were in there as well, so we played the drums and sang some songs.

Fiona: I first met Sophie in ICU as well, the day after Verena had been in. I knew the Sydney Swans theme song, so we were friends for life. It was a pretty short session, but we sang a few familiar songs. Part of our role in music therapy and play therapy is to normalise the environment. If you think about what hospital is like from anyone's point of view, particularly a child, it smells different, it sounds different, there are strangers all around you, you are in pain or you are under sedation of some sort . . .

Michelle: . . . everybody was wearing gowns to go into her room.

Fiona: . . . it is potentially terrifying, so anything that makes it normal, to connect the child to their home, is really important. Familiar songs are a great way to do that, so we sang 'The Wheels on the Bus' and a few other songs that she knew. My first impression of her was this exuberant cheeky little person who was just so full of joy. I think that you see in children their innate personality; some children are just born quiet, and there are children like Sophie who are really enthusiastic and positive and joyful.

Michelle: There was a large volume of people who went through her room, visitors, media, physios, dietitians — it can be hard to get time with any child with complex needs, not just Sophie. I saw her nearly every day that she was in, but to do an actual session — sometimes you'd go up there and it just fell to pieces because eight people would turn up at the same time. You might just stay and chat for a bit and then pop in later on and give her something to do at night when it's a bit quieter.

Fiona: Because she was seeing so many other disciplines, it made it more important that play was part of the day, that some really child-appropriate things were happening.

Michelle: I made up a timetable for her room so everyone knew what time things were happening. It was good for her structure as well, so that she knew in the morning when she got up that between 9 a.m. and 10.30 would be play and then physio. And then we started to integrate the sessions together; I might have gone up and done a little bit of play and then the physio would come in and we'd do it together. Fiona did the same thing for music — rather than just putting her prosthetics on and saying, 'Stand up', we'd say, 'Let's blow the bubbles up high and see if you can get up to reach them' or 'Let's hold the drum up and see if you can walk over here to do this', to make it more fun, to make it more rewarding for her and I guess more stimulating.

Michelle: Sophie has lots of energy; she is a very social, interactive child. She tried very hard to be positive; even doing really difficult dressing changes with her, you can tell when things have gotten too much for her but she will still try, and you can still have a conversation with her and she will still smile at you and talk about things with you. Very infectious — she would have everyone in the room laughing. She is very musical . . .

Fiona: . . . and very much a performer. I should explain first, music therapy is not about performance or teaching, so it wouldn't necessarily be the same for another child. The really dry definition is the therapeutic use of music to achieve non-musical therapeutic goals, so that means using it for things like standing up. The physiotherapist and occupational therapist needed to reintroduce the use of Sophie's prosthetics. Both music and play therapy assisted the process by creating a rewarding environment to do this in. We eventually got to a point where she wanted to stand up with her toy guitar and pretend to play and sing. She didn't know that we were doing that to get her to stand up; as far as she was concerned, we were having a rock concert. We sang a couple of counting songs where she had to throw frogs off her tray table, and as far as she was concerned, it was just counting and throwing things. She didn't realise that it was helping to build up muscle; because of the bones that had been broken she hadn't been able to use her shoulder.

Fiona: We did a lot of what she called concerts — she would spend the whole day telling people, 'We've got a concert this afternoon', and we walked around to the glass walkway so it felt like she was looking out into an audience, and just sang our little hearts out.

Michelle: She was isolated [because of the risk of infection], so it was a bit of a problem; I think she would have liked to have gone to the Starlight Room and stood on the stage and given her concert, but she wasn't allowed to go in there. They did allow her to walk on this little walkway near her ward; that became her concert space very quickly.

Fiona: Most people know about Sophie as the joyful child, and they don't see — nor should they see — there are some really excruciating procedures that she has had done, and one of them is the dressing changes that Michelle was referring to before. It must be so hard for her — and so hard for Carolyn, to hold her child while she is in so much pain. So when Michelle and I were working together it wasn't so much trying to pretend it wasn't going to hurt or do something so she didn't cry, but if she had a moment that was really painful, we would try to get her back as soon as possible to focus on something we were playing with or a song to sing straight afterwards. Sophie's injuries and the procedures she has to have are quite unique, quite specialised so that was how we managed those — it would be different for each patient.

Michelle: You can look at pain as actual physical pain and perceived pain. If you can distract that part of the brain into doing something different then you are taking away from that perceived pain, which is reducing the pain. As play therapists, you work on preparing that child for the procedure; both of us at different times also went as far as the holding bay in theatres with Sophie. Going to theatres was a real struggle for her. I remember the first operation she had once she was on the ward. I was speaking to Carolyn and she said, 'Tomorrow is going to be a really rough day, we are going to theatre at 11, anything we can have beforehand will be really good because it is a very difficult time for her'. We kept her busy right up until the minute before she had to leave. I was in the room when they called for her, so it was quite a natural thing to continue the journey to theatre with her. They have specific things they take with them to theatre and she was showing me what they were while we walked. It just kept that momentum going so she didn't stop and realise, 'Okay, this is about to happen'.

Fiona: We had a travelling concert once — all the way down to the theatres. I had my guitar, she had her toy piano and we sang every Hi–5 song, every Wiggles song that we could think of. Then her doctor, Doctor Peter, came and he had to sit down and listen to a song before he talked to mum and dad. That was what she needed to alleviate her level of anxiety; another child would have needed something else.

Michelle: Every day with her something different came out. She is an incredibly resilient child; to think she has gone through this twice, to think anyone can walk into the room and she can make them laugh ... There were times that were really tough for her as well; I sat with her in a room for about 20 minutes one day, when both Ron and Carolyn were being interviewed. Normally their nurse would have been there at that time, someone she knew from home, but on this occasion she would have been alone. I told Ron and Carolyn that I would stay; I realised at the time that she couldn't be left alone, the anxiety was just too much. She was quite distressed for a good five to ten minutes because she has an attachment with Carolyn and finds it very difficult when she leaves, unless it has been planned and the right person will be there. So for me, that was a bit of a realisation. She got through it, she was fantastic and we ended up having a great time. It makes you realise it's not what everyone sees in the public eye. What she goes through and what she has been through — I can't imagine what the burns would have been like when it was almost her whole body. But knowing the dressing changes are coming, she doesn't fight going into the treatment room; she'll go in, she knows it's going to hurt. She knows what is about to happen and she'll still walk in there and have that trust in her mother and the people she's met, that they are doing what needs to happen. That is pretty full on for a five-year-old.

Dr Adrienne Epps
MEDICAL DIRECTOR OF THE BRAIN INJURY REHABILITATION PROGRAM AND SENIOR STAFF SPECIALIST IN THE REHABILITATION DEPARTMENT, SYDNEY CHILDREN'S HOSPITAL

Carolyn Martin recalls: 'Adrienne is also part of the limb deficiency team at Westmead, so we had a relationship with her already. It was very comforting to see her head up the rehab team because you have immediate appreciation for her knowledge and skill level and know you are in very good hands.'

In the second accident, Sophie had life-threatening multiple trauma. She had a very stormy course in the intensive care ward for some weeks. She also had a head injury in the second accident. Once she came out of intensive care and got to the ward, we were able to start looking at getting her back into normal activities. The challenge for her was that she'd been in bed inactive for a long time, so she lost a lot of strength and endurance that she had achieved before. There was also a significant impact on her sense of wellbeing; she had pain from the multiple fractures and soft tissue injuries from her second accident. And difficulty with her nutritional intake — her appetite just went, and to get adequate nutrition to allow her body to heal and repair itself was quite challenging. So there were a lot of areas that needed to be addressed to optimise her recovery. Thankfully, her legs weren't significantly injured in the second accident — she didn't have any major skin loss or fractures in her legs, so we were able to get her old prostheses back on. Her endurance was limited, so she needed to rely on her stroller and wheelchair more than she had. With her previous injury she'd lost tissue in her buttock muscle, and that meant her sitting — her pelvic position — was asymmetric. That pre-existing problem plus the new deconditioning and weakness contributed to her developing a postural scoliosis [curvature of the spine], so this was a new problem we had to address. It is just so complex: she had so many fractures, abdominal trauma, chest trauma, multiple fractures, spine fractures, clavicle fracture — it was like having to go back to first base and start all over again.

The physios had to start working with Sophie to address those new difficulties — not just physical, but because of her brain injury, fatigue and lower tolerance for handling and participation in activities needed to be accommodated as well. The initial CT scan didn't show up any major intracranial haemorrhage or any sort of major damage to the brain, but we knew that because she had been hit at such high speed and because she had so many other injuries her head would not have escaped that trauma, the brain being one of the most vulnerable organs in high-speed accidents. She then had an MRI [magnetic resonance imaging], and that showed the shearing injuries [these happen when movement in the brain tears the nerve fibres and blood vessels].

Those shearing injuries can heal but it usually does lead to some residual long-term damage. For Sophie the main effect of that was probably hidden early on because of the extent of her other injuries. Fatigue is one of the major things early on; the long-term effect of the brain injury will become more apparent as she progresses with her development and schooling. She had a neuropsychology assessment done to have a look at the effects of the injury on her cognitive functioning and she has done remarkably well. With this degree of injury you might have expected it to have more significant impact on her attention, memory, processing speed — all of which are important for functioning in the classroom — but she has done reasonably well in these areas. What will be interesting is to see how she learns new things over time. One of the impacts of a brain injury in early childhood is on new learning skills — difficulty learning new information. So that requires ongoing monitoring in the classroom, making sure she has adequate support. Her brain injury won't go away, it will impact to a certain extent on her learning, but we are hopeful she will achieve to her potential.

People think of rehab as being episodic intervention — you set up goals and plans to achieve those goals. But because Sophie is growing physically and developing as a person, she will need a lot of support and she will go through a lot of transitions, so rehab will be required even into adulthood. When she moves through adolescence, finishes school, goes through further education, considers vocational options — there will still need to be assessment and support for her. This is a lifelong thing.

8
Sophie's family

Carolyn Martin's family is scattered across the globe. After Sophie's two accidents her parents, brother and sister flew in from France, New Zealand and the USA. Ron's family are mostly Sydney-based, a close extended family including his children from a previous marriage. Tragedy on this scale has a 'ripple effect', stretching and testing relationships with parents, children, brothers and sisters.

Ron Delezio and Carolyn Martin
SOPHIE'S PARENTS

Carolyn: There were so many really strange coincidences that occurred. When my sister got on a plane to fly out from Paris after the first accident, the man she sat next to was from Fairlight in Sydney. His wife had just rung him and said, 'If you hear anything on the news, it is not our children's childcare centre'. After the second accident she was already flying in to spend a week with us as a holiday. She flew in, arrived, got into a cab and heard the news on the radio. It was great that she was here already; she made sure that Mitchell was cared for and things happened at home.

Ron: When the first accident happened, my daughter Catherine came.

Carolyn: She sat in with Sophie for about three weeks, and she gave us the opportunity to sleep at night because we wanted someone to be with Sophie 24 hours a day. There was a roster of carers, our friends and Catherine — we wanted them to be with Sophie in case she died.

Ron: Dad is 80, he is less mobile than Caro's mum and dad at their age, so they stayed at home and only came in when they were brought in by my brother or my other son. I think Allan [Carolyn's father] is quite a strong person, whereas my father, he'll just burst into tears.

Carolyn: But Allan by his own admission says, 'I don't do this very well'. He would come in and read Sophie a couple of stories; he might be strong but it is also tough on him. I think with Ron's father there are not many girls in the Delezio line; Sophie was his *pupa* [an affectionate Italian term meaning 'baby'], and she adored him.

In the first accident, Mary [Ron's mother] would look at Sophie and say, 'She's all right'; I think it was Mary's way of coping. She was just hoping everything would work out. It was hard for everyone to face the reality of the situation.

Ron: I used to get upset and say, 'Mum, she's not all right'. I didn't want to make it sound worse than what it was, but that is her way of coping.

Carolyn: The second time around they knew the system a bit better. Mary would bring in party packs of food for Mitchell and boxes of Cheezels and bickies to feed the nurses, which was really very sweet of her. Ron's nephew and his wife came a lot,

Sophie's cousins, and they would bring Mary and Frank. In the end I thought, 'I'll put them all to work' — and I did. I sat them in the corridor and they opened mail and they loved it. They were very happy for me to give them tasks; that is what I did with all my friends. Sometimes you need to tell people, 'Don't just sit and look, these are the things that need to be done'.

Allan Martin
CAROLYN MARTIN'S FATHER

Carolyn's parents, Allan and Joy, lived in New Zealand when Sophie's two accidents happened. As Sophie's Journey *was being written they were preparing to move to Sydney to be closer to Sophie, Mitchell, Ron and Carolyn. Allan recalls hearing the news of Sophie's first accident.*

We were on a walking trip and well out of touch by telephone. People were trying to reach us from all over the place to tell us what had happened. It was only late in the day that we got the news and then of course we immediately had to book to get Joy over on the next available flight.

We were devastated. We didn't have the full details at that time, but it was enough to know it was very serious indeed. Joy took off next day and she went immediately to the hospital. Two or three days later she said, 'Look, I think you'd better come over', because it looked pretty grim at that stage; it looked like Sophie might die. So then I took off and got over there and went immediately to the hospital. Sophie was a pitiful sight, it was unbelievable. Her face was like a balloon, totally unrecognisable.

It was very trying and very emotional for everybody. There were a lot of friends around; there was support for Carolyn and Ron so that neither of them were left alone, and Sophie certainly wasn't left alone for any of the time. Somebody would always be by her bedside, talking to her and encouraging her. The hardest time was when Ron had to tell us about the extent of her injuries and the amputations that were going to have to take place.

There was much praying and encouraging everybody else to do likewise. There was a huge email network set up around the world with friends and relatives. Carolyn had started that off from the word go; she was very clear that she wanted this, and everybody alerted everybody and encouraged everybody. I think we were all fairly convinced to some extent about the power of positive prayer — even to this day — it may have had something to contribute. When you get into a situation like that, what else do you fall back on? There is nothing else.

I don't think this is a miracle in the religious sense, more of a medical miracle. The dedication and expertise of the medical teams at the hospitals were fantastic, and the nurses, everybody who contributed was very important. But who knows — it may have been prayer that contributed. The doctors said with 85 per cent or more burns to the body, at that age, they normally don't survive.

When the second accident happened, we were both at home this time. Ann-Louise, Carolyn's sister, had just gone back that day to Sydney to stay with her. They'd been over here for my graduation, for a PhD I just got. We were just settling down that evening, having a quiet drink, thinking life is back to normal again, when we got this telephone call from Carolyn asking me to get Mum on the first plane over because there had been this other terrible accident with Sophie. We had an awful feeling of déjà vu — the next available flight turned out to be the six o'clock in the morning and Joy was over there into it again, into the routine of running the household and looking after Mitchell and generally supporting Carolyn.

We had just made a decision not long before the first accident to move up to where we are now and take life easy at this very comfortable seaside house, and that was going to be our life from there on. It hasn't turned out that way, however. We have sold our house here and we have bought a place not far from their house, and we will be over there early 2007.

Looking at Sophie now, everybody marvels at her and she is a fantastic girl, there is no doubt about that. But because she looks so well, you are inclined to overlook the tremendous care and attention that has to go on all the time — by Carolyn, principally. It really is a demanding full-time job looking after Sophie. When you see her with her clothes off and the burns to her body and the extent of the injuries ... the operations are going to be ongoing. The dangers inherent in each of those operations, with the possibility of infection and so on each time she goes in, that is always a worrying and dramatic period.

Sophie has so mastered her legs and disabilities even at this stage, that one is inclined to overlook them — well, not entirely, you are always conscious of the fact. But it is Sophie who really takes over because she has such a personality. She has always been like that. Particularly if you look at her early pictures it seems to be showing, but I think that has strengthened throughout this period.

Sophie is coping with being in the spotlight very well; she is starting to enjoy it. I think she is a natural performer actually, she may well have been an actress if the accident hadn't happened — she is an outgoing personality. She gets tired at times and that shows, but by and large I think she enjoys it.

Ron and Carolyn are both very strong people and they come from strong family backgrounds. It was very catastrophic for them both as parents, awful, but they have come through it very strongly and determinedly to make a secure life for Sophie. And that is reflected in her recovery, the way she is acting now, and her positive outlook.

Joy Martin
CAROLYN MARTIN'S MOTHER

After both of Sophie's accidents, Joy took the first flight to Sydney to be with her granddaughter. She describes the experience of those flights.

The first one, I suppose I was in a state of disbelief, like everybody else in the family. We got the message at about nine o'clock at night and didn't get any sleep, and left the house at about 3 a.m. to get to Auckland to catch that early flight. You don't think it's real, it doesn't happen to your family. A travel companion asked me if I was going to Sydney on holiday and I said, 'No'... and then the horror of it all set in. I found it very difficult talking to people at that stage.

I think the horror of it all became manageable after I had seen Carolyn. Whilst I was prepared for Sophie's state — which was terrible; I had asked what Sophie looked like, what the treatment was, how they were keeping her alive — I had asked all those questions, but nothing prepared me for my own daughter's state. She was in a state of total shock and I was unprepared for the way she was.

You feel terribly helpless, you think, 'What can I do to help?', 'I am not doing enough, I'm not helping here'. The thing was just to be there and try and get some sort of order into this chaos. Looking after Mitchell became our primary concern. He was only four, quite little and very distressed. We tried to get some order into his life, took him to daycare each day and fetched him at the end of the day and took him home, and made sure there was some normalcy in his life.

Then when the second accident happened it was once again, total disbelief and once again, the early flight to Sydney. The same people met me, great friends of Carolyn's, and this time I felt that Carolyn would cope better. And she did, definitely.

My first reaction was, 'Not her face, I hope her face hasn't been damaged', because the miracle of the first accident was that her face was spared. When I heard about the second accident, I just thought how dreadful it would be if her face had been scarred or damaged.

Sophie is a happy child, she's gutsy and has this incredible ability to relate to people. When I'm there and come in she always has a greeting and a question: 'How's your day been?', 'Did you have good golf?', 'What have you been doing?' — she is remarkable, really. Even before Sophie's first accident, there was a huge personality there. She was always a bossy boots, from conception I think. It was such an unexpected pregnancy and there she was, she made her presence felt. Even as a tiny tot you always knew Sophie was around; she impressed people with her personality.

Frank and Mary Delezio
RON DELEZIO'S PARENTS

Originally from Malta, Ron's parents have lived in Sydney's west for many years. Now in their eighties, they have been shaken by the two blows of fate to their much-loved granddaughter, Sophie. As luck would have it, they heard about both accidents on the television news.

Mary: We heard about the first accident on the television, just like that.

Frank: Even the second one, I saw that on television. I was just about to turn off the television set and all of a sudden I saw this bulletin: 'There has been an accident and it was Sophie Delezio'. I said, 'No, it couldn't be, not a second time'.

Mary: We couldn't believe that. The way the media said it on television — 'That's not right', I said, because they said she had a heart attack. So we rang up Michelle [Ron's sister] straight away and she said, 'Mum, I'm in a hurry; we'll let you know later on, we'll ring you back'. But we were in shock.

Frank: After the first accident, we went to the hospital as soon as we could get a lift with someone.

Mary: Yes, we talked to our eldest son Emmanuel and he took us straight away.

Frank: For the first two visits we never even saw her.

Mary: But we saw Ron and Carolyn. When she started to get better we went inside and talked to her; it was a big shock for us. Our granddaughter, you know. About a week before the first accident, it was before Christmas, Ron brought them over and we had Christmas music and they were dancing, playing ... That was the last time we saw her before the accident. She was a really active girl.

Frank: She's still alive because she's got someone watching over her. She smiles so much, that's her nature. But she's gone through a lot of pain; every night of the week they have to change her bandages — and physio every night. I never put her on my lap because I'm afraid I might hold her the wrong way. They have special skin that they used on Sophie and that helped her a lot, but it's not normal skin, it's very rough skin. I know it's rather unusual for a grandfather not to hold his granddaughter but that's the reason why, not because of any loss of love.

Mary: We always say, 'We love you' and she really likes it. When they come here he plays the organ for her or when we go to her house he plays the piano and she loves the attention, she dances. She knows him as 'nannu' because that's 'grandfather' in Maltese.

Frank: Sophie is getting used to the public attention now, she loves that.

Mary: I think Mitchell took it a little bit hard.

Frank: When I go to their place I make sure that I give him as much attention as I give her.

Mary: Carolyn and Ron are marvellous people; before they had the kids they did everything for us. I think it was hard for Ron and Carolyn over the past few years. They don't tell us much, not to worry us, but we know they went through a lot. I remember Ron saying since the first accident he always wakes up at three o'clock in the morning because he can't sleep any more.

Frank: Carolyn is a very, very good mother and Ron is a very good father. They are still together, they still love each other. I said to them, 'Ron, take it a bit easy', because I can see he's got baggy eyes.

Mary: He does a lot but that's what's kept him going. Otherwise we don't know what could have happened to him, poor thing.

Frank: We don't see them as much as before; they are too far away now. The only way to go and see them is to go to Manly and to get picked up by Carolyn or Ron.

Mary: Or catch a taxi — especially now Frank doesn't drive far.

Frank: Sometimes I ask myself, 'Why is there all this attention from so many people?' I mean, there have been accidents that happen to other people but never been so much fuss as there has been with this one. But how many times do you hear somebody has an accident and they have the second accident again the same way, with a car?

Mary: It was a miracle that she was still alive. There must be something good that will come out of it; it's a miracle, like Mary MacKillop. This girl suffered so much, to be alive — there must be something.

John and Kate Delezio
RON DELEZIO'S SON AND DAUGHTER-IN-LAW

John is Ron's eldest son from a previous marriage. Now a married man with children of his own, he and his wife Kate explain how profound the impact has been for their whole family, from the time of hearing about Sophie's accident at the Roundhouse.

John: Every moment of it is so vivid still; there's not one minute of time that I cannot recall — from the phone call from Dad, being in my office getting two missed phone calls and then picking up the third one and hearing Dad just freaked out, to driving along the freeway to get to the hospital, to parking the car to just sitting there waiting for Soph to get to the hospital. It was a pretty intense day.

Kate: The weekend before her accident they came over here to visit; Oliver was a new baby so they came over to play. Mitchell and Sophie were in the sandpit — a typical four year old and two and a half year old, they like to annoy each other. Mitchell was putting sand all over her and she started to get upset in the sandpit. I said, 'What's wrong Soph?' and she said, 'Mitchell's burying my feet in the sand'. She was wiggling her feet trying to get the sand off them. When we found out that she would lose her feet, that's all I could think of: I remember those little feet because two days before that accident I was paying attention to them because they were being buried in the sandpit.

John: I think that was the most shocking thing, when the doctors were saying, 'We'll have to take this off and this off' and I'm thinking, 'How can you do that, *why* would you do that, how can she be so burnt?' In the first couple of nights I remember some big conversations with Dad; the big question was, 'Are they going to turn life support off or not?' and so that's what we spoke about. The doctors said Sophie will let them know what she wants to do, and in all of the mess she was a much bigger fighter than all of those around her. Just the way she healed — there was such an element of strength and fight.

Kate: I find it really hard to talk about the first accident because Oliver was four weeks old and William was 17 months old. It was just a time in our life that was hectic anyway and then this happened. John was at the hospital most days, most nights, and I had two tiny little babies to cope with by myself. It was a real fine balance, to say you've got to be at the hospital but I've got to cope at home with two tiny little babies. I wanted to be at the hospital with him and I couldn't because I had to be at home with the babies.

John: It did a lot of damage in our relationship. We've gone through counselling. Kate was very angry about a lot of stuff and I didn't even get it because there's no rulebook on when there's a traumatic situation.

When the second accident happened, Kate first heard about it on the television news.

Kate: I was watching the news and my sister was here — lucky my sister was here, I was eight months pregnant. These things happen when I'm having babies! We heard something about Ron; I looked at my sister and said, 'They didn't just say something about Sophie, did they?' They went straight to an ad break and my head was ticking and I thought, 'Not again, not again' — I was in denial, could not believe it. I rang John and said, 'Has your dad rung you? They just had this thing on the news, Sophie might be in an accident' and he said, 'No, no'. He tried to ring his dad and I just lost it when it came back on the news. John got home and we went straight to the hospital.

John: It was this weird sense of — all the emotion and all of the input into getting her better the first time, where did that all go? What's the point? It was so surreal. I remember getting to the hospital and seeing all the cameras, and well-wishers lighting candles — this is not more than a couple of hours after she's been hit by a car. And just the amount of people around her bed, it was like this is the most important person in the world. Doctors came from Westmead, everywhere, just to help. And seeing her on the bed — on the night I saw her after the first accident, although she was covered in foil and all that stuff, her face still looked good. But the second accident, her face was all puffed up because she'd been hit by a car. I said straight away to Kate, 'She's gone, she's gone, she can't do it again'. She's still so sick, she's got osteoporosis, her bones are incredibly brittle. When you've got that in the back of your head you realise there's not much chance of her coming through it. There was another miracle as far as I am concerned. I'm a Christian who goes to church every Sunday and I certainly believe the prayer was a big part of it.

I get a sense of being overwhelmed by the whole thing when I touch her. Touching her burnt skin is an amazing thing because she has been totally disfigured but she has got soft, beautiful, supple skin. Maybe someone will be on [Sophie's] other side and they've got her hand and you want to hold her tight but you know she's got no hand there. But it's natural for her; she allows you to have a touch connection with her, it doesn't bother her. That holding of her arm with no hand on it is just such a big thing, it's overpowering; I don't know why it's so overpowering, it's just who she is.

Kate: She's the most fantastic little girl, she lights up a room, there's no doubt about that. But I think it's hard for us to understand the whole public response because to us she's John's sister. If people find out our surname they ask, 'Oh, are you related to Sophie? She's amazing, she's touched my life.' When you're so close to a situation it's really hard to think of how this has touched so many people.

John: We've all got an element of what she's done inside of us and when push comes to shove we will fight to survive. I just don't think we get to see it very often in anyone and we got to see it in her. The fact that she's so young and pretty and the rest of her life was changed, and the fact that she's come out of it and still smiles, that's it — everyone loves her smile. That's what inspires people — and it brings me to tears. When we go over we'll play in the backyard with the boys and it's an incredible gift to be around her and to be able to push her on the swings and for her to look back at you and smile — that smile is a reassurance, saying, 'I'm okay, I'm normal'. Like I said to Dad that first or second night, 'Let's look forward to when she's walking down the aisle', because she will get to that, I know. That will be one of the pinnacles of her life: to be normal, get married, have children. Who knows what can happen — only a couple of months ago she was telling me she had a boyfriend at school. She's doing all the normal stuff, you know.

Kate: People forget that she's only five; if we go out with her people go up to her and expect to have a conversation — people she's never met before come up to her and say, 'Sophie, my daughter wants to say hello to you', and she's like, 'stranger danger'! She's had this massive impact, but we can't understand it. We've known her since she was born.

I just love the way she's alive in everything she does. Recently we went to the Wiggles birthday concert. She was sitting next to me and we were singing along. She got up during a certain song and she was just enjoying herself. And I was thinking, 'These are the moments that make all that stuff we went through, that everybody went through, just worthwhile' because she was having an absolute ball. This is the reason we went through that pain — to see her up there living life and having a great time.

John: I suppose the effect that Soph's had will stay with us forever, it will never leave us. And it's sad, terribly sad, but the joy that's come out of it will stay with us forever as well. I really just look to the future for her. I can't wait for her to turn 13, 16, 18; I want to have a beer with her at the pub and talk to her about what her future plans are. I can't wait until she's older and able to let me know her thoughts. It's like you know someone who's just got a gift and you feel privileged to be able to get to know her.

Against that sunshine is the shade — the events of the past few years have tested John's relationship with his father.

Anything like this, it just takes relationships, picks them up, chews them up, spits them out. There's a lot of history with my dad; he was divorced from my mum when I was five and there was a big gap in our relationship for a long, long time. We've got a great relationship but we're mates, we're not really father and son. When the Father of the Year award came up we had these big discussions about it — there was stuff I had to get off my chest. I'm incredibly proud of what they've both done. I look at Caro and Ron and I am in awe of the dedication they put into Soph and Mitch, I think there is no one who could have done a better job with both of them. There's no book for them to read that will answer, 'What do we do with Mitch and how are we going to do our best not to affect him for the rest of his life?' They just do their best and they've stood by each other.

There were certainly a number of years where I was thinking, 'Bloody hell, I should be compensated for this, I want to sue the driver'. Things had changed for us. Since the accident the only time Dad's family has really gotten together is at the hospital. We used to have family barbecues at least three or four times a year, but now it just doesn't happen. That's a small example of how the immediate family have changed, just the dynamics and how we relate. I recall us as a large family that came together fairly regularly, and you miss that, you think, 'Why have things changed?' — in areas you didn't expect.

Michelle Bates

RON DELEZIO'S SISTER

Basically we found out about the first accident from the news. The afternoon it happened my sister-in-law Carmen, who is my oldest brother's wife, rang me and said she just heard on the news that Sophie's been in a terrible accident and she's burnt. I said, 'Carmen, you're sure you got the story right?' and she said, 'Yeah I'm sure, they said Sophie'. With that I rang my mum; she'd already heard the news and she was a mess. So then there's this chain reaction of events; I rang my husband and said, 'I don't know if you've heard but there's been a terrible accident'. I waited for him to come home from work and we just raced into the hospital. I remember there was this little room we went into in the beginning, and Carolyn was just sitting, just gazing into nowhere and trembling. Ron broke down when he saw us, and we were hugging him. Then he got over his crying and then just carried on doing what he had to do.

Funnily enough it was the same way the second time, I found out through the news. Friends started ringing me and asking me, 'Have you heard the news?' and I said, 'Yeah, yeah, yeah'. I quickly rang Ron; at that stage he was in the car travelling to the hospital with the police escort, and he was a mess. He said, 'We don't know how she is because she's gone in the helicopter and we're going in the police car now to the hospital'. So both times the news gets to you first before you hear it from the horse's mouth; it's terrible but that's the way.

Ron and Carolyn are both very strong, determined people. Ron breaks down, but then he knows that he's got to carry on. Same with Carolyn, really. They just have this ability to handle the situation and know what to do and not dwell on what has happened, but to know what they have to do for Sophie. Even when you speak to them about both drivers in both circumstances, they've got no ill feeling towards either of them, because that was in the past and they just want to look to the future. That's just the way they are. If that was me, I don't know how I could just turn that off and not be feeling really bad against the person who did it, but they immediately didn't want to consider him or talk about him, they had nothing to say about him. All their concentration was on Sophie and that was it.

All of this has probably brought us closer, even though I don't see Ron as much as I'd like because he's always busy and everybody's lives are busy. While Sophie was in hospital after both accidents, we went and visited her and did as much as we could to help. But in the very early stages, like when she was in hospital the first time, just speaking on the phone to Ron he'd be breaking down and we shared a lot of feelings. It just brought home the fact that we love each other and that we'll always be there for each other.

With the first accident Mitchell was at a difficult age, he was at the age where he needed attention. I remember going into the hospital and we had this rather large area where he'd bring in his toys and Carolyn and Ron would always find the time to sit with him and play with him and not let that little boy miss out. They felt so sorry for him, that he had to be away from them for so long while they were living in the hospital. But they made up for it in every way they could; they kept up all his social activities and they have such a wonderful network of friends who organised this for Mitchell and that for Mitchell and of course Carolyn's mum and dad were there looking after him and he was always in the hospital as much as he could be.

I think the love of their family and the love of their friends keeps Ron and Carolyn going through all of this. More so the friends — I know that's not a very nice thing to say but I think the network of friends that they've got is a very close network; they're always doing things with their friends. There are things they look forward to — there are so many things that they've got on their plate, but there's always something pleasant to look forward to and that way you don't think about the bad side of things, the day-to-day things — it just carries them through.

I don't think Sophie is any different to what she was before. She's just very happy-go-lucky and speaks so well — she's a wonderful speaker and she tells you in exact words what she's describing. She's a very happy girl, she just gets on with it and she doesn't let things stand in her way. When she's got something in her mind she just does it. Even when she's not on her legs, even when she's on her stumps, she goes so fast. Say she wants to show you something, she just says, 'Come, come, come, come'! She's a very determined little girl, nothing stops her.

You see her injuries, obviously, but you get so used to being with her and looking at her you don't really even notice that they're there any more. She's just who she is and nothing stops her, so it's like nothing's wrong with her really. That's just a part of who she is now, and probably at this stage she doesn't know herself as being any different. I remember a funny thing Carolyn told me that Sophie said: 'Mum, I don't think I want to do ballet any more'. Carolyn said she's never done ballet in her life, she thinks that before the accident she did ballet and she said, 'No, I don't want to do ballet'. Carolyn told me Sophie said she wanted to take up a musical instrument; Carolyn thought that was rather a hard one, to pick a musical instrument that Sophie could play. So she's been going to singing lessons, and she gets a lot out of that. With these singing lessons she gets to play-act and do all these different things, which she loves — anything to do with dress-ups or anything like that she just loves. She just loves being a little girl, I think — she tries to just fit in with everybody else really, really well.

I remember when Sophie was probably halfway through her stay in hospital after the first accident. She was having operation upon operation and Ron was in there a lot of the time. She goes in and has sedation and it must have been one of these operations that was going to be a difficult one, no one knowing whether it was going to be a good outcome or a bad outcome. Ron was very upset and I remember him saying that she patted him on the back and said, 'Don't worry daddy, I'm fine, I'll be all right'. That makes me shiver when I think about it: here's this little girl going through so much and she could say that to her father.

Especially after the second accident, once she was awake she carried on as if nothing had happened. I think the public see that and think, 'Wow, what a wonderful little girl, she can get through all that adversity and still carry on and still have a beautiful smile on her face'. We visited her early on after the second accident, the day she came out of the induced coma. She was sitting up in bed; there were a fair few people in the room and you wouldn't have thought that she had broken ribs and a broken jaw and a broken collarbone. She was just talking at a hundred miles an hour to everybody. She had this little sticker booklet and everybody had to have a sticker, she'd put a sticker on everybody's hand: 'Your turn now, another one, another one'. She must have been in pain but she didn't show it at all, just amazing.

I think everything that she does in her life the public will know about. Whether that's a good thing I don't know. I think she deals with it well, and I think she realises now that she is a person everybody notices. Now that she's older she is realising that 'I am different and everybody knows me'. They stop her in the street and say hello, and they know her name.

Ann-Louise de La Poype

CAROLYN MARTIN'S SISTER

Ann-Louise lives in France; she has been there permanently since 1992. She first heard about the accident at the Roundhouse when she was woken in the early hours of the morning (2 p.m. Sydney time) by Carolyn calling her from the taxi on the way to the hospital.

Caro was having difficulty breathing, because I remember saying to her, 'You've got to breathe — breathe, breathe, breathe'. Initially Caro said something about a truck landing on her little girl. She said, 'Start praying right now'. I couldn't sleep at all after that. I spent Tuesday trying to get flights. Finally Brian, a family friend in the airline industry, managed to find one for me leaving on Wednesday afternoon. Coming up to Christmas it was very difficult to get a flight. I arrived on Friday morning and my brother picked me up [Greg, who lives in Milwaukee] — he'd been able to get a flight earlier from the States — and he drove me straight out to the hospital. Of course by that stage the big questions — about whether or not to keep Sophie on life support — had been asked. There was one big meeting with family and friends and that had already taken place. So when I came in the mood was, 'Right, let's go for it — Sophie's going to get through this, we'll all work together and she'll come through'. Nevertheless it was totally devastating.

In that period I felt that Sophie was very 'there'. What helped was just talking to her as if she could hear you. That's what all the nurses did, and that showed such great respect. The nurses would say, 'Sophie, we're just going to do this now'. And

Sophie did react — there were times you knew, even though she was in this comatose state, she was also aware of things that were going on around her.

There was another little girl in intensive care who was hooked up to breathing apparatus and to life support. She had these beautiful dark plaits that came down either side of the bed and she died while we were there. It was absolutely devastating, it was this communal pain you could just feel. We prayed every night, we would pray for Sophie and for the other little girl because that was all part of it.

Caro was so amazing. She had these meetings on how to handle the public relations side of things with the hospital. I went to one meeting with her in those first few days and she was saying, 'Right, what are we going to do, next step'. Just so phenomenally present when she herself had been through Emergency; the doctors initially thought she might have had a stroke. I remember being so impressed. Ron was a total stalwart; in those early hours he had really stayed by Sophie and Mitchell and had coped with his daughter and his wife in this dreadful space.

One of the things I've come to realise since the accident is that Caro has an absolutely wonderful network of friends. In one of her early interviews she said that with her family being away her friends have become her family. That's one of the things I've had to wrestle with constantly — the distance that I'm trying to bridge, physically and emotionally. And walking into that situation and feeling you are the sister but perhaps you're not that key person any more. Come what may, the distance changes the nature of your family relationships. I've had to work at them a lot harder and I think I took them for granted before. We can't just expect family to feel close because they're family.

I think we are all a lot closer because of the accidents. I try hard to understand what Caro and Ron are constantly going through. With phone conversations I tend to go on the sound of somebody's voice. On one level you're listening to what they're saying, but on another level you're trying to tune into the soul aspect or to reach across that distance, to feel a deeper connection. It wasn't until the end of 2005 that I had a really good chat with Caro and I felt, 'Caro's back'. Her voice was so full and relaxed and happy and that really struck me.

I was completely devastated by the timing of the second accident because we had just spent a very happy few days in New Zealand. My father had received his PhD from Auckland University so we spent a few days with Sophie, Caro, Ron and Mitchell and the family in New Zealand. Caro, Ron and the kids had flown back home on the Tuesday. I flew from Auckland to Sydney with my girls on the Friday. We arrived at Kingsford Smith, got into the taxi and I heard Ron's voice on the radio saying something about head injuries. I thought, 'No, what are they doing, is it a flashback?' then the news report said, 'Sophie Delezio has been hit by a car an hour and a half ago in Sydney's northern suburbs'. I just said to the taxi driver, 'Right, this changes our plans'. I didn't have a mobile; the taxi driver quickly called his wife in Arabic because he was due to take her to an appointment and then he kindly lent me his mobile. Funnily enough I had everybody's mobile numbers from the first accident with me, so I called around and established what had happened and dropped the kids off at Caro and Ron's house in Seaforth.

The girls were briefed not to say anything to Mitchell — this was after they'd been in tears in the taxi, we realised something was terribly wrong. So I settled things down with them and another friend, Beth, took me out to the hospital.

On that first night, I watched the news bulletin and I saw one of the hospital spokesmen sounding quite positive: 'We know she's got no serious brain injury, we know her internal organs are okay, so she's got every chance' — there was this pretty upbeat attitude. Living in France you forget that there's this attitude, it's an Aussie thing. So when I walked into intensive care with Caro I was ever so slightly smiling, I was thinking that Sophie's going to be okay. I looked at one of the nurses and I thought, 'Ann-Louise, you stupid bloody idiot'. It wasn't even a second of an exchange. I can feel my fingers shaking when I am talking about this. I looked at Sophie and I thought, 'Oh Soph, can you come back, can you come back?' I was so scared for her, I thought that she had gone. You can't really say that under those circumstances; the nursing team were working quietly away; there was not one person who left her for a second. I was aware of this professional body doing what they had to do to keep things afloat and they were working so hard. It wasn't until the next day that Sophie looked so much better, and Caro told me that the registrar said to her how hard they had to work on that Friday night, that it was really life and death.

The depth of the public feeling about Sophie struck me on that Friday night when Beth and I were leaving the hospital around 2 or 3 a.m. There was a note outside Sydney's Children's Hospital and it said, 'to Australia's little Sophie'. That is absolutely phenomenal. I don't know whether that would happen in France; there's something special about the ability of the Australian community to pull together. Sophie had been claimed by the population at large in this huge outpouring of goodwill and love. That one note — I wanted to crumble when I saw that.

The Australian public has a very positive attitude to handicapped people. There will be French people who will disagree, but the French public is just coming to grips with treating handicapped people as part of the community, not something you hide away, that you don't talk about, that you're ashamed of. Australia is light years ahead of that. So Sophie's future, what do I expect? I expect her to be funny, buoyed up by her community, supported by her community but at the same time that she will be as independent as she possibly can be. My mentor at Radio New Zealand, Denis Phelps, was wheelchair-bound and he was the wisest man in the newsroom. I'm sure Sophie will go on and study and perhaps help other people in her situation or become a psychologist or lawyer — or a comedian! Wherever she goes I know she'll make people laugh and feel happy to be alive. Because that's her lesson for us — that life is such a gift.

One of my great fears was that the second accident would affect her spirit, I thought that her beautiful shining light may have been damaged. But quite recently, it was about six weeks ago, I spoke to Sophie on the phone and she had this depth and maturity in her voice that she hadn't had before. It's that voices thing again, you have to go on those threads of information you get from a phone call, you catch on to those resonances. Sophie's voice was clear, she articulated beautifully.

Sophie is a miracle child — she wasn't expected and she arrived with a mission, guided by a sparkling light. If Sophie hadn't had this wonderful, funny strength about her she would not have got through. She was buoyed by Ron's humour and Caro's tenaciousness, by the family atmosphere and wonderful and good friends. But Sophie herself — she's just extremely special. The whole thing of being involved in not one but two accidents — how can you make sense of that? It brings us to the very core of our existence — why are we here? It exposes the fragility of existence.

I've wrestled with guilt, being away from the people I love, and I realise that I need to take more care of my friends. I want to express the surreal nature of the two occasions, especially the second one, which I found much, much more difficult to deal with than the first. I had expected to meet up with old friends and share a few glasses of good Australian wine and it wasn't like that at all. It was suddenly being confronted with the horror again, set against the most beautiful physical surroundings: Sydney in the sunshine.

Greg Martin
CAROLYN MARTIN'S BROTHER

Greg lives in Milwaukee, USA, so for him the news of Sophie's first accident came at two in the morning. Carolyn and Ron called him when they were racing to Royal North Shore Hospital.

It was odd; I hadn't been able to sleep that night. I was up pacing about the house for a good hour, so when they rang I wasn't asleep. Ron was reasonably calm — 'Sophie's been in an accident'. In the background Caro was screaming, saying, 'You pray for my little girl, you pray for my little girl'. I couldn't hear Ron over Caro's screaming; I was trying to ascertain what was going on and I said to Ron, 'What do you mean?' Ron was telling me that they had taken Sophie to Royal North Shore and now they were taking her to another hospital. I was saying to Ron, 'Where are they taking her?' and he didn't know or was blanking out. Caro wanted to get in touch with Mum but they were away for the weekend, so Ron asked me to get in touch with them or get them on an aeroplane. We went on the Internet and tuned into a couple of radio stations; we started putting the pieces together and figuring out what had happened. At that time we didn't know how badly Sophie was hurt. I was on the phone with my sister and as the night went on we got more and more of the radio reports, and I was frantically calling people in New Zealand trying to find Mum and Dad.

My recollections of those first two or three hours are crystal clear — it's not the sort of thing you forget very easily. There was that sense of isolation, because I couldn't get hold of Mum and Dad. And a sense of hopelessness because we were so far away we couldn't just jump in a car and get there. But also a sense of action — one thing with our family is that we've always got things done somehow. My sister and I both organised plane tickets through the course of the night. We also called friends and family in Sydney who filled us in. By the time I was on the way to the airport we were aware of just how severe everything was. At that stage it didn't look very good at all. Ron wanted the family members down there so he could make decisions with family input, which in hindsight was an incredibly deep thought from him at that stage — with what he was going through, to think that way. He realised maybe he would need help to make life or death decisions, so if they had to take Sophie off the ventilator he wanted it to be all the family deciding. By that stage I'd spoken to Mum and Dad and they were in a bit of shock. They got home and there were three or four messages on the answering machine. They couldn't understand much of it, so I spoke to them and told them what had happened and what little we knew. I think Mum knew how serious it was; it took a little while to sink in to Dad.

After the accident — oh, it was just horrific. Realising that a human being can have such significant injuries and still recover was pretty remarkable to me. Once she was all bandaged Soph looked a lot more comfortable but maybe that was just because it wasn't as hard for us to look at. Her injuries were covered in bandages so you could pretend they weren't there. Once they amputated her legs and the bandages weren't there any more, that's what I will always remember. Now when I see her they don't bother me but every second it reminds you of the accident.

When the second accident happened, Mum and Dad called me. They were much more emotional about the second one; Sophie had just been in New Zealand, so having just seen her, Mum and Dad were a lot more upset. It was almost déjà vu. We went downstairs to the Internet and I could hear Caro going into the hospital saying the same thing she did in the first accident, asking everybody to pray for Sophie — that got me pretty unsettled.

It was the same drill — I got the family organised, called as many people as I could. We had a support group that we sent monthly updates of Sophie's progress throughout the first accident; it went all around the world, an incredible prayer circle. So I shot off a group email to them asking for their prayers. I talked to Ron a bit more before I left and the friends who were around them, just finding out how bad the second one was.

Through the first accident and the second accident I particularly remember how wonderful people were — the warmth of strangers when a family is in a lonely place. It's something that you can't give enough thanks for: the prayers that we got, the little old lady who rode two buses to give Sophie a doll, the outpouring of emotion and the feeling that you were being comforted by people you didn't even know, whether it was a friend picking you up from the airport or someone who had dropped dinner off. Just people helping in every way.

I don't know that the accidents have changed Sophie. She has always been strong, that's one of the things about her. Sophie would never consider being second best; with an older brother, whatever he did she was going to do. A competitive spirit, a very strong-willed spirit. I think Caro has always been that way too, and I think a lot of it comes from my mother. Even when Sophie was sick in bed, unconscious, she seemed strong. When the doctors would come and move her she would start shaking her arm even when she was unconscious; she would sort of fight them off, either because it hurt or she didn't want to be bothered. I never saw her in a situation where she wasn't in control. In the first accident we left the decision up to her: 'Soph, if you want to fight, fight'. She never gave us any signal that she wouldn't fight. She was going to do it her way and her way was to fight.

I think that Caro and Ron gained from Sophie's strength some strength of their own. They felt that if Sophie was going to fight, they had little choice but to fight alongside her. Caro and Ron were both strong people before the accident; they were aware of what they wanted in life. This has changed some of the direction but not their resolve.

I think that Sophie will continue to be a fighter. She will be a champion of causes; I'm not sure what causes she will pick, I'll leave that up to her, whether it's global warming or burn victims or amputees. Whatever she does she's going to give everything that's within her to fight for that cause.

Some people have the 'it' factor; Sophie has the 'it' factor — it's hard to describe exactly what that is, but she has it. As she gets older and more on the road to recovery, or her hair gets a little bit longer, she looks more and more radiant. She was always a beautiful kid but she looks more and more beautiful with each picture we see.

9

The circle of friends

Perhaps because their family is so scattered, Ron and Carolyn have a close-knit network of friends who provided enormous support right from the Roundhouse accident and through the highs and lows following it. Each person stepped into a role: helping with media, setting up meal rosters or holding hands. Everyone did what they could. In the years following that first accident, the shape of those friendships has shifted; some people have drawn closer, while others stepped back after the initial crisis.

Carolyn Martin

SOPHIE'S MOTHER

We had a big team of friends at the hospital because everyone wanted to support us. People took on different things depending on their areas of expertise and what they could cope with and manage in their own lives. Beth [Minogue] is gorgeous, she doesn't do the hospital thing by her own admission and her husband can't do the hospital thing, but she does the ferrying of my family, organises their mobile phones, all of that, and you just know it is going to get done. You have absolute trust in your friends and know they will do whatever is needed. Dave Palmer [Louise Palmer's husband] is the breakfast man — he has breakfast with us all the time. He discovered the Tai Chi outside Westmead Hospital, so I'd go off to do Tai Chi, and he would just come and sit with Sophie.

I remember when we were staying at Ronald McDonald House, we'd said to one of the oncology mums — who were a great support in the early days at Westmead — 'How do you survive?' She said that you ride the roller coaster, you learn to live with the highs and lows, and you will soon find out who your friends are, because there will be ones you will expect to be with you and who won't be, and there are ones who will surprise you because you never thought they'd be there for you, and they are. You don't want to have expectations, but you do — because they are your friends.

Maree Thomas

SOPHIE'S 'FAIRY GODMOTHER'

Maree has known Ron and Carolyn for about 20 years. As Sophie's 'fairy godmother', she brings magic into Sophie and Mitchell's lives, donning her fairy wings and dress and waving her magic wand.

I was at the local shopping centre when I got a call from Caro. She was in a police car, unable to talk. One of our friends, Linda, was with her and she just said, 'Sophie has been in a serious accident at her preschool and Caro wants you to pray for her'. When I got off the phone I couldn't move — I was with Sophie two days before, playing being her fairy godmother and granting her wishes.

It was quite a surreal experience. I didn't know how bad she was, but if Caro was in a police car Sophie must be really bad. I went straight home; listening to the radio I heard them say on the news, 'There has been a serious accident'. I ran into the house and turned on the TV. There was a child wrapped in silver being wheeled to an ambulance and I just thought, 'Not Sophie, please God'. I knew Sophie and the family needed support, so I just started praying and praying. The next call I got was 'Caro is in shock, they are putting her into Emergency, Sophie is in a coma — it's not good, get to the hospital now'.

I felt like I was having a nightmare. I jumped into the car and started driving. I thought about how I had always felt Caro was someone special, someone with a heart of gold who cared so much for people and life. We had worked together for a few years, and I knew that she was also a woman of great inner strength.

I arrived at the hospital and went straight to intensive care, where Ron told me he had come with Sophie by helicopter and Caro was in shock down in Emergency [at Westmead Hospital]. He took me straight in to Sophie. She was almost unrecognisable, she was so swollen up, and then I saw her black little toes, and I thought, 'Oh God, please not Sophie, what's happening?' I started to talk to Sophie even though she was unconscious; I wanted her to know I was there and I loved her.

I stayed with Ron and Sophie until about 3 a.m. when the chaplain came and got me. She said Caro was still having convulsions and they could not stop them; she felt it would be good for me to be with her. As I walked down to Emergency in the early hours of the morning, the hospital felt so eerie. I was shown to where Caro was. When I saw her on the bed, her whole body shaking, that was when I nearly totally lost it. I felt the most incredible pain go right through me. I knew I was feeling her pain and I wanted to collapse myself.

I pulled myself together because I just wanted to be there for my friend, but what could I do? I started to pray and ask God to help me with my friend and I started to do a healing on her. Then miraculously she opened her eyes and asked me to get her out of there. I organised a wheelchair and signed her out. With the help of a nurse's aide I took her back up to her little girl. On the way up she looked at me in absolute shock and terror and said she couldn't take looking at her own little girl. I looked into her eyes; her pain was so severe.

This day totally changed my life. I started questioning my own life — what was it all about? What's really important in life? I had my own successful property business at the time; I went back and told my staff I wanted to close the business early — it was almost Christmas. I never re-opened. Life had a different meaning after Sophie's accident.

It was the most devastating experience, but it strengthened my faith in something greater than myself — my belief in a higher power. I have seen miracles. In something as bad as this, the amount of support from family, friends, the tremendous goodness that has come from people and the community all coming together, so much love and effort to help Sophie — it is so inspiring and unbelievable. It has helped me to see the good in so many things, rather than dwell on the negative.

I went to the hospital nearly every day for months. I would take food over for them, and I met many families having their own profound experiences. It was such a blessing to be able to give some support, be it food or a laugh, amongst their traumas. When I saw the extent of pain and suffering in others, children fighting for their lives, everything else paled into insignificance. It put everything into perspective. I don't take my own problems and difficulties in life so seriously now. I'm tremendously grateful for my own life and I have felt compelled to do something that gives happiness and help to others.

I found it very humbling to witness Sophie's courage, strength and will to live, and all I wanted to do was be with her. When she was in a coma I would sing her favourite nursery rhymes, I'd read her favourite books to her.

They started cutting bits off her that couldn't be saved because they were too burnt. I remember one day sitting in the waiting room. Ron came out and started to cry, saying they were going to cut Sophie's legs off and put them in the bin. My heart went out to Ron — I knew the pain *I* was feeling, so his must be horrific. I put my arms around him and held him; there was nothing I could say.

Sophie had last seen me as the fairy godmother with my tiara and wand, and I wanted her to have her fairy godmother. My idea was to have a magical and creative world for Sophie to experience and feel safe; a way to deal with her situation, something that would help her gain some perspective and normality in her life. I would go to the hospital dressed in my fairy clothes or sometimes in my rainbow pyjamas with my rainbow hair. She loves fairies and we would talk about my sisters the fairies, and how we would fly to the hospital at night when she was sleeping and look after her. When she got home, she had glow fairies on her wall. One day she showed me the biggest one in the middle and told me it was Magic Maree and that I looked after her when she was sleeping.

I remember the first time I picked Sophie up after the accident. I was so nervous — she had bandages everywhere, how would I hold her and not hurt her? I picked her up and she looked up at me and just beamed and moved her head on my cheek; she totally relaxed me. Sophie has been a wonderful teacher to me.

One day I was doing Sophie's hair. She was about three and a half. She looked up at me, a little concerned, and said 'Magic Aree' — she called me Aree, she couldn't say Maree — 'I don't really like my hair'; you know her head didn't have much hair on it at all. Then with the biggest beam on her face she said, 'but I am going to love it when I am five'.

Sophie wanted to show me through her photograph album. As she opened the first page she said, 'There I am in Mummy's tummy'. Then she opened up the next page and said, 'There I am as a little baby'. Then she turned to the next page, a photo before the accident, and with great pride and joy she said, 'There are my legs'. It was another lesson for me — I felt my chin quiver, I wanted to be brave for her; but she simply went on showing the rest of the photos and we had fun together.

Last year I was with her at a Day of Difference charity night. She went up on stage and was a little shy. When she came off the stage people were calling out to her; by the time she got back to me, she asked me if she could get back on stage. I explained it was a little too late for that. She's really quite a smart little girl, because this year just before she went up she looked at me and reminded me how she wanted to go back up. I told her this was her big chance and that there were a lot of people who really cared about her and wanted her to say hello to them. She was so excited and wanted to say hi to everyone. By the time she got on stage she was beaming from ear to ear and moved to the front of the stage waving at everyone. I was so proud of her.

I was in Bali on a yoga and meditation retreat when I got the call about the second accident. I didn't know where to put myself, I was in shock. I was getting calls and text messages saying that everything possible was being done for her. The best way I could think of to help was to stay in Bali and strengthen myself, to be able to fully support them when I got back and others were tired — I knew what it was like before — and so I would be there when Sophie came out of the coma.

I think you've *got* to experience some of the suffering and some of the pain to get that courage or to look beyond it to the bigger picture, but that's a really hard thing to say to someone when they're in pain. Through Sophie, thousands and thousands of people have been given peace, courage — all these wonderful gifts. At the moment I'm shaking a little bit because so much is being gained. Here's Sophie at two going out there and changing the world. I was helping Caro with the letters that were coming through from people about Sophie, about how they couldn't get out of bed because they had something devastating happen to them in their lives, but they looked at Sophie and said, 'If you can keep going so can I'. They've cut off her ear, they've cut off her fingers, they've cut off her legs, she's been burned to the bone in some areas, her skin's never ever going to grow. So people are seeing this child getting up and still smiling and still finding joy, and through that they're healing their own lives. That's miraculous, that they're healing their own lives.

Sophie and Mitchell are a big part of my life and I know I'll always be there for them. I love them with all my heart.

Katy Gompes
HER DAUGHTER, OLIVIA, ATTENDED THE ROUNDHOUSE CHILDCARE CENTRE WITH SOPHIE

My initial relationship was more with the family rather than Soph, despite the fact that Livvie and Soph were in the same room; it had 13 children in it every day, so it was quite a small community. Livvie was sleeping very close to Sophie on the day of the accident.

I was at an assembly at Balgowlah Heights Public School when the accident happened. My son was being elected a school leader and we didn't know whether he was going to get the school captaincy or not, so I promised I would be there for him. I was in the hall with my mobile phone off; a person tapped me on my shoulder as the announcements were coming and she said, 'You've got to come, I've got to talk to you'. I said, 'Can't it wait? I promised Ben I'd be here' and she said, 'No, this is really urgent — you've got to come'. I remember being told there had been a dreadful accident at the childcare centre; a car had gone into it and one of the children was killed.

I must have gone into shock; it is a very random thing to hit you. Then Robin Hardiman came up — her Chelsea and Sophie and Livvie are little buddies together — and she said, 'I've seen Olivia, she is all right but you've got to go now'. I remember driving down there, thinking people have only told me she's okay so I can drive there — obviously more delayed shock. And being told a child had died — I couldn't understand. I thought a car had run through the back of the playground; I couldn't imagine the magnitude of what had occurred.

When I got there I hit a trauma scene. I remember telling somebody where to go because they said, 'You can't go there' and I said, 'My child is in there and you can't tell me what I can do'. But when I got to Olivia I remember being very calm and saying, 'Tell me what happened' and 'What did you smell?' and 'What did you see?', and just trying to be very level about it, but obviously inside I was very distraught. Robin said when she found Chelsea and Livvie they were clinging together, cuddling under a tree. There were a lot of people sitting there singing songs with the kids, so they were being distracted. She didn't appear traumatised at that stage; I think she was just pleased to see familiar faces.

Olivia was probably the most advanced in age in the Possum Room at the time. Because she has quite a talented verbal ability she was able to communicate the things she'd experienced, whereas some of the younger ones didn't have the ability to get it out. She went into what you would describe as broken record — she just kept going over and over the same things. I remember her saying she tried to push the car away and she couldn't. Other people were being taken out and she

224

said, 'I'm here, get me, get me, I'm here too'. For about nine months afterwards she would draw pictures of broken buildings and ambulances, and she was petrified of fire engines for a while afterwards.

Two days after the accident I took her back there. I wanted to be there to honour the staff — I trusted them with Olivia's life and I knew they did everything they could. So we went back to the centre and that was a reassuring thing for Olivia, because the wreckage had been cleared out and she saw it could be reconstructed and rebuilt. I did have a sense of, 'How lucky am I', that Olivia is okay, and I felt great anguish that [other] little souls weren't okay. There was that mixed feeling — if one of them is not all right, none of them are all right.

The next morning we had a crisis session at Manly council. I went with Geata, the director of the childcare centre; we had *60 Minutes*, Channel 9 news — they all wanted to do interviews, so Geata asked me to be the media rep on behalf of the parents of the Roundhouse. The next three or four days were a very harrowing time. We'd booked a holiday so we took off, but I was being hounded by the press. Sophie's details weren't released for two or three days, so I had people ringing me wanting to know the surname and wanting to get a picture of the room where Sophie was. I felt an overwhelming sense that I couldn't allow this information out before the family were ready. It wasn't my position to speak on behalf of them, but I felt it was my position to try to protect them. I don't come from a media background; I can certainly confront things, but this was a whole new thing. I was probably in shock myself, and quite intimidated by some of the names that were approaching me. It's not easy telling people of that stature to back off.

When Caro and Ron were in a position where they could see people, I would go to Westmead and take things like beautiful noodles and fresh yoghurts, all those pampering things — nobody likes hospital food for too long. Then knowing Sophie was going to come out, I went and saw Ron and Caro and said, 'What can we do to support you coming out?' We went back to the Roundhouse and put in a cook-a-casserole program. People would bring in their casseroles and drop them at the Roundhouse and then three times a week we would transport them up to the house. Again I was aware of their personal space; we put an Esky at the bottom of the stairs and put the food in there so they didn't have to be bothered.

Sophie's got spunk, a glint in her eye and a spirit that shines from her soul. I think that is what the public sees. I also think that's why Sophie's story has hit such a nerve with the public — it could have been anybody's child. We hear about traffic accidents all the time, but the concept that you are trusting the care of your child to someone else while you work to provide for your family and that child isn't kept safe is every parent's nightmare. It was timing, the fact it happened on the day the kids were going to have their Christmas party — everything that it should never have been.

What I've come to terms with is that whatever greater source of energy there is — call it God, spirituality — Sophie is there to shine faith to others. Her recovery from both accidents is nothing but a miracle. As humans it brings us back to that fragility level; that we never know what is going to happen in life. You might think you've got everything handled, but one day something might come at you, so embrace life on a daily basis. But I was initially very angry — not at the driver, I was angry that this could have happened to her. Why her? Why does she need to go through this? And for Caro and Ron, why do they have to go through this again?

In some ways putting the infrastructure behind them after the second accident was easier because we all knew what worked. Because I'd developed a bond of friendship with the family I was happy to go to the hospital earlier this time. I saw Caro the day Soph came out of her coma; we didn't predict that, I went there to try to give Caro a bit of TLC and support, so I was very thrilled she'd come out. The first day Soph was allowed to leave her room Olivia was there, so Olivia went on her first walk with her and they ate a little bit of toast together and then hugged each other and told each other how much they loved each other. You know, that is the bond of friendship. I said to Ron and Caro, 'There might be a lot of people with you after the first accident, but we are going to be there for her twenty-first, come what may, so you better get used to us being around'.

It will be a long road, and I think that is what I find very confronting. A burns accident is not like an ordinary accident, that there is an initial accident and then recovery. I am all too well aware how many operations Sophie is going to have to go through until she is 18. Seeing Olivia jumping and skipping around in a bikini, and then Sophie swimming with all the physical obstacles that she has, I only look at Sophie and see what an amazing sparkle she has. I don't see her disfigurement now at all, but when I initially saw them side by side, I did think Olivia was very lucky to have not been hurt.

Valerie Southey

HER SON, PETER, ATTENDED THE ROUNDHOUSE CHILDCARE CENTRE WITH SOPHIE

When the accident happened, the car came through the window and through a stud wall and apparently Peter was lying just next to that stud wall. There was Peter, then another child, then Sophie, so the car went over Peter, over the other girl and landed on Sophie. Someone said Peter was the one who crawled out of a cupboard; I think a bookshelf fell on Peter and he was lucky. He had a tiny burn on his toe and smoke inhalation; he had to go to hospital to be looked at because he had soot up his nose and that was it.

You count your blessings but you also think what a random thing, it could have been Peter. They slept on the floor, they didn't have a regular spot to sleep in, so it was just the way they happened to sleep that day. It was a terrible, freaky sort of thing.

I am a teacher, and I was at Manly Vale Public School, which is close by. I'd been on playground duty; I went back into the classroom and I heard my mobile ringing, and they told me there had been an accident. I don't remember exactly what they told me, it is a bit of a blur, but I remember them saying Peter was okay and could I come. I just knew instantly it was terrible. I used to be a kids' nurse and I worked in the burns unit for a few years. The road was sectioned off but they let me through.

I had to park my car further up because there were so many emergency vehicles there and I had to run. I remember running past the Roundhouse and seeing a big hole there — I don't think I even saw the car, just a big hole. It was just chaotic, looking for Peter. They had the kids who were to go in an ambulance sectioned off with police tape. There was no smoke at that stage, just horrified people everywhere. I probably ran past Sophie on the grass, I don't really know. I remember seeing horrified looks on people's faces — that just lives with me, those mothers looking for their children. Then I found Peter and he was being cuddled by Marg, one of the staff. She said she thought he was in a bit of shock, because he was just so quiet and shut down.

I remember watching parents as they came, the look of anguish on their faces, looking for their kids. At that time we didn't know what was going on; I remember them saying there might be kids in there, they didn't know. And I was just praying that it wasn't the kids I knew, which is really awful, I wouldn't have wanted it to happen to any of them. Then I got in the ambulance with Peter and my husband came and followed us to the hospital. It took me a long time before I could even hear an ambulance or see one without going into a cold sweat. I remember we had to go back to the Roundhouse afterwards and for some reason an ambulance was there, I don't know why, and it just freaked me out. We came back to my house and we were just in this really weird sort of euphoria of, 'Thank God our kids are okay'. The kids just got on and played as kids do. Then we started to get the news of how bad it really was for the other kids. It was just terrible; I guess we had a lot of guilt.

Peter was traumatised for about a year. He came out with some awful things, like, 'The car nearly squished me'. He couldn't stand any loud noises; he used to follow me around, I couldn't be in a different room. We had a lot of thunderstorms at the end of that year and he'd be terrified of that rumbling noise — I guess it was like the car's engine. He'd shimmy up me and just shake. He was stuttering and we were seeing someone for that, and he regressed with his toileting. But I guess you compare yourself to what Sophie's parents went through and you think, 'We're all right, we're fine'. It's all relative. I'd nursed kids who were 60 per cent burnt and didn't make it, so when I heard about Sophie's burns I really prayed — and I felt awful about this — she could go peacefully. I thought, 'There is no way this kid is going to survive'.

I think her survival is down to her family. Ron and Carolyn are amazing people; that sounds like a cliché but their strength of vision and, especially, the way they don't blame — they just put all their energy into getting Sophie better. Not leaving her, just being there, talking to her when she was unconscious. I was at the classroom the other day and Ron was just watching at the doorway — it is always lovely to spy on the children and watch, we all do that now and then. I was chatting to him and he said something like, 'I wonder if it is detrimental to the other kids, Sophie being in that class'. I was just so surprised by that, I said, 'They only benefit from Sophie being in that class'. They learn more acceptance and tolerance and understanding at a very young age and that can only be good for them as they grow older.

I was at reading group this morning, and Sophie and Carolyn were there. She is such a great kid; she's gutsy, she's determined, she's funny, she's delightful. And I think that faith they've got, that really supported them too and comforted them. If it was me and I didn't have that faith I don't know if I could be that strong. The Day of Difference and everything they've done — watching Sophie's journey, it gives everyone inspiration. I just think everybody loves that kid, everybody wants her to get better and better. When it happened my daughter had a little photo of Sophie up in her bedroom and they used to light candles. Peter has a soft spot for Sophie; she came to his birthday party last year and we had Gizmo the clown. Gizmo said, 'And who is special here?' and Peter put his hand up and said, 'Sophie is special'.

I remember one day we bumped into them at Arranounbai; Peter used to go there for some OT work. I hadn't seen Sophie since the accident. I remember being shocked to see her, shocked to see how disabled this little girl was. My heart was breaking for her and her mum and also — it could have been Peter, all that emotion was still raw. When we were in the car, Peter said something like, 'Oh Sophie can't play 'cause she's got no legs'. It sounded cruel but it was harmless, just something kids would say. I yelled at him and said, 'Of course she can', and then he started to cry at my uncharacteristic way of speaking to him. It was just because I was hurting so badly for Carolyn and Sophie and he was just saying something a normal three-year-old would say. It gave me a taste of what Carolyn must have to face up to; people who say stupid things or who just say thoughtless things or don't know what to say.

And Sophie's okay, you know; today she had her legs on, other days she doesn't, and she moves pretty quickly round that classroom. You get struck sometimes — sometimes I see the aide walking out carrying her legs or something ... but she is bubbly and chirpy, she has a big grin on her face, she's happy. She was telling us today she went to a concert on the weekend and we were laughing because she just wouldn't stop, she just kept talking and talking. Golly she can talk, she is just delightful.

One day when she came and played, she had cake and was saying, 'Can I have another one?', and I thought, 'Why not?' You have to treat her like a normal kid; the thing is you don't want to spoil her. She got on Peter's trampoline — that was great, loves a good bounce. Likes animals, loves our guinea pigs, just like any other kid.

Linda Jones Meader

A LONG-TERM FRIEND OF SOPHIE'S MOTHER, CAROLYN

I have known Ron and Caro for about 15 years. I ended up living with them for a period of time when I separated from my first husband. They introduced me to my current husband, so we have very strong connections. I have known Sophie and Mitchell since they were born. There is a core group of us, we call ourselves the 'mah-jong girls'. We still play mah-jong — it used to be every week and then after babies it was about every month, and now it's about every six weeks. We even played mah-jong at the hospital.

Sophie was at my daughter's birthday party two days before the accident. Even then her spirit was amazing; she was saying at the end of the party 'come to our place for a swim now', still trying to socialise and keep the party going.

Caro rang me when the accident happened. She was on her way to Royal North Shore Hospital, I was in the car driving to Chatswood [about 5 km away] and I just turned around and said, 'I'll meet you at North Shore'. She said, 'I need you to go pick up Mitchell from school' and she told me Sophie had had a dreadful accident and she didn't know what the full story was. I said, 'I'll get Wayne to go get Mitchell and I'll be with you'. So I met her down at North Shore, that horrible blue room where we all congregated. They were trying to stabilise Sophie before they airlifted her. The thing that I will never forget is the smell of burnt flesh and seeing her wrapped in the foil and not knowing whether she was going to be okay.

I went in the police car to Westmead with Caro. It was peak hour, horrendous traffic. Ron went with Sophie in the helicopter; we didn't know what was going to happen, we didn't know if she would survive the flight. Caro got me to ring everyone in her Filofax and start praying. I just had to keep talking to Caro to keep her coherent, I'll never forget that. It took us about an hour to get there. I felt helpless, completely helpless but I was there to hold her hand and to basically do whatever she needed me to do. When we got to Westmead it was just so surreal, we didn't know whether Sophie was going to make it. The whole situation was very bleak.

I left the hospital about three in the morning, then someone else arrived to take my place — we set up a roster immediately, we slept on the floor in the intensive care waiting room. There was a whole team of us that came out on a regular basis, that was the focus of our life for a few months — as well as trying to keep our own families going. It was a very stressful time, but it was all about supporting them and doing what we could. There was a huge feeling of helplessness and not knowing what to say. We took many meals and tried to have some sense of normality at least for an hour or two a day. It was tough because my daughter had just turned five; she was starting school in February just after the accident and she was petrified of going to school. She said, 'Oh Mummy, a car is going to run into my school and I don't want to go there'. It was really tough on her, because she was and still is a very good friend of Sophie's. For us as a family it made us realise how lucky we are. Unfortunately it takes such a tragedy to appreciate what you've got yourself.

We saw Sophie in some dreadful situations — when all her organs were in bags outside her body, she was so swollen you couldn't recognise her, and day by day we didn't know if she would survive or not. That's why we had to be there round the clock; if anything happened we had to be there. Sophie just has so much strength. Also Carolyn's faith is very strong — that really came through, and I'm sure that helped a lot. There are a few of us who did some healing work on Sophie every moment we had in intensive care. We did everything we could; we read her stories, we didn't know if she could hear us — it didn't matter.

The second accident was like déjà vu — the same hospital room at North Shore where I met Caro and thought, 'This can't be happening again'. When I got the call I just dropped everything because we live so close to North Shore Hospital. I was there in two minutes; I knew what to do, I rang Sister Brigid and Father Paul. They said, 'We are going to put Carolyn and

Ron in a taxi'; I said, 'No you are not, you are going to put her in a police car because that's what we did last time and that worked'. So I was able to assist in some of those bigger decisions, and then got the whole support network happening again over at Randwick, making sure Carolyn had the things she needed. I just held her hand most of the time. I'm the hand-holder — I guess I always take a bit of a background position as well because I don't really like the media side of things.

I was the person in the first accident who did the texting. People were texting Ron saying, 'How is Sophie?' One good thing might have happened, but they'd had five setbacks at the same time, so it was a very fine line on communicating with all the friends and relatives what the current situation was. I'd say to Ron, 'What message do you want to send to everyone?' Every two or three days I'd send a text to about 60 people. I did a similar thing the second time, I just slotted into my job. I guess I've realised I can function in a great tragedy, but it's not something you want to do.

Trudy Wise

A LONG-TERM FRIEND OF SOPHIE'S PARENTS,
RON AND CAROLYN

I met Caro a long time ago, ten years ago I think. We both had miscarriages the first time round; we were both women who desperately wanted children, so that was something we had in common. Caro fell pregnant with Sophie about the same time I fell pregnant with my son, Zach, and then both the children were born at the same hospital on the same day. That knitted us a lot closer together. Caro already had a child, so she was a bit of a guidance officer for me in the first year of having a baby.

It was the Christmas party at my own son's kindy the day the Roundhouse accident happened. I was driving home and I heard all these ambulances heading down towards Manly. About an hour and a half later, my phone rang. It was Linda [Jones Meader] and she said, 'Sophie has been really badly hurt at daycare and is in a critical condition and Caro wanted you to pray for her'. I couldn't quite figure this out; I was listening to this message and thinking, what on earth could have happened to her at daycare that she is critical? I was 22 weeks pregnant at that time with Eleanor, so I was completely over-emotional. I was getting into the heavily pregnant stage, it was warm, it was getting into Christmas where you can just start to relax and let go a little bit . . .

So I rang my babysitter and asked her to keep an eye on Zach. I rang Linda back and said, 'What happened to her?' I think she said a car had gone into the Roundhouse but there were no details. I went to the church and the church was closed and I didn't know what to do. So I sat in the car and I was crying. I came home and I watched the news and I saw some children they were taking off to hospital and I didn't recognise Sophie there. Then there were two children that were in those blanket things and you couldn't see them, and Sophie was one of them.

One or two hours later the network was happening — Linda, Carolyn Reid, myself, Dave and Louise Palmer, Ron's son John. I couldn't go to the hospital straight away; I wanted to go, but I just felt too emotional and far too close to the whole thing. When you have two children born on the same day it's a bond, and when one of them gets really badly hurt, it's very close to home. I was afraid I'd just start crying and I wasn't going to go out there and do that, that was the last thing anyone needed.

Caro and Ron were giving clear instructions that I was not to go because they didn't want anything happening to me or the baby, so I went to Linda and Wayne's on the Tuesday night just to be closer. I picked up the phone at Linda's house and it was Ron; I didn't know what to say. He was crying; the doctors had told him she would lose her toes, the top of her right ear and the fingers on her right hand. The doctors must have known then though that it was going to be worse than the toes. By the Friday I had to go. I needed to see them, so I organised a babysitter and went there after work.

Ron took me in to see Sophie; she was quite puffed up in her face, all her limbs were wrapped. I only saw her two or three times before the amputations because of the risk of infection; I had a child going to daycare two days a week, you don't want to be responsible for putting any other infections in there.

Our job was to support the family. We couldn't do anything more for Sophie than the hospital were doing. At this point it was keep her alive, keep her alive — that was all anybody was thinking of at that time. People were saying to me, 'They should just let her go'. I felt a bit offended by that, because if it was my child, I wouldn't be very happy if someone was saying that to me.

I remember Ron said, 'I've got all these media people coming around', and I said, 'If you want someone to help you manage it I'll do that'. I was lucky because I was able to do something practical to contribute. So many people just wanted to know how she was, so we put out regular updates to the media.

Weeks went by; I would go to the hospital during the week, and talk to Deb [Fowler], the PR person at the hospital, and see Sophie and Ron and Caro. Sunday night I'd usually go out and take dinner; you are operating another home out there so you just need everything for day-to-day life.

Christmas was a wipeout that year, it was a very sad time. It was just such a great tragedy and it could have happened to any one of us.

You keep asking how you'd deal with it if it was your child but it's not possible to comprehend that. We put the statement out saying she'd lost the right leg from the foot, the left leg from the knee, her right ear and her fingers. I don't think people really understood until that.

When Sophie did regain consciousness, the hardest thing for Caro was that she was so sad, so very sad. Caro would say to me, 'God, I don't want a two-year-old on Prozac'. There were so many parents of children and children who had been through serious issues who end up on antidepressants, which you can completely understand.

I'd lie in bed at night with my baby in my belly and my son here and hold them and realise just how lucky I was to know they were safe. I just can't see children suffering. When she was at Randwick I heard the PR people say, 'We've got a hospital full of

Sophies here'. That's what they say at Westmead too, people don't realise. I know Sophie has horrific injuries, but she is alive; some people's beautiful little babies die. It's really quite shocking to realise how much trauma and tragedy some families deal with. We all just go on with our lives and you don't realise how so many people suffer until you see it.

When they took her out of intensive care and into the ward it was a big moment for me. It had been only family visiting for many weeks by this stage. I was going out there one Sunday, preparing for a normal visit. Ron said to me, 'You can go and see Sophie'. I was quite taken aback because I hadn't prepared for it; I was also about four weeks off having a baby. Anyway, I went in to see her. I just talked to her and said, 'Do you want to feel my big belly?' I held her little bandaged hand, and then Caro came back in and we chatted a bit. After that it got a bit easier going to see her. One night, Caro had gone away for three or four hours and I put her hand on my belly and she felt the baby move. When Caro came back she said, 'Mummy, Mummy, I felt the baby move'. That was a highlight, it really seemed to perk her up a bit.

She had a great night that night, she ate well, chatted — but the following weekend, she nearly died. Caro said to me, 'I really thought she was going to die' and you know, you could tell; you would try to read to her and she couldn't settle, she was so tired but she couldn't sleep. You'd read to her and her little eyes would almost go to sleep and then something would happen, it was probably the cocktail of drugs. Things change all the time out there, she was up, down, in intensive care, out of intensive care — it was a real roller coaster.

Louise Palmer

A FRIEND OF SOPHIE'S MOTHER, CAROLYN,
SINCE THEIR TEENS IN NEW ZEALAND

I was here at home when the accident at the Roundhouse happened. Lee [Tonelli] rang and said, 'I don't know the details but Sophie has been really badly hurt and I'm on my way to the hospital', and hung up. I think at that point I went through denial. It is a pattern of mine; I think, 'It can't be that bad'. But as it turned out, it was.

I didn't go to the hospital that night; I didn't know whether it was right to have everybody jumping on board at that stage. My husband is a bit of an insomniac, so he went in really early the next morning. He came home and then I got the feeling that it probably was a good thing to do and I went in. It was a really distressing time for everybody.

I remember the turning point for Sophie quite clearly. At one point the doctor said to Carolyn, 'There is an option to turn the life support off' and she said, 'I can't possibly make that decision without my family being here'. They are scattered all over the world — New Zealand, France and America — and they got there very quickly. But by the time they did it wasn't an option any more; as Caro said, Sophie made the choice. It seems to be like that the second time around as well. She really seems to want to be here.

In the hospital we used to go on mail duty. Masses and masses of mail arrived every day, and Caro keeps wonderful track of addresses and names so she can get back to people. Sophie would be so alert with parcels coming; she was very heavily sedated at times, but not a thing would slip by her. You'd be unwrapping something and putting it in a bag — a lot of the toys went to charities. She'd open her eyes and say, 'That's mine, is that my present?' You would just think, 'How did she spot that?' You couldn't sneak a little thing past her, she is so astute and on the ball.

Sophie had a will of iron — still has, that hasn't changed at all. Very precocious in terms of, if she wants something she gets something, and that is a trait that has served her well. I don't know how you come out of something like that unscathed, unchanged. I think it will have an impact forever, probably make Sophie a much stronger person. Undeniably her character was there originally and I don't think a lot of other children would have survived that; it was her character that got her through.

In the early days Ron was really strong and supporting Caro and then Ron fell apart and they reversed roles; Caro picked up the reins. It was almost as if one had to stay strong while the other wasn't. Emotionally they have really been through the wringer. You'd have to grow from that. They have quite a different perspective on life, in terms of what is important. When something like that happens, you realise things that seem tragic at the time are really quite inconsequential. They have a greater understanding and empathy for anyone who has any problems, I think they are a lot more compassionate. They have witnessed first-hand the shortfalls in the system as well, so they are a lot more political in terms of getting things done there. It has changed them in lots of ways.

When the second accident happened, I was pulling into Royal North Shore Hospital to pick up some diabetes stuff for my youngest daughter, who is a type 1 diabetic. I was waiting to turn into the driveway when I got a call from my husband, who said Sophie had been hit by a car. My reaction of course was denial and disbelief — I thought it was some kind of joke. He told me Ron and Caro were at North Shore waiting for Sophie to arrive. So rather than going to the diabetes centre, I went straight to Emergency. Ron and Caro had only just arrived. Neither of them knew what was going on, that was the worst part; it was almost a repeat of the first accident when nobody knew what was going on. Again Caro physically couldn't cope, again Ron took control, although he was incredibly upset. Ron knew what to do a little bit better and how to react and be assertive. And then Sophie ended up not being airlifted to Royal North Shore but going to Randwick instead. It was peak-hour traffic on a Friday afternoon, so they had a police escort to Randwick.

At that point I drove back to their house and picked up some clothes for Caro and an overnight bag and met Bec at the door; she is Caro's goddaughter who was pushing the pram. She dissolved in tears and was just beside herself. I just felt so sorry for her; she felt responsible. I just said, 'Look, I know it's easy for me to say, but it could have been me, it could have been Caro, it could have been anybody — it is not your fault'. Ann-Louise [Carolyn's sister] arrived from France that day for a holiday with her two daughters. She had arrived at the airport and got into a taxi and heard the news on the radio in the cab from the airport to Caro's house. So while I was at the home Ann-Louise turned up. She stayed there with me and the girls. At that stage Mitchell didn't know; we had to break the news. Nothing was said until Ron and Caro said he should be told.

Something like this makes a friendship, I don't think it is tested at all. I think all Caro's friends would say the same thing. It is the great leveller; things happen in your own life that you can get very involved and wrapped up in, and suddenly that is so unimportant. So it's been a blessing for all of us to have gone through it and witnessed it and experienced it.

Lee Tonelli

A FRIEND OF SOPHIE'S MOTHER, CAROLYN,
SINCE SCHOOL DAYS

Carolyn and Lee went to high school together, and flatted and worked together in New Zealand and Australia periodically up until they both got married. Lee's husband Mark Tonelli is an Olympic gold medallist and former captain of the Australian swim team, and has been very active in fundraising right from the days following the Roundhouse accident.

It's been a sad but happy journey over the past couple of years. It is quite inspirational to see how the whole family has dealt with such a situation and how they continue to deal with it on a day-to-day basis, and to see all the goodness that comes out of it. Sophie's personality makes it a real joy to be around them. You are aware of all the medications, but the reality is when we go round there, Sophie just cracks us up — she is always doing something silly or funny. Sometimes we don't dwell on the seriousness of it, because of the humour in the family — we are always laughing with Ron and Carolyn and Sophie. She is hilarious, she is very outgoing and tough and she doesn't seem to know any limits. Just before the second accident, we went over for lunch with some friends at Longueville, and their daughter and Sophie performed this dance. The next thing we saw Sophie walking up and down the stairs on her prosthetic legs and we said, 'Doesn't she know she's not meant to be able to walk up and down stairs yet on her prosthetic legs?' If she wants to do something she just does it and doesn't hold back.

When the first accident happened, Carolyn called me. She was at Royal North Shore Hospital, and she was saying, 'Lee, Lee, Sophie has been in a critical accident', and I was saying, 'Caro, what's wrong?' She started screaming and someone else picked up the phone and said, 'Lee, she has been badly burned' and said where they were. I said, 'I'll be there in five minutes' and they said to wait because there was talk she was going to be airlifted to Westmead or Randwick. So I waited where I was and ended up going out to Westmead; we were there shortly after the helicopter pulled in.

It was a very difficult night. Two other girlfriends took Carolyn to the adult's hospital because it looked like she was having seizures, so I stayed with Ron and Sophie. But it was pretty frightening; you'd go in and see Soph, and it was obvious her toes were so charred that they weren't going to heal. You didn't think it was possible she was going to live. It was all totally new territory to me; I'd never been to intensive care. It was very much a minute-by-minute scenario. Very quickly we formed a roster — we had somebody sleeping on the couches outside intensive care round the clock, probably for the first two weeks. It was so the parents had someone there with them in case of critical decisions having to be made during the night. Dave Palmer [Louise Palmer's husband], who is a bit of an insomniac, would come in about four or five in the morning and bring breakfast for whoever was sleeping there that night, so they could go home then. As time wore on and they moved into Ronald McDonald House we used to make a big feed out there every night. I would cook a roast dinner, or Louise would come in and bring her curry. But the initial period, you were just sitting on couches outside intensive care. It was really touch and go because it was pretty clear there was a chance she wasn't going to survive. Because of the swelling they had to cut her, so her internal organs wouldn't squash and they were actually exposed outside the body. You just don't think anyone can come back from that; it was pretty amazing that she did.

When I see Sophie, she makes me smile. I can understand that other people find it quite confronting, because I was like that. Prior to Sophie's accident I'd had one friend who was in a wheelchair but I've never dealt with the whole disabled thing. It's changed me enormously, because with Sophie you have to deal with it. Now I am completely at ease around disabled people. But I just see her face. I just see her character, I look at her and laugh. She is always up to mischief. One of my girlfriends from New Zealand said to me she thought she was very bright for her age, which I found interesting, with so much time missed being unconscious or whatever. Her theory is because she has had so much one-on-one adult time, her development has been quite progressed. She doesn't seem old, but she figures things out, she knows what she wants; she knows how to work an angle.

She seems to react to men better than women. Particularly athletic men, if they have gold medals or are fighting for a title! She seems to know who these guys are. She is a bit of a flirt! I think she is just a very well-adjusted kid, given what has happened to her. I don't think I've ever heard her complain about the difficulties involved with taking legs on, taking them off; the total acceptance is quite extraordinary. She complains if mum tries to take her away from a party, but she doesn't actually complain about anything to do with her.

Caro and Ron talk a lot about the power of prayer getting them through it all. I think it was largely to do with their continued network of support. Caro's mother moved over from New Zealand and she's been invaluable. They have had a fantastic network of friends; Ron would probably say he's had a lot of corporate help too [through the Day of Difference Foundation]. Caro has never been wild about cooking, but friends would cook casseroles and go and put them in the oven or go over and cook dinner. Carolyn is pretty good at asking for things if she needs it. One of the things they do appreciate is supporting them with their charity, Day of Difference. We regularly put a couple of tables together — I've got to say they are probably the easiest tables to fill at a function, but I think that supports Carolyn and Ron enormously.

Otherwise it is just life as normal, really. We go over there on Sundays and have barbecues and nothing like that has changed. Ron still burns the sausages, he still runs out of gas, Sophie and Mitchell still get in the pool and swim with the other friends' daughters and sometimes we'll have a couple of bottles of wine too many. For a long time Caro was just with Sophie the whole

Sophie proudly displays the carousel cake made for her fifth birthday by one of her many supporters.

Jeff Fatt from The Wiggles pays Sophie a visit for her fifth birthday — a big treat for a keen Wiggles fan.

First day at school
— Sophie in her class at Balgowlah Heights Public School.

Paralympian Karni Liddell is a strong supporter of Sophie, but says that Sophie gives her much more: 'Sophie pumps my heart up when I need it most.'

Sophie with a group from Arranounbai School. Principal Garry
Smith is at the back of the group.

Sophie loves the beach, and being in or near the water.
Here she is with her friends the Miller sisters at the
Australian Interstate Surf Lifesaving Championships
held at Queenscliff in 2006.

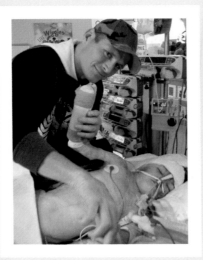

Boxing champion Danny Green visited Sophie in Sydney Children's Hospital when she was still in a coma after her second accident.

Charli Delaney from Hi–5 with Sophie in Sydney Children's Hospital, just after Sophie regained consciousness.

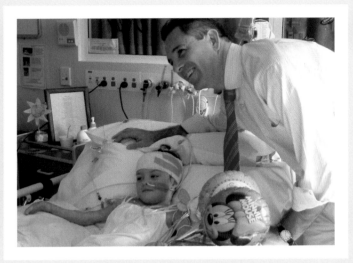

Paediatrician Dr Jonny Taitz — now best known as 'Dr Jonny' — with Sophie at Sydney Children's Hospital. He has been involved with Sophie's care since her first accident.

Sophie knows television newsman John Mangos as 'Johnmangos' — just one word. He first met Sophie at a Sydney Swans game and has become a good friend.

Pat Barraclough is one of the home carers who helps to look after Sophie. The home carers do everything from bathing Sophie to making meals and picking Sophie up from school.

Singer and Australian Idol finalist Anthony Callea pays Sophie a surprise visit. Sophie loves music, so the pair spent the afternoon playing games, dancing and singing.

Ron and Carolyn with Dr Michael Novy, who was part of the
CareFlight helicopter crew that treated Sophie after her second
accident.

Sophie's Uncle Greg
on a visit to the family
in November 2006.
Greg Martin lives in
Milwaukee, USA.

Sophie's grandmother Joy Martin is an important part of the team looking after Sophie's day-to-day needs.

Olivia Gompes attended the Roundhouse Childcare Centre and was sleeping close to Sophie on the day of the accident; she and Sophie are still good friends.

time. Then after 18 months or so we were over there for dinner one night and she actually sat down and ate her dinner without carrying Sophie around. We recognised her sitting and eating dinner with us as a step forward. They still do normal things; they went away at Easter time camping with friends at Budgewoi and Sophie rode a quad bike at Cooranbong! I guess it will never be normal, but it is normal-ish.

10
Milestones in a day

There are some areas of Sophie's life now that are very ordinary: she goes to school, she has a dog, she enjoys swimming, she plays with her brother and her friends. The flip side is far from 'normal': the Delezio home buzzes with nurses, carers and physios, there is a never-ending schedule of operations and medical procedures, and there is always intense media interest in the family's activities. In the midst of it all, Ron and Carolyn try to give their children the best life they can — and they admit that it is sometimes a struggle.

Ron Delezio and Carolyn Martin
SOPHIE'S PARENTS

Carolyn: It is not uncommon for there to be eight adults in this house. We have a nurse, a therapist, Mum and Dad, grandma — there is a big team of adults. There are so many people involved in Sophie's care, I would love to have continuity of care at home. We haven't achieved that yet, though we've had some very good long-term workers. It is a transient casual-based industry so you get a lot of coming and going. It takes an adjustment for everyone: Sophie has to adjust to new carers, and that is tough on a young child.

Ron: It takes a long time to train someone up to what we expect. Some people don't get it, some people come and sit down on the sofa when I'm trying to talk in private here, but generally they are pretty good, we have a few issues and we sort them out.

Carolyn: They don't like the dog or don't want to fold Ron's undies — and they are all real issues for some people, so they are obviously not the right people to be in our house. It's not just about caring for Sophie, it is actually caring for the family, so it is a uniquely diverse role. There is a lot of media attached to it. And even if you plan each day something always happens differently to the way you had it planned, and you have to adjust to that.

Ron: What they forget sometimes is we don't like it either — it's not what *we* want. It is also being aware of our relationship too; we might want to have an argument!

Carolyn: And the carers have to cope with the fact that we want to yell at each other sometimes! It is really multi-faceted and awkward to manage efficiently and as well as you can all the time, but you learn to say that's okay.

We are all trying to cope with the grief of the accident along the way as well. After the first 12 months someone said to us, 'Well, you haven't even had a chance to grieve, you have been that busy in terms of medical care'. I don't know that we have ever really had the time. I think that we move through areas of it. The life that you had before is lost and not only do you grieve what was, you grieve the change. You have to get on and you adapt, it is the way it is and we always said we would take the positive out of the situation and move forward.

Pat Barraclough

HOME CARER

Much of the intensive day-to-day care that Sophie receives is provided by nurses and community support workers from Noakes Nursing Service, part of Wesley Mission. They do everything from bathing Sophie, changing her dressings and putting sorbolene cream on her scars, through to making meals, washing, ironing and picking Sophie up from school.

The first time I met Sophie was before her fourth birthday. I had read about the story in the *Manly Daily* when the original accident had happened so I knew about her, and I'd been given a briefing by Noakes on what to expect.

I'd only been with Noakes Nursing a couple of months when they asked me to go in to Sophie. I'd been looking after my grandchildren and they moved up to the Gold Coast. I was at a loose end, so I decided I'd do some nursing work. I did a Certificate III in nursing; before that I used to lecture at technical college and teach — I have a degree in English and Sociology. I wanted something a couple of days a week but at the moment I do every day except Friday and alternate Saturdays, because some of the staff have dropped out and I've covered other shifts.

I come in at 7.30 in the morning and organise Sophie for school, depending on what stage she's up to — she may still be in bed or she may be up having breakfast. She needs cream and oil on her body and her prosthetic legs put on. I make school lunches, do the washing. I do most of the household stuff for the children, like all the nurses that come in here. Sometimes I take them to school; most times Carolyn will take her. I picked her up from school today, and tomorrow I'll take her. There are certain days when Carolyn has regular commitments and I take her; other days we just decide who's taking her on the day. I also went up to Byron Bay with them for a week in September, just before Sophie's operation. I had a room with the two children and Carolyn and Ron had their own room, so I was looking after them there.

The second accident was quite horrendous. By then I knew Sophie so well; I look after her after school from three o'clock to eight o'clock every night, so I was quite close to her. I was in the car driving to the city; my mobile phone rang and it was Carolyn. It was a Friday, which is the only day I have off, otherwise I would have been picking her up from school. At first she didn't say anything about an accident, anything about Sophie, she just said, 'Can you pick Mitchell up from school?' I was thinking, 'Oh, it's my day off', and then in the next breath she said, 'Sophie's had an accident, she's been knocked over by a car'. She was worried about what would happen to Mitchell, so I said yes and I was here until about two o'clock in the morning.

One of the people from Noakes took all the nurses in to the hospital to see Sophie. We didn't get to see her that first night, but we saw Carolyn. It was dreadful, awful, because at the time — I don't know whether other people thought it, but you wondered if Sophie was going to survive. You don't say that to anyone but you think it. Carolyn's sister had just arrived from France . . . so I was here to let her in. When I came back from the hospital she went in to visit and I stayed here with her children and Mitchell. The following night I went in when I finished work at eight o'clock. About every other night I went into

Randwick to visit her when I finished work. Carolyn and I used to sit by the bed and talk to doctors about what was happening. It really was horrendous seeing her lying there in the bed, all strapped to machines. Carolyn said to me, 'It's nothing like last time, you know, it's nowhere near as bad as last time' — I suppose she is sort of used to it after the first accident. It's all relative, isn't it. Sophie looked awful: she had drains coming out of her lungs, she was just lying there in a drug-induced coma.

When she came home after that accident the hours were longer because the shifts went from eight in the morning 'til ten at night. There were more things you had to think about after the second accident. When she came out of hospital she had a pump attached to the back of her head, like a 3-metre tube with a battery backpack. You had to carry it around and follow her when she was up and about.

Friends of mine used to say, 'Doesn't it depress you going in there?' and I'd say, 'No, it's just the opposite'. You might be worried about something or have some slight problem of your own, then you go in there and see what she's got to put up with and you think, 'What am I worrying about?' Despite all her disabilities she's a very happy child, she's always smiling and laughing. She has her moments when there are tantrums and what have you, like any normal child, but the actual disability doesn't seem to worry her, it's just something she accepts. When I first used to go in to kindergarten with her they'd be doing songs where you had to clap your hands and she had only one hand, or singing, 'Put your left leg in', and she wasn't wearing her legs. I'd think, 'How can they do songs like that?' but she just gets along with it and doesn't worry.

Jenny Berry

Jenny is a community physiotherapist who works with Sophie twice a week at her home.

I saw her for the first time on 23 June 2004, the day after she came home from hospital. I was quite deeply affected by the extent of her injuries — to see that first-hand was almost confronting. This is not an injury that you find in your everyday work life.

I see Sophie twice a week at home. For a short period of time after the second accident it boosted up to three times. My goals are to help her to function as normally and as independently as possible within the scope of her physical abilities.

I think Sophie is an absolutely amazing person. She has incredible courage and enthusiasm and she really takes on a challenge. Even if she doesn't actually want to do something when you are first introducing it, I find it is like you are planting a seed and she will often have a go at it the next time.

I try to involve Mitch when he's around, if he wants to and if it's going to work. It has been difficult along the way, there have been times where it just couldn't work but I've always tried to allow Mitch to be part of it because he's a great kid and it's all part of life. If there is a sibling around I try to include the sibling if it's feasible because I think that is a very good way of making what's happening acceptable, and not something very special just for one child.

Carolyn tends not to hang around through the session. Children sometimes don't respond quite as well when a parent is around. There have been periods along the way where Soph would just want to cling to Carolyn rather than doing what we were doing, particularly in the earlier days when it was very tough going, so she tended to be in a different room, just come in and out. But we always feed back after the session; when Carolyn's around we usually chat before and afterwards, talk about what we are doing. It is really important for the family to know exactly what we are working on because it is not just the hour or hour and a half that you are there that counts, it is what is going to flow through the rest of the time. We have a little exercise book where I write notes at the end of the session, and I usually try to communicate with the nurse who is on as well. It all becomes part of daily life, so the things we might be aiming at become part of her program in general.

Sophie's second accident had a huge impact on me. I was in the car driving along and I heard on the radio there was an accident and I thought, 'Gee, that's close to Sophie's, I wonder what that might have been'. Then my phone rang and it was a friend of mine who had just seen it on the television. She said, 'Jenny, are you driving at the minute?' and I said, 'Yes', and she said, 'Pull over', and I pulled over and she told me. To say that I felt devastated would be an understatement. That something so horrific could happen again was just so unbelievable. I was desperately upset.

It had a huge impact on Sophie in terms of our work together, but again she has been working her way back steadily because she is such an incredibly gutsy kid. I guess it is helpful we had a working relationship from before the accident so she was happy to continue on, but it was a huge setback.

I do most of my work with children through play. I think I'll probably end up being known as the whoopee cushion lady. In the earlier days when we were trying to get some active work done, I introduced whoopee cushions and Sophie would kill herself laughing by making them make their atrocious sound. It made it fun and it gave her an incentive to work. I try to make therapy as fun as possible and for it all to happen through play. We went through quite a phase when she was into the Little Mermaid, so we'd go outside and play the Little Mermaid. She was Ariel and I was every other character in the show. We adapted the foam blocks that she's got outside to make up the scene. We needed to do some work on trunk balance, for example. One of the foam shapes is a dome-shaped block; it is now called Crazy Rock because if you turn it upside down and sit on it, it rocks, so we were able to start getting nice trunk work happening. But it was all fun because it happened while we were playing Little Mermaid. Those sorts of things are pretty cool.

For 26 years I've been working purely in paediatrics. Working with children — particularly the younger ones — I find if I can get to work with them in a fun way, using all sorts of imaginary things, that they enjoy it, it's fun and everyone gets on. I just adapt whatever scenario we are in to fit the therapy goals we want to achieve. So I am constantly thinking on my feet, or my knees or my bottom — wherever I have to be to make it work. You may not seem to be doing a lot at some stages, but you end up with such amazing cooperation that in the long run you achieve a lot more.

All children are fantastic to work with and it is wonderful working to achieve the best outcome for children, whatever that outcome may be. Soph is a really cool kid; she's enthusiastic, she loves having fun and she really tries very hard most of the time. Like all children she will have her days when that is not on, but it is great to achieve these goals that we've got with Soph, in particular. Her strong fighting spirit absolutely captures your heart and it is that smile that has captured the whole world.

Sophie started in a preschool class at Arranounbai School in the Sydney suburb of Frenchs Forest in 2004. As Ron and Carolyn explain, it was the perfect place for Sophie, bringing together children with special needs and those without special needs. It was an important step for Sophie, allowing her to get on with her life — and to be a child, just like the others.

Ron Delezio and Carolyn Martin
Sophie's parents

Ron: Arranounbai is a very special place, we were extremely lucky to have it five minutes up the road.

Carolyn: The nurse who is part of the physical ability unit there, Maxine, worked at Westmead in the burns unit. To find a paediatric burns trained nurse out there in the community is like striking gold and she was five minutes up the road.

At Arranounbai Sophie could integrate into a little preschool class. When she first started, there were three of them with special needs and the rest were just siblings or people from the local community and she was in this fantastic environment. She would go out to do physio and OT and the nurse would do any burns dressings with Maxine, and then she'd do hydrotherapy in the pool, then back to preschool, as opposed to having a multitude of people in an external preschool environment. It was all very 'normal' — to be in a wheelchair was not abnormal in that environment, it was just the most beautiful place for her to be.

Garry Smith
PRINCIPAL OF ARRANOUNBAI SCHOOL

Arranounbai is a special school for students ranging from preschool through to Year 12. Most of the students have a physical disability or some kind of chronic health condition, which means they need smaller class sizes, closer attention, and a personalised welfare and education program.

Sophie originally came here in 2004. Our early learning program is a group of visiting preschoolers if you like, attached to the school. Sophie was in that preschool program from the time she was discharged from the hospital after her original accident at the Roundhouse. Last year she was fully enrolled as a student. It was understood that she would attend and participate when she was available, when she wasn't in hospital having surgery or the like. A lot of her rehabilitation was done here; we have a hydrotherapy pool next door to us which she used, we have the health department team that took over her physio and OT focus, and the nurse here was able to look after a great deal of Sophie's health care needs.

Our program brings together children with special needs and children without special needs. We are based on an integrated model using the children without special needs as role models, and children with special needs as role models about diversity and difference. That was right up Ron and Carolyn's alley.

My first impressions of Sophie were that here was a girl who didn't show signs of being robust — in fact you would have thought she is very frail and fragile — but she proved herself to be otherwise. Mainly through her psychological resilience — she wanted to try everything, she wanted to be in everything. She knew her limits though; if she was uncomfortable or in pain, she'd cry and that was fair enough. But there were lots of opportunities where she could have given up yet she didn't. I think my very first impression was of her physical appearance, but I got over that very quickly. I've been in the disability game for a long time now, and I'm not taken aback by any particular physical condition or injury. That wasn't such an issue for *me*, but I was concerned about how the other kids would respond to her and her appearance. It was quite remarkable how she answered their questions — because they had questions, particularly the children who didn't have disabilities in the preschool program. They asked, 'What happened to your hair?', 'Where are your feet?', 'Why are your hands like that?' And she had the answers. The staff in the classrooms were prepared to manage that interaction, but she had answers all ready. I think she had had a bit of practice at answering those types of questions.

One of the main obstacles she faced at that time was her pain threshold, and letting other people know what boundaries they should observe in relation to her physical wellbeing and tolerances. The mobility issues were significant, but again her resilience showed through. She worked out ways of getting around on her knees and joining in as best she could with everybody else. She was delayed in some communication issues; there had been quite a stop put on her social interaction with her peers when the original accident happened. She took a little while to join in social aspects of the classroom, but once she worked out what the interrelations should be with the individuals in her group, she was leading the group in many ways.

She definitely has a leader personality. Sophie is quite assertive at times, has definite ideas of what she wants to do and how she wants to do it — whether or not that is what the teacher wants. I've certainly witnessed her ordering other kids around — 'You should bring that toy over here', or 'It's not time to play with that now, we should be playing with this'.

She was being plucked out regularly to do therapy or hydrotherapy or have her prosthetic limbs fitted or to have a dressing changed or whatever it might be, so there was always that fear that she was going to relate better to adults than to her peers in the classroom. So we had a focus on maximising interaction with the other kids as much as we possibly could.

We also wanted to extend the amount of trust she had with as many of the staff as possible in the school. It would have been easy just to leave her with a teacher and a teacher's aide all of the time, and she related very well to those two people, Lisa and Robyn. But if there was an issue out in the playground she needed to talk to someone out in the playground, so it was important everyone understood about Sophie's condition. We briefed the whole staff and we had paediatricians and people from the burns unit come to make sure we all understood where Sophie was coming from, how we could relate to her, what we needed to look out for.

I didn't find that any of the staff here were significantly affected by Sophie's high profile. In fact there may have even been times when people joked about it and it just became quite ordinary. And to be candid, she was a centrepiece for the school while she was here. When we were starting our push to buy a new bus, we used a number of students as the face of Arranounbai, and Sophie was one of them. We were very cautious not to make Sophie *the* Arranounbai girl.

It wasn't long after she got out of hospital from the second accident that she was in here with Carolyn to see her teacher from last year and to sit and chat with the kids who were in that early program group. It was great to see her; once she'd been in and visited the school everyone just marvelled again at how resilient she is. And how resilient Carolyn is as well. She has been so good for this school on a parent level; she has been inspirational, almost as much as Sophie has. Carolyn always communicates well, irrespective of how traumatic current events are. She is always happy to talk and to tell you what you need to know about Sophie's situation and then to supplement that with the work for the Day of Difference Foundation, ideas she has for exemplifying tolerance. Well, not tolerance — Ron says, 'No more tolerance' — acceptance, if you like. I guess that is what we are on about here, too — we don't tolerate our kids, we accept them for what they are, as we did with Sophie.

One picture that always comes to mind for me is Sophie getting around in her wheelchair. Irrespective of prosthetic limbs she was going to need a faster way of getting around. The first day it came here I was amazed at how she just pushed her way through everybody, got up into the wheelchair, strapped herself in, took over the controls and headed off down the corridor independently. The seat of the wheelchair raises and lowers on command; she came to a classroom door and she just lifted herself up to have a stickybeak through the glass to see what was going on, and then lowered it down again and off she went. Obviously she'd had some previous orientation in using the chair, but to see her get in and out of it and control it so independently, so quickly, was pretty eye-opening. There is a great confidence there; cheeky behaviour to be applauded, not to be condemned. The other thing that struck me about Sophie was how much she did of what the other kids did. No problems with her hands or her legs or anything else, she just wanted to be like the rest — and basically she was, and still is.

Cathy Meaney

ASSISTANT IN NURSING AT THE PHYSICAL ABILITY UNIT

The Physical Ability Unit (PAU) is a service of the Child & Family Health Team of Northern Sydney & Central Coast Area Health. It is located in rooms at Arranounbai School in Frenchs Forest. There, they have use of two spacious therapy rooms, a playground and a hydrotherapy pool. The unit is a tightly knit team that works closely with the community to help children with physical disabilities and motor delays with their physical development.

Sophie was referred here through the PAU nurse, Maxine Amies, who contacted Westmead Hospital, and she has attended here since she was discharged from hospital after her first accident. She comes here for physiotherapy, hydrotherapy, occupational therapy and any other service we are able to provide.

Sophie came here first with her mum and dad and grandma to have a look at the preschool that's attached to Arranounbai. I think her parents were most impressed with it, and for Sophie we borrowed one of the children's electric motorbikes and she drove around the playground in that. They've since bought one for her because it was just a trendy little item for her to get around in. Sophie attended the preschool when she wasn't in hospital and we would just pull her out of class for therapy sessions.

When she started swimming with us, we were worried about putting any sort of flotation on her — her skin was so fragile. We actually put her into a little rubber ring that had no seams on the inside. Fortunately for us, she was a water baby before the accident, so she just got in and took off and we can't stop her now. Up until the second accident, she would have been swimming 10, 15 metres of basic overarm freestyle, and probably the same in backstroke. At one stage we were told she had 90-degree elevation in her arms, which is basically to her shoulders. I said to her mother, 'Well, how come we've got her doing backstroke with her arms coming up to her ears?'

She is very easy to work with and in the water she will try anything. She is very competitive — we had her in a group situation last year with some older children and whatever they were doing, she had to do — she would give it a go. There were times we had to rein her in a bit — she wanted to dive and we had to work out ways she could dive from her knees into the pool.

In January 2006, my 13-year-old niece was a member of the New South Wales Surf Life Saving team competing at Queenscliff, and Sophie came to watch. Top athletes in surf life saving were competing. It was an eye-opener to many people at the carnival: Sophie was on the beach, playing, wrestling, rolling, and not letting anyone walk — we all had to have knee races. Everyone sees her in a dress, they see her at functions; a lot of people had never seen her getting in and playing like any other child. That is what she is, a child who loves to be involved and play. She loves the beach and she just had a great day.

In the next section, other members of the Physical Ability Unit join Cathy to talk about their work with Sophie. Absent from the group is physiotherapist Janet Pickering, also part of the PAU.

Cathy Meaney (Assistant in Nursing), Maxine Amies (Registered Nurse), Michelle Appleby (Physiotherapist) and Pauline Hole (Occupational Therapist) at the Physical Ability Unit

Michelle: Our work is integrated into the children's program rather than withdrawing them out of the classroom or preschool group. Her preschool was interrupted enough with visits to hospital and surgeries and things like that, so to limit the interruption was really good — and it was much more fun for Sophie as well.

When Sophie originally came she was having some individual sessions in physio. She wasn't able to sit by herself; she couldn't get down onto the ground, so she needed some help in re-establishing those skills and getting her mobility under way. Once she had her artificial legs fitted, we did a lot of work helping with mobility — playing in the playground, walking on different surfaces, going down slides and all those fun things. One of the greatest things about Sophie is that she never says 'no', she says, 'Let's see what we can do'.

Pauline: Once Sophie was mobile we were able to integrate her into our community groups which was really lovely, she was with her peers. We'd often start with something messy and she was just delighted — anything from shaving cream to sorbolene. One day she mixed them all together — her idea. She is the queen of slime and anything messy, she loves those things.

When she first came she was in plaster, so the children's hospital made her a splint, and it didn't take very long at all before she was drawing — and with her left hand! [Sophie was originally right-handed.]

Maxine: She has very good verbal skills, she will always tell you exactly what she needs and when she should have it. One of the things that impressed me the most about her is her sense of humour. It is quite advanced; you could joke her out of most things.

Pauline: One of the things I remember, she was with Maxine having her dressings changed and she was undressing Barbie. I just had to take a second look and think, 'Wow, that is amazing' — she had very limited movement. She does have excellent problem-solving skills and a real drive to achieve.

Michelle: It is interesting, when people meet Sophie they find it really confronting. We first met her when she was in hospital and we went in and they were doing bathing and things like that, and it is very confronting. But only a few weeks later and you don't even see it. Most of the children accepted her, they just took to her. She was Sophie and that is how she comes.

Maxine: One of the little boys — who wasn't trying to be unkind — said to her, 'Why do you look like Spiderman?' She said, 'Oh, my brother Mitchell just loves Spiderman'. She would make something positive out of it, most of the time. There were a few times when she went home and said, 'I've had a sad day because someone said something', but most of the time she was very positive. We have a couple of mirrors in the room and sometimes she'd check herself out and you could tell she liked herself, she saw who she was on the inside, not on the outside. She would gauge people's reactions as they came into the room; she expected adults to accept her straight away. I think with adults it wasn't so important to her, but on first meetings with young children she would just watch them very closely to see how they were going to react. But she likes who she is, you know, which is a great quality.

The amount of attention she has focused on her, I would expect her to be not a very nice child. Some children who have disability and a lot of focus on them don't have those nice social skills. It hasn't seemed to have affected her in the slightest. She cares too, she'll try to say things in a grown-up way so she doesn't hurt someone's feelings; she does care about other people. It's not what you'd expect from someone with that much attention. I've seen children who have accidents or disabilities and the attention — they are different, they are not kids any more.

The thing about Sophie is we have gained so much more than we have given, just because she is amazing. You just think of her — we are teary at the moment, but normally you think of her and you smile or laugh.

Cathy: She was invited last year to a sport carnival for a special school and didn't have her legs for some reason. There were wheelchair races and running races and she made her mother get down on the floor and have kneeling races. When I had her at the beach everyone playing with her had to be on their knees — that was the rule, Sophie's rule.

Straddling a quiet suburban street, Balgowlah Heights Public School is a school of two halves. It's not just your standard school: ramps replace steps, doors have been widened, air conditioning, new bathroom facilities and soft-fall surfaces have been installed.

Sophie's arrival in 2005 precipitated extensive work to the physical structure of the school. A lot of thought also went into preparing the children and the staff to welcome this new student — but from day one, Sophie made it clear that she was going to fit right in.

Ron Delezio and Carolyn Martin
SOPHIE'S PARENTS

Carolyn: The shift to school was huge. That was six months in the planning, because of the physical work that had to be done. It was all completed in 2005, so there was a lot of integration from that side of it, even testing that Sophie had to undergo: the type of teacher's aide and how she would fit into that community.

Ron: We had a lot of support from the education department. They spent over $400,000 on Balgowlah Heights school — they did it for Sophie, but the good thing is they did it for everyone to benefit.

Carolyn: The other schools in the area were not accessible. So it made sense for the education department to spend money on Balgowlah Heights, to make it the accessible school in the area with all the mod cons.

Ron: We didn't want Sophie to go to the same school as Mitchell anyway. There was too much media attention and too much fuss — the last thing he needed was to be at the same school as well.

Craig Davis
PRINCIPAL OF BALGOWLAH HEIGHTS PUBLIC SCHOOL

Anne Murray
SOPHIE'S KINDERGARTEN TEACHER AT
BALGOWLAH HEIGHTS PUBLIC SCHOOL

Craig: It would have been early 2005 when Sophie's mum and dad made contact with the school. Ron and Carolyn are walking, talking medical dictionaries, they know quite extensively what Sophie's needs are. They were also aware the school needed to make modifications if Sophie was to attend, so we needed a reasonable lead-in time to incorporate architects, the department, physios . . . a whole lot of people. To Ron's credit, he was saying, 'Whatever we do has to be of benefit to everybody, not just Sophie'. Is a ramp better because everyone can use it, or is a lift better where only one person can use it? The architect went on the philosophy that whatever improvements were in place should benefit Sophie directly but also everyone else.

We all did an observation of Sophie up at Arranounbai. What they did in her preparation was extensive; she came to school very ready for school. We were more concerned for her physical needs — and that would have occurred for any child coming to their local school. We wanted her to feel comfortable in the environment, which meant a lot of work in terms of thinking about how we could integrate her into the school. Asking Anne to be the class teacher was one of the first moves, because Anne is somebody I feel 100 per cent confident in. She supports the kids, so all the other children were able to cope with Sophie's arrival.

Anne: She had the flu when she first came so she was only here for half days. A couple of the other kindy teachers said that some of their children didn't know how to cope with this, so one afternoon when Sophie was away we brought them all in. We talked all about the accident, we just talked and talked. I said to look at her face; if you look at her face and you look at those eyes, you get past everything else. I'd say within a week, Sophie was just another child in the classroom and the playground.

Craig: That is the amazing thing, she doesn't set herself apart.

Anne: ... or make excuses — 'I can't do that'. Kindergarten is a very special year. They all like to please their teachers — not just me, their library teacher, their science teacher. I'd say that she could be more retiring with all she's been through and give up, but she does have a strong personality and a strong drive to get her where she is.

Craig: I think adults stand back and think she is quite amazing, in that she has overcome a lot of obstacles. She climbs over them; she doesn't stop and say, 'That was a problem', she just moves beyond it. For her classmates Sophie's just one of the kids they play with. They are quite acutely aware of her differences, but it doesn't seem to get in the way of their relationship at all, and it doesn't get in Sophie's way.

While Sophie has very obvious needs, she never seems to falter at giving something a go — often to Anne's dismay. We were telling someone the story the other day about dance, when she had her prosthetics on and all the kids took their shoes and socks off to dance.

Anne: We nearly died; she wanted to take her shoes and socks off like everybody else did.

Craig: We didn't know how good the prosthetics were, whether they would give her the grip she needed, so we debated it and Sylvan [the teacher's aide] ran down to find out what we should do. We said, 'Let's ring Mum and ask'. By the time it was sorted she already had her shoes and socks off! When she was starting school we thought we'd have to put her in cotton wool and she resists that. We are always around her but not in her way.

Anne: I think she loves coming to school because this is a normal life for her. At home there is a physio, there is an OT, there is swimming ... Every other adult in her life is doing something to her or with her or expecting something from her, and we're just giving her a taste of normality.

Craig: And the way both Ron and Carolyn approach Sophie and the school gives us confidence too. I remember, Sophie went on an excursion — we do risk assessments for those sorts of things — not just for Sophie, for everybody on the excursion. As they were all being bussed away I said to Carolyn, 'Are you all right letting her go?' and she said, 'I've got to let her go sometime'. In one way, their strength is our strength. Also they are very cognisant of everybody's needs, not just Sophie's needs; they will be concerned about Anne, about the teacher's aides, about the other kids, about the other parents of the children ... they met the P&C [Parents & Citizens' Association], and said, 'We are Sophie's parents, this is Sophie's story. If you've got any questions, we would rather you be informed and ask us. Here's our number and don't hesitate to call us.' Their approach to life, and their approach to Sophie's life and education, has made it easier for all of us.

You might think that Sophie's two accidents would make children fearful of cars and roads — but the children seem to take it in their stride.

Craig: Not from the children's point of view, probably from the adults' point of view — it is something the adults have been acutely aware of, but the children haven't shown any fear. Nor has Sophie; children cross with adults, and she is across this road every other day.

The amount of public interest is something I've never experienced in my many years of teaching. After the second accident we had phone calls from Western Australia, we had phone calls from children in Brisbane, Victoria ... It was lovely because a lot of schools were feeling the anguish we were feeling. I had an email from somebody in Canada, an expat who had been doing a search on the news on the mining disaster in Tasmania, and came up with the story of Sophie's second accident. She was devastated, she said, 'I'm just hoping to give you a message that even though we are in Canada and we're so far away, it has impacted on us as well — and if it has impacted on us, it must have really impacted on you'.

Anne: It's because she is a little girl, and really none of this is her fault. It has all been something that has happened to her, through no fault of her own; she has been a victim both times. Two car accidents, two old men — the second accident, we thought it was a hoax.

Craig: I'm not sure what it is about Sophie; I don't want to use the word luck, but for me it's a sense of unfairness that it happened again and that it happened in the first place. For a person who through no fault of her own has to deal with this legacy — but once again, that is the adults putting all this emotional stuff on it. She's not carrying any baggage, or she doesn't show she's carrying any. And that is what is special. There are children with disabilities here at the school who are similar to her in that they don't talk about being profoundly deaf, or having uncontrollable tics. I think that's what's touched people. And we've been with her since she was three, really, everyone has shared her growing up from the time of the first accident — she's had a very public growing up.

The staff here have been incredibly professional because they are really aware of not drawing too much attention to her, to be

271

equitable in their conversation with kids. So in one way we have absorbed her, rather than adopted her. She is in the playground today; the teachers and the teacher's aide supervise her but they keep their distance, keep her in eyeshot all the time but don't overload her with too much TLC.

Anne: She had a whole term off after the second accident; some of us were going back and forth to the hospital to see her and work with her. We kept the children in the class up to date, and when she came back, it was really like she'd never been away.

Craig: Once again she is probably moving a little bit faster than I'd like. She is wearing her stockings out at the knees, playing with the kids on the floor in a very confined space together; the other children are brilliant.

Anne: She seems to have got her strength back this week. She was a bit fragile week one, coming back after the second accident. I picked her up yesterday because we were doing a warm-up for sport, and I said, 'Sophie, you have been eating too much, you are getting heavy'; she laughed.

Craig: I'm really aware when new kids arrive at the school that a lot of children may not have had a lot of exposure to kids with disabilities or kids with special needs. That hasn't been an issue either; we've had quite a few children in and out of the school and nothing has struck us yet. It is unrealistic to think it won't happen at any stage but I'm hoping that if it does happen we have the skills and the structures to support children through that.

Anne: Again I think that is our adult projection — children just seem to be able to see through to the heart of the person instead of what they physically look like. We've got this little puppet in our room called Mike who goes home every weekend to someone's house and has a play. A little boy who was in the Roundhouse accident with Sophie had Mike the day of Sophie's second accident. His mum just happened to say, 'Do you think it might be nice for Mike to go to hospital to be with Sophie?', and he said, 'No, she's had her turn'. And I thought, 'Out of the mouths of babes' — here was an adult thinking this would be nice and the child said, 'No, she's had her turn'. So I then had to get Michelle, who is the other puppet — she went to hospital. That's how the children are. They know they have to be careful walking around her when she is on her knees, but Sophie is just one of them. If she's bossy they'll say, 'No, I don't want to do that'; they'll walk away. They treat her like they treat anyone else.

Craig: I think it is Sophie's courage that amazes everyone — even the doctors speak very emotionally about her, not clinically. From a medical point of view it is something beyond their expectations, and she certainly exceeded our expectations at a school level — and probably will continue to do so. There is that sense of ownership of her, emotionally, and I think we've bought into that too.

Anne: She'll always be mine. They all are — your class is very special.

Craig: Anne is very balanced with that but you've got a bigger responsibility. Sophie is never far from her thoughts in terms of where the next step might be and what we need to accommodate it. Just seeing her this week, she is a lot further down the track than I thought she'd be this week, than she was last week — and she keeps doing it to us.

11

A catalyst for hope

Sophie is Ron and Carolyn's little girl; she is also Mitchell's little sister, she is a niece, a cousin, a granddaughter, a friend. As well as that she is 'our Sophie' to thousands of people across Australia and across the globe. The public support for Sophie and her family has been overwhelming: cards, emails, gifts and donations have flooded in. Sophie has also attracted a team of high-profile supporters who have used their influence to smooth her path, and to boost the work of the Day of Difference Foundation, which Ron and Carolyn set up to support the prevention and control of burns-related disease.

Ron Delezio and Carolyn Martin
SOPHIE'S PARENTS

Carolyn: An elderly lady who sends us $10, that is so sweet and so thoughtful; it is the same as the person who hands over a $25,000 cheque for the Day of Difference Foundation. The amount doesn't matter, it is the thought that counts. We have been working on a database to send thank you notes; I would say 60 per cent of the cards and letters we were sent had addresses and we are up to 3000 on that database alone. Then on the

Wishes for Sophie [website] database, there are more than 16,000 messages — people took the time to do that.

We know we are extraordinarily lucky with the enormous care and love people gave to us and the opportunities we've been presented. We accept every one of them because we know how fragile life is and it can be gone in an instant. My children deserve all they are offered because their life is far from 'normal', it will never be 'normal'. If they get to go and meet the Swans after a match, or say hi to the Hi–5 team or play games with The Wiggles, great. What is quite extraordinary is these people are so casual in terms of themselves, they are just gorgeous people who have a very heartfelt connection, and we are enormously appreciative of that because it helps us.

Sophie is very black and white [in her expectations]; The Wiggles came to see her early on, and they were supposed to come and see her at Randwick too. She asked, 'When are The Wiggles going to pop around, Mum?' I said, 'Sophie sweetie, it doesn't work like that!' Very fortunately we got tickets to see them at their fifteenth birthday. I don't think Sophie really had an understanding that that is not the normal way it goes.

Ron: I remember Danny Green, the boxing champion, visited Soph when she was in a coma. I invited him to stand behind her for a photo and he leant forward and said something like, 'I love you, Sophie'. A smile broke across her face and with her eyes shut she reached behind to him. That sort of support is very special. It is definitely a privilege being with some of these people, too. You think, 'Wow, fancy sitting down here and talking to Jack Thompson, Andrew Denton and all these people, it's amazing!'

Carolyn: You realise there are a lot of really good people out there who do a lot for the community and we get to meet them because of the nature of our foundation. But you look at it on the basis that you never know what is around the corner — so when people say, 'Do you want to do this?', we say yes, if we can do it.

Ron: We've had to learn how to accept this and enjoy it. At first you say, 'I don't want to do that on the back of Sophie's injuries', but now my attitude is we've been through enough, let's enjoy it, let's just take the fruits of life.

Carolyn: Sophie loves the Swans, she dresses up and has the teddy bear that sings the song, she is a full-on advocate and has been since last year, when we got invited to the box. She loves the vibe of it, she just loves it with all the passion in the world. If that gives her a moment of joy, then great.

Alan Jones

BROADCASTER, PATRON OF THE DAY OF
DIFFERENCE FOUNDATION AND FRIEND

Sophie's tragedy overwhelmed everybody and her spirit captured everybody's imagination. As a broadcaster I have a responsibility to provide appropriate and sensitive narrative to my audience. There was a lot of interest in Sophie's wellbeing, but equally I felt a profound understanding that these were very difficult times. This was a kid fighting against extraordinary odds; she had to be given her space. I think it was important not to create false expectations. I took the view that we would only tell the good news on air; I didn't want to regale listeners with the details of the difficulties, because it tends to overwhelm people, and I thought that the goodwill of the public and their prayers and understanding were central to any hope that the family might have. So I suppose my first job was to mobilise that hope and through that, enable the parents to understand that they weren't fighting this battle on their own.

In the early days the medical team were very cautious, and rightly so. They were very difficult and deep waters. Then as some legitimate hope emerged, I spoke with some of the medical team who gave authority and authenticity to the narrative comment that I was making. Through all of that long and torturous battle, I didn't speak to Ron, because I didn't think it was right at the time to be publicly canvassing their grief and their struggle. The maudlin preoccupation with a family's grieving can be very invasive for them.

Then of course the good news was that Sophie would be coming home, which was just unbelievable. It was the nature of the fight and the quality of the fight that endeared Sophie, because her burns were horrific beyond any capacity of anybody to contemplate. This is a young lady of just amazing dimension and internal reserves.

Several things touched the public. One is that they did have a fairly comprehensive understanding of what had happened to her. And then the fact that in spite of this she prevailed. Here's this young girl with the most angelic smile on her face, wearing her difficulties and her burdens with a freshness of spirit — that really highlights the limitations of us all as we whinge about the one or two difficulties that cross our path. In many ways the struggle has given her some sort of strength to share the triumph with others. We're not sharing the injury, we're sharing the triumph.

I'm the patron of the Day of Difference Foundation, and whenever I can we do fundraisers. They're all gala affairs; we put a good night on so that people get value for their money — you can't ask people to pay money in a fundraiser if all they're going to get is a rubber chicken. I recall one fundraiser at the Town Hall — it was a great night, Rhonda Burchmore sang and everything was terrific. I asked little Sophie to draw the lucky door prize. I came off the stage where I was broadcasting and went down to see that Sophie was ready. Before she said hello or anything, she said, 'What do you think? I've got lipstick on tonight.' Here she was pointing to the lipstick, and then she said, 'And eyeshadow'. I just burst out laughing.

I'd offered the Delezios my property in the country so they could have a holiday whenever they wanted to and so Sophie could go and meet the cows and chooks and all that sort of stuff. I asked them to regard it as theirs, but even so I hadn't really met them. But after the first function at Luna Park, I met Carolyn and Ron and Mitchell and they felt they knew me better and I knew them better. My PA is also my niece; she has three children and Hunter is about Sophie's age. We'd all go out and see the family at home and have afternoon tea. Sophie was showing us all her toys, and it was then that Ron said he was going to put this foundation together, and he asked me if I would be the patron. Well I said yes, happily I'd do that. So that's where that started and the association has just continued since then.

I remember where I was when I heard she'd been knocked over at the pedestrian crossing — I was doing a fundraiser in

Brisbane, and I couldn't believe it. We'd done a few big fundraising gigs, so Sophie and I had got to know one another. I'd say things to her on the phone and I'd interview her on the radio and she was always lovely, so she got to know my audience as well and I got to know her. I went into the hospital when I came back from Brisbane, and there was little Sophie in intensive care. My God, there were marks all over her and she was plugged into everything and I thought, 'I can't handle that'. And then I realised the extraordinary resilience of these two parents. I mean, what do you say? It's obvious that you're praying for Sophie to get better and wondering whether it's humanly possible. But what kind of reservoir of hope and faith must these people have that they can stand there, day in, day out, hour after hour and support their child — and yet graciously communicate an understanding to the public. They understand the public treat her as 'their' child as well.

The Delezios have dealt with it well. They understand that in some strange spiritual way she is more their daughter than she would ever have been as a result of this tragedy, and yet because of the tragedy she's less their daughter and more the community's heroine. So there's this ambivalence in all of this. It gives you faith, it gives you hope, it makes you believe that anything is possible.

I think Sophie's got a very big future. I think she'll grow out of these circumstances — although she'll always have them; it's a bit like someone who's blind, isn't it? She knows nothing else now, so this is normal for her. At this stage there's been a double triumph in the face of adversity and I think that the parents are trying to recognise both their need to look after Sophie and also their need to respond to the public. She's got to be allowed now to have her own space, her own identity. She's a bright young girl with an amazing adaptability so I think she'll be very, very successful. After all, her mind is good, her verbal skills are outstanding — in the world of broadcasting, for example, she'd be quite outstanding. There are no impediments to that.

John Mangos
Television newsman, currently Senior Anchorman for SKY News Australia

I met Sophie vicariously before we actually met. My 'real' job is as a newsreader at SKY News. The last few years I've also been filling in over the summers for John Stanley on Radio 2UE. I was on the air working on John's show when we broke the story that there had been an accident at the Roundhouse Childcare Centre ... My ears pricked up — one because it was an accident, two because we were on air live and we had a reporter very close by, so 2UE were the first at the scene. I live at Seaforth so it was around my neighbourhood; you feel a little more connected with it. We dropped everything and focused around the story for the rest of the shift. Here I was, new at radio, but I felt very close to the story.

It was the AFL footy season; I do a lot of work for Sydney Swans — I've compered every chairman's club lunch for the last 16 years. One particular day I'm sitting in this box with other guests and in walks the Delezio family. I'd spoken to Ron over the air, I felt close to them, and suddenly Mitchell and Sophie were right there. When kids walk in, I welcome them. Mitchell walked in first and I said, 'Hello, are you a Swans supporter?' and he said,

'Yep'. The second kid was Soph and I put my hand out to kiss her little hand, as I do, not knowing it was Sophie. As I kissed her hand I realised and said, 'Oh, it's you', and I got a big smile out of her, as most do. I spent the rest of the afternoon playing with Sophie and ignoring the football, which is rare for me! We just spent the whole day playing and singing the club song.

In the course of the afternoon we realised how very close we lived to each other. I said to Ron, 'If there is anything I can do, just don't hesitate; I've done fundraisers for every hospital in Sydney, I've been a patron of Make a Wish, I feel this is in my backyard'. Sure enough, he said, 'We've got a dinner coming up in a few weeks' time, will you compere it for us?' Straight away I said yes. I've got a few wealthy mates around town, so I made sure we got a table together with people who are good spenders. Our table spent a fortune — I knew they would. I stayed in touch with the family, and I took my wife around to their house and we met the kids and the dog and brought them Christmas presents and we just got on. Sophie calls me Johnmangos, one word — 'Hello Johnmangos'.

In the preparation for the dinner, Ron asked if I'd make a DVD at the hospital. At past dinners they had doctors talk about the hospital to try to pull on people's heartstrings, and this time they wanted to add some visuals. I suggested I rope in my colleague, Susanne Latimore, whom I read the news with at SKY. So the two of us went to the hospital. We started at Concord and we went to Westmead, and we interviewed all the doctors and looked at all the equipment we hoped to buy with money from Day of Difference, and Sophie was woven into the whole thing. We did these lovely shots of Sophie running around and falling over and hurting her leg and she'd start crying, and we'd play this little game of let's do a kiss for the camera.

After we met at the footy, I said to Sophie and Mitchell, knowing they lived close by [SKY News was at Frenchs Forest at that time], 'Would you like to come out and see a TV station and read the news with me?' The kids got all excited, so I organised it with Ron and Carolyn and they brought them out. We put Sophie and Mitch in the newsreader's chair and they mucked around on the monitor and stuff. Sophie was brilliant at belting out the national anthem and the Swans theme song.

Then of course the other accident was just around the corner from our house. I was at a meeting in the city. One of the producers from SKY News, knowing I was close to the Delezios, rang and said, 'There has been an accident in Seaforth; a little girl has been knocked over. They think it's Sophie Delezio, can you find out?' I rang Ron immediately; I knew straight away, I could tell in his voice. I said, 'Is it true, is it Sophie?'. He said, 'Yes, the helicopter is just about to arrive'. 'Is she all right?' 'I don't know, mate, I'll call you later.' I confirmed with the newsroom it was Sophie; the newsroom knew not to broadcast anything until the hospital issued a statement, but at least they were prepared; we had file footage ready until the hospital released something. Then I rang my wife and we dropped whatever we were doing and jumped in the car and went to the hospital. We didn't see her that first night; we saw Ron and Carolyn. We gave it a few nights and went back in. Soph was semiconscious then. She could detect voices, so Ron took us in. I said, 'Hello Soph, it's John Mangos', and her little hand went like that; it breaks your heart. We said hello, we gave her a little kiss; we didn't know if she was going to survive at that stage.

The following Sunday when they said she was sitting up and a bit brighter, I went in. She was still pretty battered, but she was more conscious. It was a lovely Sunday morning and Ron and Caro were there. I've come in and given her a little kiss and had a chat and a few laughs. I brought her some presents and others had given me presents to bring, balloons and things. Sophie was sitting there with a fairy wand and I picked up the wand and I pointed it at her and said, 'Soph, if I can make a wish with this wand, I would turn you into a princess'. And she smiled at me and took the wand and said, 'If I could make a wish, I'd turn you into a frog'.

It's the smile, the spirit. I went around to their house last Sunday. Mitch is playing basketball and Sophie says 'Johnmangos, do you want to play husbands and wives?' Her room is like a toy shop, she's got a little kitchen and a little bathroom. She says, 'Can you put the bathroom there and the kitchen there', and I went, 'Sure, Sophie'. She said, 'It's not "sure, Sophie", it's "yes, honey"!' It is these little things that make her totally magnetic.

Sophie is the centrepiece of a wider cause and she is a little girl who loves it. I sometimes worry about all this media attention, I wonder how it would affect any child her age. But the remarkable thing about Sophie is that she seems to handle it. The fact she has a naturally extroverted personality means that she kind of embraces it, but I've seen her shy away and not want to do stuff, and I guess it is also relative to her pain levels on the day. I can see when she is starting to hurt — the Delezios can see it about half an hour before anyone else can see it and they start wrapping things up. When we were filming out at the hospital she got so excited to show me all the different wards in the hospital, she knew the place back to front. She had me by the hand and we had the camera behind us; she ran ahead of me and tripped and fell. She had her legs on and she hurt herself, she really cried and cried and cried. She was so excited to show me — and that is Sophie, she gets excited and wants to perform.

Karni Liddell

PARALYMPIC SWIMMER, MOTIVATIONAL SPEAKER AND MEDIA PERSONALITY

In 2004 Sophie's mum called me. At that time I was raising money for the Paralympic team to go to Athens; we were trying to raise a million dollars in four months. The Delezios were in the process of starting the Day of Difference Foundation, so our first conversation was mainly about fundraising. As the conversation progressed Carolyn said to me that Sophie was having a few problems with pushing her wheelchair and asked would I meet Sophie and show her how to use it. I was so excited; I'd seen her on *60 Minutes*.

We organised for me to surprise Sophie at her kindy. It was Christmas, so they had a concert; I wheeled in and Sophie was up the back with Carolyn. Sophie was pretty shy at the start; I had a bit of a chat to her and I gave her a wheelchair Barbie. Of course she was pretty excited to have Barbie in a wheelchair! Then she wanted to race me in the chair — it just progressed from there.

I was in love with her straight away. She pumps your heart up a lot, being around her. We went back to her house, we spent all day playing Barbies and just hanging out. Sophie was so young, she didn't really get why I was there. She didn't know I was a Paralympian, she was just happy I was there to play with her.

Sophie and I were really close from the start. I'd go to Sydney every month for work [Karni lives in Brisbane] and always go to see the family. For some reason, I just wanted to be around Sophie as much as I could. She gave me more than I could ever give her.

Before the second accident she was doing so well; I'd watched her progress from being not very good at pushing the wheelchair and at walking on her legs, to putting her legs on and pushing me around in my own wheelchair! We were at Seaworld one day for the Bravehearts award [*Take 5* magazine's award for children who have shown courage in the face of adversity], and Sophie and I were playing and carrying on. I hadn't seen her for a couple of months; she was really good at walking with her legs and she decided she wanted to push me in my wheelchair, so she was pushing my wheelchair, up ramps — unbelievable. Then she wanted me to take her to the toilet. Now, I'm really weak, I have a muscle disease; I don't know how I did it but I lifted Sophie onto the toilet. I think she tested me a little bit to see what I can do!

I really believe the reason I met Sophie was to be able to see what my parents went through when I was a child. I've always appreciated my parents, I've always talked about them in my speeches, but to see it in action — kids are demanding enough as it is, but when you have a disabled child who needs someone to take them to the toilet or get a drink of water, and you add that to the equation ...

It has also been great for me to witness what Mitchell goes through. My younger brother Brent was always really hyperactive, an amazing little character, and you can see now why he was like that. It gave me a bigger appreciation of why my brother feels a bit like Mitchell does, a bit left out. To a child it can seem that when your brother or sister has a disability it is so much better because they get so much attention — everyone wants to push them in their wheelchairs, everyone wants to help them, everyone gives them presents. So to Mitchell it looks like Sophie gets more; he doesn't understand her life is going to be much harder. One day he's going to realise, 'Thank God I'm like this', but right now he is too young. So for me it was like being able to rewind the clock 25 years.

At Seaworld I met all these other kids with disabilities; they were all gorgeous in their own way, but Sophie has something that makes her stand out. My mum said I was always so loud and it was a way to make sure people didn't treat me any differently. I think Sophie is going to be okay because of her personality, and I think that's why we have that bond. We are very similar; when I was a child, it was exactly what I was like, thriving and loving the attention.

I don't think you are ever given anything you cannot handle. Everyone's threshold is equivalent to what they are given. I didn't know Sophie before the accident, but I've met Carolyn's friends and most of them say she was very special. Even now, Sophie is so matter-of-fact with how she deals with everything. I know other children with disabilities who aren't like that; they are very embarrassed about their differences, whereas Sophie is very strong and enthusiastic, she is really leading the way. Sophie is definitely not shy!

When my mum was pushing me in my wheelchair, she would whisper to me all the time, 'Look at everyone looking at you because you are so beautiful', or 'They are all looking at your gorgeous shoes'. I've told that story to Carolyn and she does similar things with Soph. Children are a product of their parents.

I really did believe that people looked at me because I had nice shoes or because I had a pretty face. Ron is great too; he is always telling Sophie she is beautiful, and hopefully it is getting through. Something is obviously working as she is really happy and very confident at school.

Carolyn said to me — which is very moving for me — the reason why she has involved me in Sophie's life is for the future. Now, we play Barbies, she talks to me on the phone — all I'm really doing is showing Sophie there is someone else out there in a wheelchair. However, in the future when she is going through teenage years, that's when someone like me will need to be around. They are really tough years, especially when you are trying to meet boys and go to school dances and no one asks you to dance and you don't know why — as you've done all this work on your hair and makeup, so you think you look great! All the kids at school loved pushing me around in my chair in primary school, but in high school it's a little bit different as it really is not as 'cool' to push your friend around in their wheelchair.

Sophie will always have good friends, as her smile and personality is infectious. What will really be hard for Sophie will be boys. I never got asked to dance at the high school dance, I have made up for lost time now, but at that time it really was a big deal. I never got teased at school; however, I really never felt pretty, as I didn't get the same attention from the boys as my friends did. It was only when I got out of school and started modelling and receiving attention for my sport that I started to pay attention to my appearance. Sophie has such a beautiful face, and an amazing spirit, I hope that teenagers will be able to just focus on that and forget about her differences. As you get older, men become more open-minded with disability but those high school years can be tough; I plan to be with Sophie during those times and beyond. That is of course if she is not sick of me by then! Ron and I constantly talk about sport for Sophie, so she meets other people with disabilities. That's what happened to me — I met boys on the team with disabilities who gave me attention, which boosted my self-esteem; I think without that I would have been a different person. Sophie is a good swimmer; I was quite surprised at how well she can swim. It doesn't mean she has to be a Paralympian, it just means she will be able to start going away with sporting teams where she can feel comfortable and 'normal'. I despise using the word 'normal' as it's such a boring word, but everyone really wants to just fit in and be treated equally; I guess that is 'normal'. That's the great thing about the Paralympics; all of a sudden you are part of the majority, not the minority.

I was born with a disability. I don't have any idea what it is like to run on the beach, I don't have any idea of what it's like to be spontaneous and jump out of your car and run to the toilet, or run through the rain. Sophie will have no memory of before the accident and in some ways it may make life a little bit easier. At the same time it really is hard to say it will be easier. When I saw Sophie in the hospital after the second accident, strapped up to all those tubes in intensive care, her little body covered with gravel rash — there is no way I could ever say that it's better that it happened when she was younger.

Sophie is very patient, which is quite rare. When she had the VAC pump in her head after the second accident, she couldn't move for so many hours a day. I didn't realise that she couldn't move around on her own as she needed a nurse with her all the time. Sophie's usually up and about, but when I was over at the Delezios' house for a visit we just sat in the lounge room for hours and talked and read books. I'd just given her a fake mobile phone from America; I had bought her lots of presents from the US and all she loved was this $5 phone. She was pretending to ring everyone, including Nicole Kidman, whom she's met. I said to her, 'What was Nicole like?' and she looked at me very carefully with her big eyes like she wanted to say something to me but didn't know how to say it. She said, 'She's very pretty, but not as pretty as you' — she was trying not to offend me! We just talked and talked for hours; she never once said, 'When is this going to be over?' or 'When can we go and play?' I only realised that she was not able to move when her carer came over and said, 'Okay, now you can move, Sophie'.

I think about Sophie every day; whenever a bad thing happens in my life I think of her. She has definitely changed me. Sophie pumps my heart up when I need it most. I am so grateful that she came into my life when she did; I don't think I would have chosen to do speech therapy if it wasn't for Sophie. It's not an amazing thing I'm doing for Sophie at all, it is just a friendship but it made me realise what I want to do with my life. Most of all Sophie makes me laugh.

Nicholas Karandonis
THE DELEZIO FAMILY'S AGENT AND PUBLICIST

I went to Sydney Children's Hospital at Randwick some six times after Sophie's second accident. Each time, Ron and Caro would encourage me to come into Sophie's room and always made me feel welcome. Poor little Soph was obviously out of sorts and in pain and I would often say hello and then leave her be. She had so many visitors at that time, I thought the last thing she needed was a new friend. She would sometimes say hi, but more often than not she would just look up and smile.

When Sophie was discharged, the hospital was alive with media. The New South Wales Rugby League team had chosen the same day to make a visit to distribute toys and presents to the children, so the scene needed some management. It was an absolute scrum outside. Soph was meant to be wheeled out in a chair, but she decided that instead, she would walk. I told her that there were a lot of people outside with cameras and that they were all there to see her. She boldly announced that she would like to walk out to them and would I get her a butterfly to wear — they were being sold by the hospital to raise funds on the day. On this day my job was to manage the media and ensure the family made it safely to the car, so I didn't have the chance to talk at length with Sophie.

Thankfully, everything went well and a couple of days later, I was at the family home for a TV story being filmed by the Seven Network. I was met at the door by Carolyn's mother, whom I hadn't met previously, and as we walked along the hall talking, an excited voice yelled out, 'Hi Nic!' I turned to my left and there, sitting on the lounge with Mitchell, was Sophie. I said, 'Hi Soph, hi Mitch — I wasn't sure if you'd remember me, Soph'. She looked me right in the eye and said, 'Of course I do, silly. You came to visit me in the hospital' — and my heart just melted. That evening I was treated to a 'Strawberry Shortcake'

DVD, a story about fairies — made up by a very creative and talented little girl — and a concert, where Soph sang a number of her favourite songs. In actual fact, she sang the same verses of her favourites again and again — as is her way — until she felt everyone appreciated her skills and that she had properly captured the songs. Ron playfully teased her by singing along, which prompted howls, of 'Don't, Dad!' and that in turn, encouraged Mitchell to start up. It was an evening I will never forget, because I had the enormous privilege (and that is what it is) of being welcomed into an amazing family — chiefly by its spiritual leader, Sophie.

Julia Parker
MANAGER OF THE DAY OF DIFFERENCE FOUNDATION

When I got involved in the Day of Difference, I had just moved to Australia [from the US]. My sister-in-law-to-be took her son to a playgroup, and Carolyn and Mitchell were in the same playgroup. She got a call from Ron and Caro saying they wanted to start a foundation and did she know any kindy mums who might be able to help build a database. At the time I wasn't working so she said, 'Actually, I do know someone'. I agreed to see them through the start-up; Christmas was coming up, so there was no point in trying to job-search in Sydney at that time of year.

They wanted to do a launch of the foundation six weeks from the day I was hired. They were hoping to have 400-plus people, prizes and entertainment and all kinds of things. At that point there were just business cards with lists of names and a rented room in the Four Seasons. My original intention was to get them through that first event, and because my background was human resources and systems, I'd help them recruit a person from the field. After the first event we sat down and talked and they said, 'We don't want to do this with somebody else', and I said, 'Good, because I don't want to go somewhere else' — and there we were.

Sophie is our catalyst. Sophie is the reason we exist. However, as a foundation the money does not go to Sophie. The focus of our organisation is to help other kids and in order to do that, we have to enable the hospitals to have what they need to treat kids. We have to ensure the research happens, and we need to educate people on a million things to prevent these injuries. If we can't prevent them, we have to make sure that the hospital is equipped to adequately treat them. A lot of our motivation comes from Sophie's daily experiences. If someone is rude to her or reacts a certain way to her, then it is happening to other people. In the grand scheme of things we are hoping things will be better for her, because when she goes into hospital, the hospital is equipped; when she needs some type of surgery, the research has been done; when she meets people on the street, the attitude adjustment has been done. So in an ideal situation it all benefits Sophie, but her as one of many children.

Her parents have said a thousand times that in order for this not to be in vain, something good has to come out of it. I hope that we are that 'something good', and I hope that what we can do will make some kind of difference. There is no justifying or quantifying what they have been through, but if we are able to make things a little bit better for somebody, then something good has come of it, it is not in vain.

When we first started out, we were in an office above the garage at their house. It was Ron and me for the most part, Carolyn when possible, and then when Tara [Sophie's guide dog] came on board it was Ron and Tara and me! For the first year we worked out of their home and then we were fortunate enough to have these offices donated to us [by the Motor Accidents Authority of New South Wales]. I love coming to work in the city rather than riding my pushbike and parking in their garage. But I miss my tea parties with Soph and my daily scare from Mitch — he used to hide and scare me. And Tara and the nurses and Carolyn ... that is the part that I miss, being in their house every day, seeing their adventures and challenges and triumphs.

I remember, when I got the job, talking to my fiancé and saying, 'I really hope when I see Sophie I don't cry, it really breaks my heart and I don't want to do that'. There was zero chance of that happening. The second day Carolyn walked in with Sophie and introduced us. Before I could even react to her, she was sizing me up and literally giving me the head-to-toe once-over. I started to crack up because she was so bold about it, and I just said, 'Okay, I see you are checking me out, but as of tomorrow we are friends, so get it out of your system'. She just kind of smiled, and the next day we had a tea party and we've been best friends ever since.

There is something about Sophie that just wins you; before you even know it you are sucked in, you would be giving her lollies out of your pocket, whatever she wants. There is a spirit in her and that is something people can relate to, something they want to find in themselves. I think it is something she was born with. Take a look at her parents, there is no question of their strength. She is not going to be a weak child, Mitchell is not going to be a weak child. But I think maybe the accident has given her an old soul; some of the things she comes out with you don't expect from a child her age. I remember my first Christmas working for the foundation. I had baked gingerbread boys and girls. I saved a perfect little girl and perfect little boy for Sophie and Mitchell to go on top of their presents. As I was getting out of the car I dropped the girl and I started to cry because I'm thinking, 'How can I give her this — it is broken, her head has come off. What if she thinks that's how I see her?' It's overthinking but I was really caught up by this. So I go Soph, 'I'm really sorry, I broke the little girl cookie'. She just looked at me like I had six heads and said, 'That's okay Julia, I'm sure it will still taste good. Because it is a cookie, that's all it is.'

She wants to be the one to explain things to you; if they go on vacation, she'd break the news to me. She forgets she's not the adult. I'm sure there are other children like that but there is just something about the way she does it.

Sophie is just beautiful, I absolutely love and adore her. I think she has the world's most expressive face. I always say the greatest gift was that that perfect little face wasn't touched because it is absolutely how she communicates. If she's unhappy there is no masking it, if she is happy there is no masking it. I'm lucky to know her, I'm better for knowing her.

I got to meet Sophie when she had already survived; I got to fall in love with her when she was already recovering. I got to meet the family after they'd been through the worst, but the second accident — what we've done couldn't have begun to prepare us for the second one because we were all about burns, and the second one had nothing to do with burns. The second one was all about road safety. Of course there is that freakish fact it was an elderly man driving, again it was an innocent unsuspecting child and another adult ... But there was nothing that could have prepared us for that. As a result of that we will expand beyond burns to trauma, including burns. We already work with the New South Wales Rural Fire Service and NRMA's Kids FireWise program in regard to fire safety, so perhaps we can do something in regard to road safety. As much as Sophie may be the great love of our lives, she is one of many children impacted by these terrible road accidents. But it does bring it to light how important it is.

One of the benefits we have at the foundation is with Sophie as our catalyst, a lot more people know about us. As a result of that we have been able to raise a lot of money to help a lot of children. The down side is that people don't realise how small we are, so you get all these calls, anything from an old lady calling to tell you why she loves Sophie to someone who wants to come help out or volunteer. Because we have the affiliation with Sophie, we have a constant stream of people who want to know things about her, to get in touch with her. People say, 'My son would like to visit with Mitchell', 'My daughter would like to meet Sophie'; even though it doesn't have anything to do with Day of Difference, it still has to be handled. So it is busy, it's full on — but it's good, because the worst thing as a charity would be sitting here with the phone not ringing.

Paul Francis

CHAIRMAN AND FOUNDER, HUMPTY DUMPTY FOUNDATION

When Sophie had her initial accident in December 2003 she was rushed to Royal North Shore Hospital to be stabilised before she was moved to Westmead, and a lot of the equipment that was used to keep Sophie alive had been bought by Humpty Dumpty and our supporters. Through a mutual friend, Mark Tonelli — who is a big supporter of our charity — I approached Ron to see if Ron would be happy to speak at one of our events in May, the Balmoral Burn; this would be his first ever public speaking engagement. When I met Ron, he asked if I'd like to come out and meet Sophie at Westmead and I said, 'Yes, I'd love to'. So my wife and I went out a couple of days later — I must say with great trepidation. Everybody was aware of the terrible injuries she had suffered and what she was still going through; I wasn't quite sure how I'd react when I first met her and neither was my wife. We met Ron and Carolyn outside the room and we walked in, and straight away Sophie had this huge smile on her face and you just felt quite at home with her. She was just like any other little girl, except she was going through enormous pain. It was just incredible to see her going through what she was going through, and to see the care that she needed, and she was still able to smile and have fun and be as normal as she could be. My wife and I went in there very nervously and came out having experienced one of the most inspiring moments I've had in my whole life.

She's a unique girl. Other people have had more misfortune; Ron would say that when Sophie was in hospital they met so many families that had lost their children, they were at the hospital and their children hadn't made it, and Sophie was one of the lucky ones that had made it. But there is something really special about her, without doubt. You look at her face and it's so bright and alive. I quite often read books about people who have been through things, they've had a terrible illness or they've been injured or whatever it may be, and it reminds them of what the important things in life are. All of a sudden you're not waiting: what would you do tomorrow if your time was limited? It would be a lot different to what you'd do today — you'd spend more time loving people and you'd spend more time with the people you care for, and you'd probably spend less time working and less time doing self-indulgent things. When you look at Sophie you see she's full of love and full of happiness — and she's been to hell and back. If you talk about feeling like you're in the presence of a saint, I think that's as close as you can be.

Sophie's second accident was on the fifth of May, and I remember that very well. We were getting organised for our Balmoral Burn dinner again. Ron and Carolyn were due to be at the dinner that night. I went home to get changed to get down to the function early, and I had just got out of the car and I was walking into the house. As I got to the front door my mobile rang. It was Ron, and he said, 'Mate, Sophie's just been hit by a car'. I actually pulled the phone back away from my face and just looked at it, and I thought, 'Hold on, what's going on here — this has already happened'. I thought I'd gone into some sort of time warp. I put the phone back to my ear and I had to repeat it back to him, and he said, 'Yeah, Carolyn and I are in the city, we've just come out of a meeting and we've had a phone call to say she's been hit by a car. The ambulance is on its way and they're going to take her to Royal North Shore Hospital. Can you ring the hospital and let them know that Sophie's on the way?' — because we've had a fair bit to do with North Shore Hospital. So I rang the hospital; at that stage they weren't aware she was on the way and they had to make sure they had a team prepped. Then Ron rang me back and said, 'They've changed their minds, they're going to take her straight to Randwick [Sydney Children's Hospital], can you ring them?' which is what I did. Randwick already knew she was on her way at that stage — that was just after four o'clock.

We had our dinner on that night and Ron and Carolyn were going to be our guests; they'd become quite close to the people at our functions. Ray Martin was hosting it with Phil Kearns, so I had to get on the phone and speak with both of them — because they knew the Delezios very well — and say, 'I don't know what we're going to do, because Sophie's being rushed to hospital and she's really, really struggling'. I found it pretty traumatic, because Ron was upbeat but the doctors I was talking to weren't so positive about the outcome Ron was hoping for. I said to Phil and Ray, 'We've got 400 people coming, a lot of them know Ron and Carolyn closely and it's going to hit the news very shortly. I don't know how we're going to run the function.' How do we have Vince Sorrenti on stage making everybody laugh? I was in tears at that stage. So we got together and we were debating whether to have the function or not. We agreed that's why we needed to have the function, for kids like Sophie, so we decided to go ahead with it. I was struggling because my phone was going off — not just from Ron but from doctors and from our supporters who wanted to find out what was going on.

Everyone was in tears, including a lot of the doctors. Ray got up and he was just sensational, he did a job that only he could do and just reinforced to everybody that's why we're all there — to help Sophie and kids like Sophie. A lot of the doctors who were supposed to be at the function were working on saving Sophie. As everyone arrived everyone was just crying, but as the night went on the news became slightly more positive. The night ended up raising one million dollars, and I think part of that was because of what had happened with Sophie that afternoon.

Afterwards we were in at the hospital and there were hundreds and hundreds of letters and presents coming in for Sophie. Ron and Carolyn asked us and another couple to open them and categorise them, and it was incredible to sit down and read the letters and the inspiration that she was to other people. The four of us sat there with tears rolling down our cheeks, reading letters from people of all ages that she had done so much for — purely by being who she is. It is just by being her, and by dealing with things and by sticking her chin back up again. We were at a birthday party with them recently and there she was with her new legs on, walking down the stairs into the garden. You get adults walking around complaining they've got a sore back — well, sorry, she's lost both feet, she's six years of age, what's wrong with you? [laughs] You're having a bad day — that'd be a great day for her! She's helped people to focus on other people and not so much on themselves.

That family is just the most perfect example of how people make the most of whatever card they're dealt; that makes Sophie and her whole family an inspiration to us all. I include Mitchell in that; I think what a hard dig it is for him. The whole family has made the most of an exceptionally difficult situation, where they could have said, 'Why me, why us, what have we done to deserve this?' — and a lot of people would have done that. I think because of Sophie and her family less people do that today. They look at Sophie and they go, 'Hey, my day's not too bad,' because she's still managing to smile.

Father Paul Coleman

PRIEST AT THE MARY MACKILLOP CHAPEL, NORTH SYDNEY

While Sophie was being cared for at Westmead, a web of support built up outside the hospital walls. Father Paul Coleman had known the family since before Sophie was born, and led the prayer efforts at the Mary MacKillop Chapel.

I remember when Sophie was born; that was a time of great joy to us. The baptism was a very happy day for everyone, and then they went off and led their lives. And then the great day of tragedy came. I got the news and rushed straight up to Royal North Shore Hospital, but because she was so badly injured they had airlifted her to The Children's Hospital at Westmead, so I missed her but I did talk to the chaplains. From then on it was the saga of praying here at the shrine. Ron and Carolyn both had a great connection with Mary MacKillop, who featured prominently in their struggle to keep Sophie alive. Carolyn and Ron had the Mary MacKillop picture on the pillow and little Sophie would look at the picture and get the energy and courage to fight on. So that's my part in it, very slight really, not in the day-to-day struggle. I did go out to the hospital, they had a room there, and their courage was wonderful. Sister Brigid was one of the sisters here; she formed a great bond with Carolyn and Ron and she would go out a lot and see them.

My main role was in prayer. I wasn't able to be out there physically comforting them all the time, but we would be praying for her with the whole community of faith here. We would have a healing mass or a thanksgiving mass and Ron and Carolyn would talk about what it meant for them; they were inspiring moments. The support of having Mary MacKillop Place with a shrine as a focal point and people praying for her; a tremendous amount of prayer went up from this chapel on a regular basis. Every need was put before us and we would pray for it by name.

When the news started filtering through that this was a very life-and-death situation — we don't know whether she will live, feet have to be removed — that puts you in a quandary, but you pray that whatever is best for Sophie and the family, God allows it to happen through the ministry of the doctors and nurses and the faith of the people. The ripples that have gone on from this event — it has been a painful one for her parents, and an extremely painful one for her, but it has demonstrated the power of the human spirit. Then add the component of faith, and the component of Mary MacKillop, Australia's blessed one — you've got an extraordinary coming together of the elements that just make human beings be human.

Why does God allow this to happen to an innocent girl? That's a natural question and it's a struggle, no matter who you are. I believe that everyone on this earth has their own unique mission to fulfil in whatever way they can. It seems to me Sophie has this mission: that she can rise from this terrible tragedy, and can show courage, hope, the triumph of human spirit over affliction and tragedy and hurt, and just continue to go on.

Ron and Carolyn are marvellous — their composure. But the thing about them is genuine faith, a genuine belief that God and Mary MacKillop will save their daughter. It's not just showy, pious stuff, it is real human suffering and pain and yet expressed with that note of hope. That is really the story of all of us. Christ suffered and died on the Cross, but He rose. And that is what happens to human beings; we go down but we need that extra gift of faith to rise.

I am very reserved about the word 'miracle'. I believe in the faith and the efforts of the people involved. Her parents are wonderful people, the doctors and the burns people have shown skill and dedication and commitment, and God is working through that. A miracle is a technical term, I don't like using it. I can just say that it is God bringing goodness out of this.

These events make people think, maybe start a little movement in their minds or hearts. The spirit of God lives in everyone and just because people don't reflect on it, because they've got other agendas in their minds and hearts, it doesn't stop it. Everyone gets the gift of God, the spirit of what we call G O D, but it is the spirit of love, spirit of hope, human endeavour — all those wonderful things, the spirit of reaching out. God is at work in the world. I know terrible things happen, wars and so on, but that is due to humans being blinded to the real way of God. Wherever you've got genuine love, there is God, and you meet it all the time. People may never go to church, they may have no religious belief, but God is in their lives even if they don't know it.

What has transpired to date — the two great sorrows, the courage of the family, the courage of Sophie, the element of faith and the spirit of God, the impact on the nation — that has uplifted people, it has helped people to think of a spirit beyond them, it has helped people to go beyond the bounds of their own self. That is something that is good as a result of all this, and that can't be taken away. Now, where the future goes, none of us can say.

Jeff Fatt

MEMBER OF CHILDREN'S ENTERTAINMENT GROUP, THE WIGGLES

Sophie was a big fan of The Wiggles when the accident happened. We got a call through Diana, our publicist, saying it would be great if we could get down to the hospital and pay a visit. We do a lot of hospital visits for sick children or children who have been injured and we get a huge kick out of doing that. So we paid a visit to Sophie at the hospital. You really felt as though you were intruding on their personal space, but the bottom line is if you can help out in any way, that is a great thing. You really don't know how to react except go along with what the parents want you to do. I think just being there helps.

There were a few visits. The next time was when she was conscious and that was when you really got to see what an amazing spirit Sophie had. She was a little bit reserved and a bit shy at that stage. For any child to see The Wiggles in reality can be a bit traumatic, because we are not in the typical Wiggles environment, the TV or video. She did eventually come around; we had more photos taken with her and that was fantastic.

Knowing that she has gone through such a horrific ordeal and seeing that she has this great bubbly personality is really inspiring. She always seems to be so vibrant. There is something there that you don't find in any other child; she has this gift of being so bright and happy and so positive.

She absolutely does have something special that sets her apart, and it's to the full credit of Carolyn and Ron and how they are managing her through this whole process. They certainly don't give her any slack in terms of letting her get away with stuff. By the same token, she has missed out on so much, they are balancing that by allowing her to do things over and above what a normal child would do.

I thought of her on her birthday, just before the second accident. I remember when I saw her earlier in the year she was showing me her new legs; it was like no big deal, it was just part of her and she totally accepted all that. When I heard the news about her second accident, we were overseas. It was one of those things that just twists you, it makes your gut really wrench, and I guess the whole of Australia was feeling that as well. We really loved seeing her at The Wiggles fifteenth birthday party at Luna Park, to see that she had come through that second ordeal and to all intents and purposes she was okay.

Because of her personality you only see Sophie for what she really is rather than the injury. You do notice it but it is not the main thing about Sophie. Her face wasn't affected by the whole ordeal, and her face is just so expressive of her personality. She doesn't appear to let the whole ordeal worry her — although we don't see behind the scenes, the impression we get is that she is riding above it all.

I think the greatest moment for me was seeing her with her new legs, and to see she was actually walking. That for her was a great milestone; she had the mobility and I was just so happy that she was mobile. I think every time you see her, she lights up your life, that's all I can say.

Charli Delaney
MEMBER OF CHILDREN'S ENTERTAINMENT GROUP, HI–5

It all started when we saw Sophie on the news, and we thought we saw something from Hi–5 in the background. I was so touched by her story I just took it upon myself and got a Hi–5 pack together uninvited. I found out she was a huge Wiggles fan, but I didn't care! I made my way in and asked if I could see her and give her some gifts. I spent some time with her in the hospital. The moment I saw her, those eyes — I thought there is something so special about this little girl. She must have been in so much pain, it was so soon after the accident, but I thought if I could bring some relief, just a bit of joy to the day, that was all I wanted to do.

I was very touched by that meeting and was fortunate enough to meet them again doing a *Backyard Blitz* show. It was lovely to see the family again; I was also inspired by both her parents in the way they were coping. With the media attention it has drawn, it can only be a positive thing. Ron said this at the gala the other night: people walking along won't whisper, and say what's happened to this little girl or woman, they'll just say, 'It's Sophie'.

When the second accident happened, my family and I were talking on the phone and we were all just crying. We think Australia cried that night — everyone shed a tear that night. For lightning to strike twice, it just didn't seem fair.

Just after she came out of the coma after the second accident — I don't know why, I had to do it — I went to the hospital again, just to leave a little gift for her at reception. The lady at reception said, 'Can I just call them and let them know you are here'. Luckily Carolyn said, 'Come on up'. So I bolted up, couldn't go fast enough, and I was very fortunate enough to see Sophie. Truly that little girl, she is the most inspiring child I've ever met. That face is so beautiful and there is something so deep in those eyes, she touches everyone's hearts. It is like she is an angel. To be as strong and high-spirited as she is in these times is incredible.

My involvement kicked into another gear when my sister Casandra found out about an event called 'Ride for Sophie'. She got stuck into that and got me and my parents involved. At Anna Bay, where my family live, we created a fundraiser: 'Day of Fun for Sophie'. We had bands and camel rides and I did signings for a gold coin donation, photos and things, to raise money for Day of Difference. I got everything I could off Channel 9, and we auctioned off all these items. For a month my family were completely devoted to this event; without ever meeting Sophie, they wanted to do everything they could. Mum was going around the streets of Port Stephens and putting out jars and making up signs for windows. Motorbikes and vintage cars rode from Anna Bay and then we met the Sydney Ride for Sophie motorbikes and drove in convoy to Harbord Diggers to present the cheque to Ron and Day of Difference. That was an amazing thing to be part of; you feel so hopeless when you know someone is in pain or suffering, and you feel like there is nothing you can do. But what you can do is raise money for foundations like Day of Difference, to help others in Sophie's situation.

This little girl has touched so many people that she doesn't even know about; my friends and family feel like they know her, even though they hadn't met her at that time. For a child to be able to do that on a camera lens — which is all we'd seen her on — there is something so special about her. We believe she will be a woman of our times; she will grow to be a woman with such a story to tell, she is just destined for something great.

I saw her again at a gala the other night and I was so touched because she said, 'My boyfriend kissed me' and I thought, 'She's got a boyfriend!' — it is just so cute. I believe she will grow into something so special. She already is, but she has touched the hearts of Australia in a way that we haven't been touched before. For example, my sister grew out of this situation. Doing this fundraising took her on a journey; she couldn't sleep because her brain was ticking about how we could help. I've never seen my family like it — they pulled together in a way that I never thought I'd get to experience. The repercussions on so many people ... How can one little girl be so inspiring if she is not destined for something great on this earth? I feel so fortunate that I am in a children's group, that I am able to go to the hospital, to hug her and kiss her cheek and bring a smile to her face, and see this brave little girl is doing so well.

12

Sophie today

There's no doubt that Sophie Delezio is as bold as brass and strong as steel. But she's also a little girl who loves her dolls, teases her brother and is sometimes scared of the dark. Two years after her second near-fatal accident, she and her family talk about how life has moved on for them, what the future might hold, and the things that bind their family together.

'Look!' Sophie proudly holds up a bandaged arm to show me. A week earlier she had been in hospital for operations to fix contractures where the skin was tight on one of her fingers and fusing on her left ear, and to remove a staple in her hip. These had been her first operations in a year — a long gap after having had two years of one operation after another.

Ron explains: 'You very easily get used to not having operations, so it was something that I was a bit concerned about. Before Sophie goes for an operation she has what we call "wobbly medicine"; it's just a pre-medication to zonk her out a bit, so when they put a mask on her she's not too scared. But she doesn't like the mask and she doesn't like the gas. This time we got these masks that were sent across from Perth's Princess

Margaret Children's Hospital. They are clear plastic masks with a strawberry scent. She really took to them, and we brought one home and used it with her dolls. Sophie decided that she didn't want to have a pre-med this time. Normally she gets taken in to theatre on a trolley, but this time Sophie wanted to walk in without assistance. Sophie put her prosthetic legs on and walked into theatre. She went in and was put on the bed; then she grabbed the mask, put the mask on herself and went to sleep. I know that a lot of other kids do similar acts of courage, but she is my daughter and I'm very proud of her. It's a pretty gutsy thing to do.'

Sophie gives a bright description of her strawberry-scented face mask, but pauses when I ask her what it was like to be back in hospital again. 'Mm, yeah ... I was feeling a little bit scared. But — I didn't feel anything! Anything at all! They had to break my finger, but I didn't feel it.' She adds in a singsong voice: 'I was f-a-s-t asleep!'

Carolyn describes the shift in their lives over the past year as huge. 'When you go back to hospital after this period of time, you become a bit contemplative of where you have been. You recall the times when you were in hospital previously. But the good thing is that we've been having various appointments with specialists and the like, and they're saying, "We don't need to see you for another review for one year" — two years in some cases. And that's all fantastic. Sophie's getting more medically well and there's less to manage on a daily basis, although we're continually reviewing her. We don't have to have the same intensity of care, and that opens the time for Sophie to do other things, like have friends to play and join a drama group. So she can do a few things which children at that age generally get involved in, even if it's just having a friend to play. Sometimes that wasn't an option before, just because there was no time.'

Sophie tells me proudly about her drama class: 'I go on Mondays after school. We do plays, poems, dances — all of those kinds of things. I'm best at plays — I like making people laugh.'

Sophie also loves sport, despite the physical limitations she faces. Carolyn says, 'She said to me, "Mummy, I want to play soccer, I want to go back to ballet" — which is interesting because she never actually went to ballet, but she's quite convinced that she had! So we suggested that maybe not ballet, but she could try jazz ballet as an option. And we're looking at including a little gymnastics class into her physio, which is just a group that meets early on a Saturday morning. Every time Sophie comes home she's got another idea for something she'd like to be involved in — and I imagine the list is going to get longer and longer!'

Along with Sophie's physical progress comes a growing confidence. 'Her increased independence and mobility is lovely to see', says Carolyn. 'She gets great satisfaction when she's made her own bed and put her oil and cream on her body. Don't ask me how she does it … I don't go there with her because I feel if she's made the effort to do it, I don't then go and reapply anything. I think to myself, well, we can just double up this afternoon with whatever's been missed, because I think it's important for her to gain that confidence. When she does get up and get dressed and make her bed, I just think that is of more importance at this stage than the other things. So whilst previously we were always assessing things on a medical ground, we're now assessing things on a holistic ground — looking at Sophie growing and maturing and gaining independence.'

The Delezio family no longer has quite the army of support people, carers, nurses, etc, they had in their home initially. 'About this time last year, I stripped that right back to give us some family time and so we didn't have to rely on having additional care', Carolyn explains. 'The focus was just on the family managing and having to do what other families do in the morning — get up, get breakfast, get to school, all under your own steam, which for Sophie just takes that little bit longer. I thought it was important for her to have little duties that she's expected to do as part of the family routine as much as anything else. And she gives it all a go. So some days we don't have carers; we shaved off probably half of the care. Having said that, we're reliant on my parents, who moved permanently to Australia from New Zealand at the end of 2006. And some people contribute a lot in terms of their time at no cost to us — babysitting or chipping in when I can't get to Mitchell in time because I've got Sophie tied up at hospital, things like that. So we've still got a bank of people who are prepared to help out, but it doesn't involve a carer in the home. That's working fairly well for us. I recall a conversation I had with someone early in the year saying that your needs will change over time, and that's what we're experiencing — as Sophie gets more medically well, and ages, we have different elements that come into play. It's ever evolving — but with that comes a great excitement with the fact that we *can* change things round to suit Sophie's needs and lifestyle.'

At the same time, there remains concern over Sophie's head injury from the second accident. Ron explains: 'There's been

311

continuous testing on how her mind is working. We have realised that her mind fatigues a lot quicker than it did before.'

Sophie's paediatrician, Dr Jonny Taitz, says that though Sophie is performing well at school, the neuropsychological evaluation shows that she's probably a few points down from where she was before the second accident, but she is still within the average range. 'She probably had a severe form of concussion and some bleeding on the brain during the time of the second accident. When we did the initial testing in August [2006] we were concerned that the results of the neuropsychological evaluation may have been misleading as it was too close to the second accident, but in fact a year on it does show some subtle changes from her previous score. How that translates into school performance is something that we're going to have to keep a close eye on. The plan will be to test her annually for at least the next few years. Compared to the average population she's fine. But given her other limitations and disabilities we obviously want to maximise her scholastic potential.'

Carolyn and Ron still find they move through areas of grief, despite their determination to focus on the present. 'It never really leaves your mind', says Carolyn. 'But probably the grief lessens in time as you adapt. I don't think you ever lose it because life is never the same, but you find joy in other things. [Long pause.] It's a hard one to describe … the more you focus on the future and things you want to do in life, the less you tend to contemplate what's been. And that's always been our focus. One of the reasons we took the trip [a three-week holiday in France] was that Sophie was medically well and we've learned to seize those opportunities because it changes very quickly. And with

Sophie's operation last week — you kind of wish that wasn't going to happen, but at the end of the day you know that it is and when she gets past it, that's one down, one less that she has to go through. You'd rather not have to experience that, you'd rather not have to see your little girl go through all the pain and suffering that she's going to go through yet again. But that's not how this works.'

The family still has the support of people like social worker Sandra Spalding, who meets with them all on a regular basis. 'Sophie has certainly moved on in many ways, but she still quite regularly feels a need to re-engage with some of her early experiences — particularly the hospitalisation period and medical procedures. Sophie isn't morbidly preoccupied with these — it's more like an acknowledgement of them; they are a dot-point in her journey. But what I see is that her "tool bag" of coping skills is expanding.

'Sophie sometimes struggles with her frustration at not being able to do manual things easily, and I see her giving up on tasks — she quite often abandons what she is doing. This is understandable, but I do try to bring her attention back to the task and get her to think through how she could get the job done — to problem solve — but I don't often succeed in this. My concern is that she could develop a practice of giving up, and this needs to be carefully monitored.

'Sophie does recall small snatches of the first accident, but she has fragmentary auditory recollections rather than a coherent memory of it. She's no longer terrified by her recollections, but any reference to them makes her pensive and quiet for a moment, and then she redirects her attention to the present. The issues around the accident will quite likely need to be addressed at various times as she matures. It'll be important to respond to her need or interest in talking about the accident in an open and honest way.

'Sophie obviously knows about the second accident, but she appears to have no recall of it. Carolyn once suggested that Sophie saw the admission following the second accident as an extension of the first; she's probably correct, because when I'm working with Sophie she doesn't bring up the second accident.

'Sophie continues to amaze me. She remains an absolute delight — she's engaging and has a delightful sense of humour. She has enormous courage and resilience — she can still be cheeky and bossy. She can also show enormous empathy and compassion, qualities I am seeing more and more of as she matures. I still look forward to seeing her with anticipation — never quite knowing what to expect!'

Ron quietly explains how he is inspired by his own daughter. 'I know she's got a lot of courage and I know that she's a person that just gets on with things. That happened in the hospital, when all we were worried about was making it as easy as we could for her. But instead of Sophie following, she led the way. She went beyond taking the operation in her stride. She went a lot further than I gave her credit for. She's a very insightful girl too; a friend of ours, [asbestos campaigner] Bernie Banton, just died. Sophie was saying her prayers last night for Bernie, and she says, "Oh, he's going to heaven shortly". And this morning he died. This sort of thing has happened before. I think she's been there, you know? We're religious, we believe in God, and I think God had her at one stage and gave her back to us, but in the process she's now got a connection. It was so uncanny; we'd been saying prayers [for Bernie] for a while, why would she say it now, that Bernie's going to heaven shortly — and then at one o'clock this morning he dies.'

As I speak with Sophie, Carolyn and Ron at their house, there's a buzz of people coming and going, but the overriding sense is of a home full of calm and affection. Phones ring; Ron gulps down a sandwich before heading to the airport for a trip to Melbourne; Pat Barraclough, Sophie's carer, works quietly around the house in the background; Ms Wright, a teacher/tutor, sits with Sophie in the kitchen for a while, helping her catch up on schoolwork she missed while in hospital the week before. A neighbour drops Mitchell home from school and stays to chat, showing us photos of a beautiful but damaged gum tree that was recently cut down near her house.

Sophie clearly adores her family — Carolyn says, 'She'll just come up to you and give you a great big hug and say "I just want to tell you how much I love you"! I often think to myself, we should all do a bit more of this!' When pressed on the question herself, Sophie explains that 'Daddy teaches me to punch. Mum's kind, and Mitchell is silly'. Mitchell is sitting in Sophie's room, crunching crackers; he gives a cheeky grin, and acknowledges that Sophie is a pretty good sister. About his family, Mitchell says, 'It's pretty much a well-behaved family. We learn and my dad teaches me how to do a good job when I do my homework. Mum does most of the work, but we have to do our chores. I make my bed, clean my teeth, get dressed, and — this isn't my chores but sometimes I do it — I help make my lunch'.

Carolyn describes the closeness between Mitchell and Sophie with an example from their recent holiday in France. 'We were in a museum and Soph was going, "Pick me up, mummy, pick me up" and I was saying, "No, I'm not picking you up Sophie, you can see through the glass there, you know exactly what you want to look at." Next thing you know Mitchell's whizzed over to her and lifted her above the railings so she can get a better look! I'll just point out that there's only a four-kilo difference in their weight — there's this 26 kilo eight-year-old boy who's a bean pole, lifting his fairly hefty little sister up above the railing so she can have a glimpse! So he can be extraordinarily loving and caring. They can be competitive as siblings often are, there's the normal rivalry — it can get a bit tiring, but they can play beautifully together and it makes up for the noise and chaos that's sometimes coming from the back of the car!'

'Mitchell is travelling pretty well', says Ron. 'He still goes through his sad periods every now and then. With Sophie's last operation, he got a bit emotional and a bit upset about the whole thing. We believe that they'll ask if they want to know something; Mitchell asked what was going to happen in the operation and I explained it to him. I think it's starting to sink in a bit with Mitchell what an operation actually is — that it involves a knife and cutting the skin and more. He might have felt that he asked too much. So I feel sorry for him there, but at the same time you've got to be honest and as compassionate as you can with your answers.'

Many people, both those close to the Delezio family and in the wider arena, have expressed concern about the impact the family's high profile will have on Mitchell and Sophie. Mitchell sums up how he feels about people paying his family so much attention: 'When people do, it feels like I'm a busy person but when it's not happening, it feels relaxing.'

Sandra Spalding's take on it is that the children are quite used to the media attention now — 'but they are really just children who want to get on with their daily lives. I know that Ron and Carolyn are mindful of the potential intrusion of the media, and they'll keep an eye on the impact on the children as they grow older — that's the time when they may resist involvement'.

For Ron, the media focus is not just about their family, nor is it something the children just put up with. 'They're aware of what we do with the charity and a lot of the time they mention, "This is for the other kids who are in hospital." It gives them a sense of pride that they're doing something as well. If Sophie says "I don't want to be involved" or "I don't want to have my picture taken", I say to the press, that's it, you've got to be quick otherwise the opportunity isn't there any more. And we're very aware of what Mitchell goes through — to make sure he's included as much as we can.'

What does the future hold for Sophie and her family? First up is a new house — the move is planned for early 2008, so by the time you read this the boxes should be unpacked. 'I'll tell you all the rooms that we have', says Sophie. 'Four bedrooms, one playroom, and a garage, a balcony … and guess what? On my new bed, this is where the pillow goes', gesturing widely. 'If you press the button — this is the button — it can go like that!' gesturing up. 'And when you press it, it goes down. And it can go just halfway — anywhere you want. So you can sit up to read a book. And I'll show you how long my bed is — see where that chair is? It goes from there to here. I've got a long bed because I have to have a hand to get up. It's a bit hard. And I usually sleep with my mum because I'm a little bit scared of the dark.'

The vision for their new house started with two simple requests, Carolyn says. 'One, I wanted Sophie to be able to walk to her front door easily; and the other was for her to be able to wheel in her electric wheelchair into the rooms and not bump into furniture, which happens here. I just wanted her to have a degree of mobility, particularly in the summer months — she doesn't manage heat well so we stay at home a lot, or have people over because it's easier to manage her in a controlled environment. So we've designed it so there are lots of interesting little areas to go to which are destinations in their own right, little spots that she can visit and hopefully will give her a different atmosphere. I think it's going to be fantastic, and who wouldn't love to live in a brand-new home? It backs onto Sophie's school, so she'll be able to just go out the door, round the corner and be in the school grounds. She'll be with a carer but in future she'll be able to manage on her own and that's why we bought where we did. There's a bus at the door and shops up the road, and those things are all considerations in her future independence.'

Stability is the thing that Ron is looking forward to most. 'We just want to get into the new house and settle down, get a routine in place. There are a lot of things that are going to make it a lot easier for Sophie and the family. No steps, the right sort of air conditioning for her and for the family, the right communications in the house if she needs something, it's got a lift, it's got all that sort of stuff. So there's a lot to look forward to. And I think the operations she's just had will do a lot of good for her. It's going to be nice to see when all of the bandages get taken off. We've got some more operations coming, but we know they're going to be really positive operations.'

Sophie is also getting a new set of legs. 'They're just in their final stages of fitting at the moment, so that's a step forward as well', says Carolyn. 'As she gets a little bit taller her feet get bigger — so she gets a lot of new shoes! Talk about going shoe shopping — you know, it's not all bad!'

Dr Jonny expects that as Sophie matures, she'll start questioning more and more what happened in her first five years of life. 'That's going to impact how she starts viewing herself when she becomes an adolescent and a teenager. That's the time when most kids struggle, and I think with her disability that may pose some increased challenges for her and her family. Right now I think she has a degree of innocence, which will change with time.'

Although no one can predict the future, Sandra Spalding says, having children means that family dynamics shift and change as the children grow and mature. 'This is also true for parents, of course, who go through their own developmental changes at the same time! High and low points happen along the way — I expect there will be a lot of these for the Delezio family. What I can predict is that critical developmental stages are likely to be most challenging — especially adolescence and young adulthood, when body image and self-esteem can become major issues. In general, parents' emotional wellbeing mirrors what is happening to their child or children, and I suspect this will be the case for Ron and Carolyn. While Sophie and Mitchell are doing relatively well, they will too — and so as much as I anticipate some tough periods for Sophie, I expect Ron and Carolyn to have their difficult periods too.'

Further down the track, Mitchell has plenty of ambitions. He wants to be a professional sports player when he grows up — 'either soccer, tennis or swimming. Or baseball'. And if he had a magic wand to change the world, he would fix the pollution. 'Especially in Paris'. And he would make sure that no one gets sick.

Sophie's aspirations are closer to home. She wants to be a teacher when she grows up. I ask her why, and she gives me a look that is both incredulous and condescending. 'So I can teach kids.' Of course. And it does make sense — after all, Sophie is teaching us all so much already.

13
Wishes for Sophie

One of the most powerful things about Sophie Delezio's story is the way in which it has drawn people together. The website www.wishesforsophie.com has received over 16,000 messages from people offering their support to Sophie. Here, some of Sophie's friends and supporters share their wishes for Sophie. They describe the magic that they would weave for Sophie, if they had a magic wand, and if they had a crystal ball, what they might see.

John Mangos

TELEVISION NEWSMAN, CURRENTLY SENIOR ANCHORMAN FOR
SKY NEWS AUSTRALIA

My 'realistic' magic wand is to make the journey as comfortable as possible. If it was the 'mega' magic wand it would be no pain, no discomfort or no torment at all, but I don't think that is going to happen. I feel for her now; I feel for her when she enters puberty; I feel for her when she has her dark moments and looks up and says, 'Why me?' — one day she will say that, and it breaks my heart to think about it.

The magic wand is for all of them — so Mitch has this normal upbringing, so mum and dad have as least grief as possible. They've got plans to build a new house; they had to buy a block of land that was totally level so the house has no steps. As Ron said to me once, this is the house Sophie will probably live in for the rest of her life. It will have all the equipment she'll need now and also anticipate the things she'll need as she gets older. I know that they get frustrated sometimes in their private moments; when some people hear about all this money that goes to Day of Difference, they think it is to buy things for Sophie. I know that hurts them tremendously, because they are comfortable, but they are not rich. And even if they were rich, no amount of money could pay for what they have gone through and continue to go through.

I'd like to see in my crystal ball that Sophie miraculously recovers. That is not going to happen; we have to face up to that. Tragedy does impact on different people in different ways; some people are geared to deal with it and turn it into a positive, and Sophie is one of those people.

Alan Jones

BROADCASTER, PATRON OF THE DAY OF DIFFERENCE
FOUNDATION AND FRIEND

I just want Sophie to be happy and to be Sophie. Not Sophie, the little thing that was injured, Sophie the little thing that triumphed. That has to be put behind her. Carolyn is a very powerful force for normalcy. And Ron, he's a dad and dads spoil their daughters and that's what Ron will do — and she needs that as well. I think they feel they've been blessed: they've been blessed with two beautiful children, they've been blessed with an angel on Sophie's shoulder and it's guided her from impossible circumstances to exceptional triumph. I think that might be symptomatic of the life that exists for her ahead. She's an exceptional young girl and I think that she's going to have some exceptional triumphs.

Paul Francis
CHAIRMAN AND FOUNDER, HUMPTY DUMPTY FOUNDATION

It's easy to say, 'I wish her the best and I wish her a future where everybody treats her as their equal' — but she's not their equal [laugh], she's better than everybody else! She's shown that already; I just hope that she continues to do the wonderful things that she's already done; I think that's what she'll want to do.

Siobhan Connelly
FORMERLY BURNS AND PLASTIC SURGERY CLINICAL NURSE SPECIALIST, THE CHILDREN'S HOSPITAL AT WESTMEAD

She has such strength behind her and such a supportive family that she is going to be able to do whatever she wants. I just hope she's happy because she can deal with the physical, it is the emotional. When I do school visits for people who have had hand or face burns, it is always one of the main things you have to walk people through, because it is quite confronting. The good thing is she's had such a public profile that she isn't looked on as strange. If she goes overseas where people don't know her, I hope that that goes with her — not the fact that she has a high profile, but the fact she can deal with the situation she's been placed into. We look at Sophie as a gorgeous little girl, the apple of her family's eye; Australia sees her as an amazing child who survived. We had a boy from overseas and we couldn't send him back because he would be ridiculed and made a pariah. I hope for Sophie — and all children surviving an injury or disease which leaves obvious physical effects — that the world will adapt and be less superficial.

Maxine Amies
REGISTERED NURSE AT THE PHYSICAL ABILITY UNIT

Long-term friendships; that would be huge. She needs kids her own age all the way through to stick by her, because she can support them just as much as they can support her. People who aren't there because they are therapists, they are there because they are her friends. If we had magic wands we'd make the whole world better; I would use it more than once. I can assure you, we've often wished for one.

Sandra Spalding
SOCIAL WORKER, THE CHILDREN'S HOSPITAL AT WESTMEAD

I would wish happiness for her, and success in whatever she chooses to do. I think Sophie is going to do some good things for others out in the community because of the profile she has, she does have that opportunity, but it has to be her choice. I hope Sophie can have as normal a life as possible; she talks excitedly and expectantly about her wants and hopes, and I hope those dreams come true. And I hope those dreams are not really modified because of her injuries — I hope that she always finds a way around any obstacles. I hope that she doesn't feel that she has a responsibility to others, that she can just be and do what she wants to do.

What I wish for Sophie is that the world allows her to 'just be Sophie' — a truly beautiful human being, but human all the same — and we all have human failings and weaknesses. The public shouldn't expect too much from Sophie; she will 'struggle' through her adolescent years like most young people and quite likely challenge her mum and dad in the process! She will always be one of those patients whom I will never forget. As much as I may have had an impact on her young life, she has impacted on mine, both professionally and personally. I will always be interested in her journey and hope that her life is punctuated by mostly 'I happy today!' days.

Garry Smith

PRINCIPAL OF ARRANOUNBAI SCHOOL

No more major incidents in her life — if I could foresee that, I'd be a happy person. I can already see in my crystal ball that the support will always be there for her; I can see she will always remain that fairly resilient kid. It would be nice to live long enough to see her grow into an adult. Through curiosity, sure, because not too many people survive what she went through and it would be nice to see how things end up for her. One day last year we were doing a photo shoot about our new school bus, and in one of the photos Sophie was in the bus hanging her head out the window and waving to the camera. I was supporting her at the time and it struck me then just how damaged her body is, and how much her body is going to need to be adjusted for her — not naturally, but unnaturally — how serious her future is.

Rebecca Myhre
CAROLYN MARTIN'S GODDAUGHTER, WHO WAS PUSHING SOPHIE'S STROLLER WHEN IT WAS HIT IN THE SECOND ACCIDENT

I just hope that Sophie and the family live the rest of their lives to the full, that they continue to be so strong and full of love, and that she can achieve anything that she wants to. I want the world for her, really — I love them loads!

Ann-Louise de La Poype
CAROLYN MARTIN'S SISTER

If I had a magic wand — oh gosh, I would wish all Sophie's pain away. I would wish all the pain away for Carolyn and Ron too, and for all the families and children who suffer in the world. The accident has really helped me understand what suffering is. That raw nerve, it's the underside of happiness. You suddenly understand what an Iraqi family might feel when their daughter's been tortured; suddenly you're there, suddenly you know what it is for a family to be dealing with a child who's got cancer; you understand that, you can share in it.

Greg Martin
CAROLYN MARTIN'S BROTHER

That she doesn't remember any of the accident and that she doesn't suffer any long-term pain from the accident. And that she takes things from the accident and utilises it with the personality she has to do good.

Michelle Bates
RON DELEZIO'S SISTER

It would be lovely to say that one day she could marry and lead a normal life. That very well could happen, that would be lovely. And to have children.

Katy Gompes
HER DAUGHTER, OLIVIA, ATTENDED THE ROUNDHOUSE CHILDCARE CENTRE WITH SOPHIE

I would give Sophie a world of acceptance, and a world where she is empowered and passionate to make a difference. She is going to live a remarkable life and has so much to contribute, so I want her to have an environment where she will be supported and listened to.

Linda Jones Meader
A LONG-TERM FRIEND OF SOPHIE'S MOTHER, CAROLYN

We talk about our children all flatting and going out together, and my daughter Lillie saying to Sophie, 'Come on, put your legs on, we need to go out now'. We hope she can have a normal life, and there is no reason why she can't. I hope she gets to have a lot of close relationships with very special people. I can see her being a great motivational speaker about overcoming disabilities. Sophie has a knack of saying the right thing to the right people at a very young age, and she touches your heart every time you see her.

Louise Palmer
A FRIEND OF SOPHIE'S MOTHER, CAROLYN, SINCE SCHOOL DAYS

I would love for them to have as normal a life as possible from now on. They are very much in the public eye and always will be, especially considering Sophie is going to do something huge, but just for them to have time out and be able to relax and not have to worry about Sophie so much. Certainly financial security so that is never a problem, because it is an enormous cost to cover all her special needs. For them to never ever have to worry about those issues, to see her grow up and achieve her potential.

Adelle Pink

PASSER-BY AT SECOND ACCIDENT

What I want for her is to experience all the beauty and joy and happiness. To have children, to fall in love, to travel, to feel beautiful. That's what I wish for her.

Carol Inkson

FAMILY FRIEND

I would wish that it would never ever happen. That it never happen to Sophie, that it never happen to anyone. And I pray every day for that magic wand.

Katrina Brayshaw

FAMILY FRIEND AND DAY OF DIFFERENCE DIRECTOR

I'd just wish for Sophie anything that she wishes for herself. And I will support her 100 per cent in achieving whatever that is.

Rod Smith

THE DELEZIO FAMILY'S SOLICITOR AND
DAY OF DIFFERENCE DIRECTOR

What I want to see is that Sophie achieves all the dreams that any little girl would have. Any girl growing up dreams of meeting a wonderful man, having beautiful children, a lovely family, seeing them growing up with that love around you. And I think she'll do it.

Maree Thomas
SOPHIE'S 'FAIRY GODMOTHER'

What would I wish for Sophie — that everyone would treat her normally, that everyone would see her as the gorgeous little girl that she is. For her good body to be back! That she always keeps her joy, her loving, her openness, her compassion. That she always keeps the beautiful qualities that she has now, looking for a rainbow in every day.

Ruth Edwards
(DUBAI, UNITED ARAB EMIRATES) —
WISHES FOR SOPHIE WEBSITE MESSAGE

What an amazing little person you are ... Such courage in the face of so much, and at such a young age too! You truly are an inspiration. May your life be filled with happiness and good fortune.

Domi
(SYDNEY, AUSTRALIA) — WISHES FOR SOPHIE WEBSITE MESSAGE

Dear Sophie, get better and live your life to the fullest because I'm sure you see how precious life is. Get better for all the people that love you. And get better for yourself, you have been through so much and you are what reaches out to so many hearts worldwide. Everyone loves you, Sophie, and never forget to love yourself.

Umesh
(MUMBAI, INDIA) — WISHES FOR SOPHIE WEBSITE MESSAGE

Just can't imagine what you must have gone thru, my heart goes out for you and I wish I can take the time back and save you from all the two accidents. But I cannot do that, I can only pray for you. I must say that you give hope and courage to millions who know about you. May god be with you.

Mike McAuliffe
(PERTH, AUSTRALIA) — WISHES FOR SOPHIE WEBSITE MESSAGE

Best wishes to your whole, wonderful family. I have wept for what you have gone through but in many ways you are blessed because tragedy has brought the very best out in you all. Best wishes now for a life that gets better with every day.

Alistair and Jordan
(NEWPORT, RHODE ISLAND, USA) —
WISHES FOR SOPHIE WEBSITE MESSAGE

Dear Sophie, we are sorry you are hurt. We are sending our thoughts and prayers to you and your family and hope lots of good things happen to you in the future!

Paula
(Southampton, UK) — Wishes for Sophie website message

Darling Sophie,

If I had only one wish in the whole wide world, then it would be for you to be better as soon as possible and back to the way you were before.

Thang Tri Nguyen
(Ho Chi Minh City, Vietnam) — Wishes for Sophie website message

Best wishes for you Sophie. I saw your face on the news, you always smile, you made me stronger Sophie. I hope you will get better soon. You are brave and strong Sophie. My hero.

Sophie's people

More than 80 people contributed their story to *Sophie's Journey*.
Many more have played a role in Sophie's life. This list includes
the people represented in this book, as well as some key people
who do not appear in these pages. There will be others not
listed here too, because the circle of love and support for
Sophie spans the globe — we also thank all the people who
have cared.

Maxine Amies	Registered nurse, Physical Ability Unit
Michelle Appleby	Physiotherapist, Physical Ability Unit
Dr John Awad	ICU specialist, Sydney Children's Hospital
Pat Barraclough	Home nurse
Michelle Bates	Ron's sister
Andrew Berry	Child Flight NETS crew
Jenny Berry	Physiotherapist
Scott Black	Passer-by — first accident
Wendy Bladwell	Child Flight NETS crew
Gordon Boath	Fire inspector, Manly Fire Station
Lauren Bradford	Theatre nurse, The Children's Hospital at Westmead

Katrina Brayshaw	Family friend and Day of Difference director
Brown family	Family friends
Dr Michael Bryden	Head paediatrician, The Children's Hospital at Westmead
Lisa Carnovale	Play therapist, The Children's Hospital at Westmead
Brad Ceely	Nurse practitioner in PICU, The Children's Hospital at Westmead
Lisa Charman	Sophie's preschool teacher, Arranounbai
Peter Clark	Second accident — driver of stationary car
Sarah Clarke	Burns unit nurse, The Children's Hospital at Westmead
Megan Cluff	Pain clinic team, The Children's Hospital at Westmead
Father Paul Coleman	Clergy from the Order of St Joseph who supported the Delezio family
Dr John Collins	Pain clinic consultant, The Children's Hospital at Westmead
Siobhan Connelly	Burns clinical nurse consultant, The Children's Hospital at Westmead
Melissa Cook	Roundhouse mum
Dr Carolyn Cooper	Paediatrician, Royal North Shore Hospital
Joan Cottrell	Volunteer, The Children's Hospital at Westmead
Jeff Darmanin	Photographer
Craig Davis	Principal of Balgowlah Heights Public School

Ann-Louise de La Poype	Carolyn's sister
Charli Delaney	Member of children's entertainment group, Hi–5
Ron Delezio	Sophie's father
Frank Delezio	Ron's father
Mary Delezio	Ron's mother
John Delezio	Ron's eldest son
Kate Delezio	Ron's daughter-in-law
Catherine Delezio	Ron's daughter
Manuel Delezio	Ron's brother
Mitchell Delezio	Ron and Carolyn's son; Sophie's brother
Jan Donohoo	Chaplain, The Children's Hospital at Westmead
Michelle Driver	Play therapist, Sydney Children's Hospital
Joyce Duncan	Volunteer, The Children's Hospital at Westmead
Cameron Edgar	Ambulance Service NSW paramedic
Victor Eisenhut	Lives across the road from the Roundhouse Childcare Centre
Dr Adrienne Epps	Rehab specialist, Sydney Children's Hospital
Jeff Fatt	Member of children's entertainment group, The Wiggles
Debra Fowler	Public relations officer, The Children's Hospital at Westmead
Paul Francis	Chairman, Humpty Dumpty Foundation
Amy Gaffey	ICU nurse, The Children's Hospital at Westmead

Wade Laverack	Firefighter, Manly Fire Station
Helenne Levy	Nurse in PICU, The Children's Hospital at Westmead
Karni Liddell	Paralympic swimmer
Kam Soon Lim	Anaesthetic registrar
Catherine McKersie	Social worker, Sydney Children's Hospital
Dr Peter Maitz	Head of burns unit, Concord Hospital
John Mangos	Television newsman, SKY News
Carolyn Martin	Sophie's mother
Greg Martin	Carolyn's brother
Joy Martin	Carolyn's mother
Allan Martin	Carolyn's father
Cathy Meaney	Assistant in nursing, Physical Ability Unit
Beth Minogue	Family friend
Anita Mudge	Physiotherapist, Sydney Children's Hospital
Anne Murray	Sophie's kindergarten teacher at Balgowlah Heights Public School
Dr David Murrell	Anaesthetist, The Children's Hospital at Westmead
Rebecca Myhre	Carolyn's goddaughter, who was pushing Sophie's stroller when it was hit in the second accident
Dorothy Napper	Volunteer, The Children's Hospital at Westmead
Richard Nest	CareFlight pilot
Johanna Newsom	Burns physiotherapist, The Children's Hospital at Westmead

Jenny Nickolas	Home-based carer for Sophie
Dr Louise Northcott	Paediatrician, The Children's Hospital at Westmead
Dr Michael Novy	CareFlight doctor
Neil Nutley	Lives across the road from the Roundhouse Childcare Centre
Dr Matthew O'Meara	Head of Emergency, Sydney Children's Hospital
Louise Palmer	Family friend
Julia Parker	Day of Difference Foundation manager
Janet Pickering	Physical Ability Unit team member
Adelle Pink	Mum who stopped at second accident
Dr Arjun Rao	Senior specialist — Emergency, Sydney Children's Hospital
Carolyn Reid	Family friend
Dr Gary Sholler	Cardiology consultant, The Children's Hospital at Westmead
Dave Simmons	Police officer in charge of scene at the Roundhouse accident
Garry Smith	Principal of Arranounbai School, where Sophie attended preschool
Richard Smith	Family friend and Day of Difference director
Rod Smith	The Delezio family's solicitor and Day of Difference director
Lyn South	Ward granny, The Children's Hospital at Westmead
Valerie Southey	Family friend
Sandra Spalding	Social worker, burns unit, The Children's Hospital at Westmead

Constable James Sykes	Officer attending second accident
Dr Jonny Taitz	Paediatrician, Sydney Children's Hospital
Cheri Templeton	Burns physiotherapist, The Children's Hospital at Westmead
Maree Thomas	Sophie's guardian and 'fairy godmother'
Lee Tonelli	Family friend
Karen Upton	Theatre nurse, The Children's Hospital at Westmead
Skye Waddingham	Occupational therapist, Sydney Children's Hospital
Trudy Wise	Family friend
Lauren Wood	Dietitian, Sydney Children's Hospital
Anna Young	Occupational therapist, Sydney Children's Hospital
Amanda Zimmerman	Childcare worker, Roundhouse Childcare Centre

acknowledgements

Sophie's Journey would not have been possible without the support of my family — most of all Rob, Bethany and Sophia. Jan, Pete, Ross, Lisa, Nic and Stephanie — you provided a place to stay when I needed it and encouragement all the time — thanks.

Thanks, too, to Kate Rossmanith for conducting additional interviews with such charm, and to Janette Doolan for transcribing a mountain of interviews.

Sally Collings worked in book publishing for almost twenty years and is now a freelance writer and editor, working on books and magazines. Her work focuses on stories of inspiration in the broadest sense — from portraits of life after loss to accounts of academic excellence. Sally lives in Brisbane with her husband and two girls.

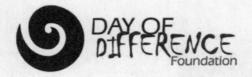

DAY OF DIFFERENCE Foundation

Day of Difference Foundation was founded by Ron Delezio and Carolyn Martin, the parents of Sophie Delezio, who received third-degree burns to over 85% of her body as the result of a terrible accident in December 2003. Sophie and her family lived at The Children's Hospital at Westmead for over six months and during that time, they saw that government money could not adequately fund all of the vital research, specialist equipment and necessary building works. As a result, Day of Difference Foundation was founded as a health promotions charity which works to raise funds that are used to ensure that optimal care is available. A share of proceeds from this book will go to the Day of Difference Foundation. For more information about the Foundation, please visit www.dayofdifference.org.au.